Property of Bill McGinnis

To
Love
and
Be
Loved

This is, or should be,
everyone's goal.

In this provocative new book,
Dr. Allan Fromme explains
what love is and tells how you
can develop your ability to
love more freely and live
more deeply.

D0018972

Books by Allan Fromme

The ABC of Child Care
The Ability To Love
Our Troubled Selves

Published by POCKET BOOKS

P *Are there paperbound books you want*
              but cannot find in your retail stores?

You can get any title in print in POCKET BOOK editions. Simply
send retail price, local sales tax, if any, plus 35¢ per book to
cover mailing and handling costs, to:

MAIL SERVICE DEPARTMENT
   POCKET BOOKS • A Division of Simon & Schuster, Inc.
   1230 Avenue of the Americas • New York, New York 10020

Please send check or money order. We cannot be responsible
for cash.   *Catalogue sent free on request.*

Titles in this series are also available at discounts in quantity
lots for industrial or sales-promotional use. For details write our
Special Products Department: Department AR, POCKET BOOKS,
1230 Avenue of the Americas, New York, New York 10020.

TOM BRUCE

The Ability To Love

Allan Fromme, Ph.D.

A KANGAROO BOOK
PUBLISHED BY POCKET BOOKS NEW YORK

**POCKET BOOKS, a Simon & Schuster division of
GULF & WESTERN CORPORATION**
1230 Avenue of the Americas, New York, N.Y. 10020

Copyright © 1963, 1965 by Allan Fromme

Published by arrangement with Farrar, Straus & Giroux, Inc.

All rights reserved, including the right to reproduce this book
or portions thereof in any form whatsoever.
For information address Farrar, Straus & Giroux, Inc.,
19 Union Square West, New York, N.Y. 10003.

ISBN: 0-671-80884-2

First Pocket Books printing July, 1966
10th printing

Trademarks registered in the United States and other countries.

Printed in the U.S.A.

*This book is dedicated to
Babs and Pam and Steve
because I love them*

Preface

This is a book about our efforts to reach each other and develop meaningful relationships. It is a book about love—love as we experience it and fail to experience it in everyday life. It is not about the great lovers of all time but about you and me.

Too often we regard love as some distant, inexplicable grand passion and allow our daily expression of it to go unexamined and, worse yet, unimproved. The result is that even our partial encounters with it in our daily contacts with people, not to mention our dreams and fantasies, frequently fail to break the pattern of our essential loneliness.

Certainly love merits deliberate study. This is what this book attempts to do: to study love, but in such a way that we see how we ourselves improve or impair its role in our lives. Such insight can not only ennoble our common expressions of love but it can endow our special loves with the longevity and grandeur in reality that we all desire.

Naturally, writing a book such as this required the loving help of others. Dr. William Kolodney, Director of the Kaufmann Auditorium, sponsored this material initially as a series of lectures. Roger Straus encouraged their adaptation to book form. Margaret Sheffield provided valuable editorial help.

Ruth Goode deserves special mention. Her literary skills helped preserve my intent and meaning through all the difficulties of conveying them. Her assistance was creative beyond the usual boundaries of editorial work.

Harold Roth was of enormous help in the re-working of the manuscript into its final form. The quality of both his enthusiasm and judgment turned a chore into a most agreeable task.

Finally, my wife makes it a pleasure to be interested in love. She adapted herself so willingly to the whole undertaking that it became truly a labor of love.

Allan Fromme
New York, New York

Contents

CHAPTER ONE

What Is Love?

LOVE IS A familiar subject, as old as the study of human nature itself. Human nature has been dissected, analysed and studied in great detail, but love for the most part has escaped this intensive study. It has more easily inspired poetry and music than scientific investigation. The result is that we have a wealth of beautiful poetry and music but not much understanding of love.

It is far easier to tell stories about love, to savor love in one or another artistic form, to muse and dream about love than actually to answer the searching questions we all raise about love. What is love? Why do we fall in love? Why is love so often associated with anguish, disappointment, and disillusionment? Is love different for men and women? What can we do to maintain love, to make it grow? And where does the power of love come from, that it arouses such deep feelings in us?

Even more urgent are the troubled questions that keep many lying awake at night. People in love, husbands and wives ask themselves in the small hours of the morning, "Does he (or she) love me enough? Do I love him (or her) enough?" Mothers, and sometimes fathers, ask, "Do I love my child enough? And what is enough love?"

Today we think and talk more about love than perhaps in any previous era in history. We have been taught love as a religious doctrine; we have dwelt on love as a romantic dream. Today we examine it critically, even clinically, for we realize that love, the ability to form meaningful and satisfying relationships with other human beings, is the only way we can live our lives successfully.

And so we are all interested in love, although we do not

always behave lovingly. Jesus did not confront the most co-operative multitude when he enjoined them to love their neighbors as themselves. Yet the values he taught have lived on with us whether we profess his religion or another or none at all. Clearly, love is not a simple reflex, a built-in part of us. Nobody beseeches us to breathe, to sleep or to eat; we need not be reminded to go out and earn a living. But there are many times when we have to be reminded to be more loving. Despite our desire and our need for love, there are obstacles within us which prevent the fulfillment of these longings.

Experts on Love

There have been all kinds of experts on all kinds of love. History is full of them. So is literature; Plato, Sappho, Casanova, Don Juan—each of them wrote as an expert on some kind of love. The Renaissance statesman Machiavelli has never been described as being an expert on love; his little book, *The Prince*, is ordinarily thought of as a rather cynical discourse for princes on how to rule. But in it he cast a perceptive eye on the subject of love.

In those days, it was customary to curry favor among the powerful by giving them costly gifts. Machiavelli had no great wealth, but he was ambitious and he wanted to be well thought of by the powerful Medicis. And so in the foreword of his book he wrote that he could not offer gold cloth or fine Arabian steeds but he could give something of value to a prince, the result of his years of study in history and politics. Knowing that the prince would have little time or inclination to read, Machiavelli proceeded to write a concise digest of government, choosing only those subjects that have the sharpest significance in a ruler's life. One of the chapters bore the title, "Of Cruelty and Clemency and Whether it is Better to be Loved or Feared."

That is a question that would catch the eye even of a Medici. And Machiavelli's answer was that it is best for a ruler to be *both* loved and feared. His reasons constitute an interesting commentary on love, by no means romantic. On the contrary, his evaluation of this tender sentiment is as realistic as it is cynical. The trouble with love, he said in effect, is that the loved one, even though a prince and all-powerful, is not in control of it. People are fickle, said Machiavelli, and because of this and other defects in their character, the bonds of affection are easily broken. Unfortunately, fear seemed to be more reliable because of the threat of punishment. Furthermore, a ruler could manipulate the amount of fear he wished to instill in his subjects, whereas love did not lend itself so easily to his control. In a word, Machiavelli saw love as desirable, but unreliable. Yet despite his Machiavellian recommendation on the value of fear, he cautioned rulers that they must do everything to avoid being hated.

Everyone an Expert

Today, 400 years after Machiavelli, 2000 years after Jesus, contemporary psychological science once again underscores the value of love. The ability to love is recognized as one of the important signs of the well-adjusted individual. And still we ask: what is love?

In a sense, anyone can answer this question; everyone today is an expert on love. Each of us feels in his heart that he is a good lover—or that he could be if only he had the right person to love or the right atmosphere for love. It is very much like what we feel about our ability to drive an automobile. No one says, "I'm a less-than-average driver."

And so it is with love. No one admits even to himself that he is a less-than-average lover, or merely an average lover. Each of us thinks of himself as tender, sensitive, full of insight and understanding, capable of great passion and complete devotion. We may admit certain reservations about our capacity for love, but usually because of defects in the object of our love or in the circumstances, and never, or hardly ever, in ourselves.

Yet despite this expertness we automatically claim for ourselves, none of us is really deeply sure. If we listen carefully to conversations on the subject, we cannot help but notice how expert everyone is on *others* and how silent, confused, and uncertain each one is about himself.

We all have our doubts. On the one hand, we say, "Everyone knows what love is," and on the other hand, we ask, "Am I really in love? Am I loved? What is love?"

A Cool Look at Love

What, indeed, is love? Putting aside our feelings about it for the moment—but only for the moment—let us take a dispassionate look at what we encompass in this word.

The strong interest a man has in a woman is what we generally call love. The strong interest a man has in his business, his golf game, his hi-fi set, watching television or reading murder mysteries or collecting art books—all these we call by other names: vocational interests, avocational interests, hobbies, leisure time activities, anything but love. And yet we also say that the man simply loves to watch television or loves to play golf or seems to have a passion for making money.

Is this merely carelessness in the use of the language? Not really. When we use a variety of words—interests, hobbies— we are making distinctions, and of course there are distinctions. The interest a man develops for a member of the opposite sex generates far more intense, more complex emotions than his interest in these other objects and activities. Yet there are also differences in the way a man loves one woman and the way the same man loves another.

On the other hand, when we say the man loves golf, loves his hi-fi, loves his wife, we are underlining something else about all these loves. We are saying that, although of course they have differences, they also have similarities. When we use the word *love* for all these relationships, we are acknowledging that they have a common thread.

Let us trace this common thread in all our loves. Let us call it, for the moment, *attachment*. This is a bland word, an emotionally neutral word. When we say of all these loves, hobbies, activities, interests, that they are attachments, it is at once easier to see an essential common ingredient in the love a man has for golf and the love he has for his wife.

When two things are attached, they are two things brought together and bound to each other in some way, whether it is two pieces of wood fastened with nails and screws or two people joined by common interests which they pursue together, or an individual and an activity to which he is linked by some interest or desire within him.

The interest or desire within an individual may be the force that brings together and forges the bond of attachment. But an attachment does not necessarily begin with interest or desire for the object. A man may begin to play golf merely to be sociable, or to advance his business connections; he may not care for the game at all. He may never come to care for the game itself, and yet continue to play it for the original reasons that brought him together with it. On the other hand, if he plays frequently, and especially if he comes to develop some skill at it or to feel some challenge in it, he is quite likely to increase his attachment to the game.

In the same way a man and woman may be thrown together willy-nilly in a business office, on a vacation trip, as professional colleagues at a conference—or, as frequently happens in the movies, they share a series of harrowing adventures through a night or a week or several months before they discover that they are attracted to each other. A man finds, as did Professor Higgins in *My Fair Lady,* that he's "grown accustomed to her face." He finds that he has an interest in the woman. He has formed an attachment.

Now this attachment may continue to give him joy, satisfaction, comfort, pleasure, as in his first awareness of the attraction it promised to do. But it may turn out quite the other way. We all know loves, and some of us have experienced them, which bring us grief, pain, frustration, everything but pleasure, and yet we remain attached. Like two pieces of wood, we continue to be joined together. Indeed, when two people do wrench themselves apart by divorce, often they do it not out of a genuine effort to improve their lives, to rid themselves of a source of unhappiness, but rather out of vindictiveness. Divorce is the most emphatic way to say to one's wife or husband, "I don't love you." If they were interested only in breaking the attachment, surely they would accomplish their divorce in the smoothest, most expeditious way possible. But they drag out the proceedings, battle over the terms, and frequently they continue to fight long after they are legally parted. Though the marriage has been dissolved, the attachment has not, in fact, been broken.

Even when two people continue married, and continue to feel love for each other, their love is not always enjoyable. They suffer friction, disappointment, frustration and sometimes merely dullness with each other. A man who loves his work also suffers dullness and drudgery, yet he does not abandon his work. The romantic lover at the very height of his love suffers as much anguish as happiness and sometimes even more.

In all these instances the attachment remains, whether or not it gives pleasure.

Thus our cool look at love has illuminated some significant aspects of it. All our loves, all those bonds that we describe toward an object, an activity, a person by saying "I love—," have in common this one ingredient of attachment. Even bonds that we do not describe thus positively with the word love, but that bind us nevertheless, are also attachments. Our attachments do not always give us joy, whether or not we call them loves.

If they do not necessarily bring us joy, happiness, pleasure, why, then, do we remain attached? If not a simple desire for happiness, what desires do our attachments satisfy? Or do they satisfy any desires at all? Do we, perhaps, form our loves for other reasons, out of other needs and motivations? How do we come to love, how do we form attachments in the first place?

To find answers to these questions, we must look again at ourselves, the lovers.

Love and the Lover

In *Alice in Wonderland* one of Alice's strange experiences involves a Cheshire Cat which sits smiling in a tree. She is chatting with him, and all at once the cat begins to disappear, tail first, until little by little the whole cat has vanished and only his smile remains. Alice objects; she has seen cats without smiles but never a smile without a cat.

We too may wonder whether it is possible to answer questions about love or to study love without the lover. The only way we can profitably come to understand love is to study people who love and how they love. Unlike the cat in *Alice in Wonderland*, we will not let our subject disappear from view. Our effort to understand love begins with understanding ourselves as lovers.

It goes without saying that we all experience many other things in life besides love. All our experiences have an effect upon us and in turn upon each other. We cannot isolate any one set of our experiences and study those exclusively. Love exists only in the context of our total experience. This is another way of saying that the better we understand human nature, the better we are potentially able to understand love.

The psychologists, then, should have the answers, since it is their profession to study human nature. Yet 2000 years of writing on the subject have failed to come up with these answers. One reason for this is that for many years psychology was only a branch of philosophy and physiology. Not until the end of the last century did psychology finally gain its independence and take on its present day form. We all, of course, recognize today that the man most responsible for shaking psychology loose from its previous bonds was Sigmund Freud. Interestingly enough, it is also Freud who wrote more on the subject of love than any other writer in history.

Most people identify Freud's name not with love but with sex, but actually Freud was principally interested in love. He saw sex merely as the soil out of which love arose; love was his basic topic.

Freud believed that an individual could best be understood in terms of the history of his love, that the love life of an individual was his best psychological biography. Freud also believed that any neurosis was basically some kind of impairment of the ability to love.

When Sigmund Freud first stated his ideas on human nature some 70-odd years ago, he had a most explosive effect upon the world. It was a time when Victorian values were at their peak. Some felt that even to talk about love, to examine it objectively as Freud did, would kill it. They felt it should remain sacred and beyond question. Freud's assertion that sex figures so prominently in our motivation was especially repulsive. Worst of all, he ascribed sexual feelings to innocent little babies and children. And what kind of sense did it make to tell people that many of the things they said and did, a vast part of their day-to-day behavior, came from feelings they were not aware of, from experiences they did not remember, out of some part of their minds of which they were not conscious? If we had to think of man as an animal, couldn't he at least be a rational animal?

Not only uninformed laymen, but many physicians and scientists were shocked to have human beings, themselves included, exposed in such fashion. Seventy years are a brief period in the history of a science and yet these ideas, which were initially regarded as preposterous, today are generally accepted.

People were also critical of the automobile, which appeared roughly at the same time. We do not like everything about the automobile: its toll of human life, its daily cost in dollars, and the exasperating experience of traffic jams; but the automobile is here to stay. There are many, many points in the writings of Sigmund Freud which still generate controversy and disagreement, but his general point of view has permanent acceptance. One does not have to be "orthodox," one does not have to call oneself a Freudian, as I myself do not, to subscribe to the interpretation of human nature that Freud evolved. He has not only increased our understanding but he has lent dignity to the therapeutic efforts of clinical psychology and psychiatry, and unquestionably they have achieved salutary results with millions of people who suffer from emotional illness. Before Freud, such emotional sickness had been essentially untreated.

Is Man a Rational Being?

The prevailing view of human nature in Freud's time was that man was motivated by reason. People thought of themselves as rational beings who pursued pleasure and good and avoided pain and evil at the dictates of their rational, conscious minds. This emphasis upon man's rationality dominated all social thinking up to the end of the last century—in fact, until Freud offered his revolutionary propositions. It was granted that men might be lacking in education or intelligence, and their reasoning powers might consequently be imperfect, but that man was essentially rational was not questioned.

Freud himself began with the same belief in man's rationality. At the outset he was not even interested in psychological matters, but spent the early years of his career as a research physician, winning considerable recognition in the field of anatomical research. Freud enjoyed laboratory work and did much of the pioneer experimentation that led to the anesthetic use of cocaine. He also identified certain childhood neurological diseases, his descriptions of which are part of modern medical literature.

By a stroke of good fortune, Freud received a traveling fellowship which allowed him to go to France and study under two distinguished French medical psychologists, Charcot and Bernheim. Charcot was then the head of the clinic of the famous Paris hospital, the Salpêtrière, where his treatment of patients by hypnosis had attracted worldwide attention.

A century earlier, the German physician Franz Anton Mesmer had introduced hypnotism into France. He called his discovery "animal magnetism"; others called it mesmerism. He had great popular success, but the French Academy of Medicine discredited him for his theatrical abuses of hypnotic technique and he retired to Switzerland, where he died in obscurity in 1815. Now the great Charcot had revived this mysterious method and was using it with patients suffering from hysteria.

The Fashionable Sickness

Hysteria was a widespread, baffling illness in the late 19th century. Just as there are styles governing the way we dress, there are fashions or modes of illness. From about 1885 through World War I, there was a wave of hysterical symptoms, something like what we nowadays call psychosomatic symptoms, except that our psychosomatic symptoms are not quite so dramatic. An emotional disturbance which causes and is expressed in the form of *bodily* symptoms—headache, heartburn, ulcers, colitis, for example—is called psychosomatic today. The typical "psychosomatic" symptoms of those days tended to be various kinds of paralysis or loss of function. An arm or leg, or perhaps both legs, would become limp, flaccid. Or the limb would suffer what we call a spastic paralysis, a rigidity of the muscles. With the comparatively limited diagnostic techniques available to them at that time, physicians assumed that there were some organic cause for these symptoms, some pathological condition of the nervous system itself. Massages, baths, and other physical types of treatment were employed, but all to no avail. Charcot's approach was different.

Charcot placed such a patient under hypnosis, which is essentially a state of extreme suggestibility. In this sleep-like trance, the patient is awake enough to hear, answer, and obey commands. Charcot would command the patient to move the paralyzed arm, to get up out of the wheelchair and walk on the supposedly paralyzed legs. Under hypnosis, the patient would obey, and appear not to suffer from any paralysis in the affected limbs. Or Charcot might suggest to some of these patients that when they were awakened, they would be able to use the arm or to walk. And when he woke them from the hypnotic state, they were indeed able to do these things.

Now this was very dramatic. Charcot's hypnotic demonstrations were performed, furthermore, in a large medical amphitheater before many interested spectators, students and physicians and distinguished professors from all over Europe. The theatrical setting actually played a part in Charcot's success, for such a setting facilitates hypnosis.

True, Charcot's feats were not really cures; they turned out to be discouragingly transitory. Sooner or later the same patients came back with either the same or similar disabilities, so that they required periodic treatment by hypnosis. Yet the demonstrations were striking, and they also indicated convincingly enough the absence, in most cases, of any organic disease. If there were any physical damage to nerves or muscles, the patients would not be able to make the paralyzed limbs function normally merely in response to a command given under hypnosis.

For Freud, Charcot's work was especially impressive because he himself had gone to the opposite extreme in his own teaching. He had previously disparaged any departure from the strictest organic interpretation of such "hysterical symptoms." Now, demonstrated before his very eyes, he had repeatedly witnessed the dramatic evidence produced by something other than physical treatment.

"I Just Had to Do It"

From Charcot's clinic Freud next went to Nancy. Here, in another part of France, Bernheim was doing work similar to Charcot's but in a less dramatic fashion. Bernheim had a research laboratory rather than a clinic, for his purpose was not to demonstrate hypnosis but to investigate it. He had devised some simple experiments which he called modestly enough, the "A" experiments and the "B" experiments. He would, for example, place a patient under hypnosis and then say, "Now I am going to release you and, two minutes after you are released, I want you to walk across the room, take the umbrella out of that stand and open it."

Surely enough, about two minutes after he had been awakened from his trance, the man would walk across the room, take the umbrella out of the stand, and open it. This was Bernheim's "A" experiment, which, in today's language, established the fact of post-hypnotic suggestion.

Then Bernheim proceeded to question the patient. In his "B" experiments, he would ask, "Why did you do this?" Invariably the individual would have an explanation, such as, "I wanted to see if it worked," or "I thought it looked like rain," or any sort of answer that seemed for the moment sensible and reasonable.

But the professor would not accept these answers. He would persist: "No, that's not true. Why did you open this umbrella?" And presently the subject would break down and admit, "I don't know why—I just had some kind of feeling deep inside of me—I just had to do it."

Then, finally, as Bernheim continued to ask, "Why did you do it? Why? Why?"—suddenly the patient would know. The truth would come to him apparently from out of nowhere and he would answer, "You told me."

Freud watched these demonstrations again and again. During the journey back to Vienna he thought deeply about what he had seen. His was the genius to see "a world in a grain of sand," to trace the vast potentialities of this work which had escaped Bernheim. Freud never returned to clinical neurology. His subsequent writings never once mentioned a nerve cell. From that time forward, his thoughts moved along psychological channels to the highly original areas of understanding that we associate with the name of Sigmund Freud.

Freud Continues the Quest

First of all, Freud pursued the possibility of unconscious motivation. He said to himself: if Bernheim places an idea in the mind of an individual, and the individual can act on this idea and yet have no awareness of it, then how do we know how many times in the course of a day we may perform actions for which we think we know the reason but actually we do not! We may, Freud perceived, do countless things in exactly the same way!

We all know that when we ask someone, "Why are you doing that?" he always gives us a good and reasonable answer. But as we also know, after Freud, what we offer as reasons are often rationalizations or justifications.

When someone tells you why he votes Democratic, why he votes Republican, why he is moving to the country, why he is moving to the city, why he is marrying, divorcing, changing jobs or leaving college or never in his whole life would eat oysters or wear a green tie, his spoken "reasons" are generally intelligent and frequently persuasive.

But these "good" answers are strikingly like the answers Bernheim elicited when he asked his experimental subjects why they opened the umbrella. They were fine, plausible answers; when a man says he opens an umbrella to see if it works, he sounds rational, intelligent, even as if he might have a scientific mind.

The answers we give, like the answers the hypnotic subjects gave, all reflect credit on us, on our intelligence and rationality. But also like those of Bernheim's patients, our answers are not necessarily true. In the laboratory the truth emerged only when the individual ran out of rational answers and said, "I just had to do it."

In other words, we are not the highly rational beings we like to think we are. We believe that we consciously deliberate the pros and cons of our choices *before* we make them, but Freud saw that we more often do our rational thinking *afterward*. The initial idea might not actually be at all good for the individual; yet it compels him to do something, and he then explains or justifies the act plausibly, with a "good" reason.

Our choices spring from more imperative stuff than thoughts. They spring from the rich volatile inner core of our being. According to Freud, we use our rational capacity to make these choices look acceptable to us and the world.

Certainly love, too, involves choice and soon we shall see how much more we can understand about love, once we recognize that our choices are not necessarily based on reason. Man is *not* a reliably rational animal and we come to understand his behavior better and better as we search out motives below the level of his conscious, "good" answers.

Freud pursued this line of thinking further. It might be, he thought, that if we persist in asking our patients why they do certain things, and why they cannot do certain other things, then we too could get to this truth. If we push the inquiry back far enough, Freud thought, we might even help the patient discover who put the idea into his head or how the idea originally arose. Not long after his return to Vienna, Freud had another lucky encounter. In Vienna there was a somewhat older, well-established physician, Dr. Joseph Breuer, who was using hypnosis to treat some of his hysterical patients. Unlike Charcot, he did not suggest to a patient under hypnosis that the patient would awaken cured. Instead, Dr. Breuer made use of the hypnotic trance to get his patient to answer questions, or to talk at random about his experiences in general. He found that under hypnosis people would talk very much more freely, either about matters on which he questioned them or about anything they chose. He observed that people released tensions in this way and seemed to benefit from what was soon called "psychocatharsis." Patients discovered again and again that many of the experiences and ideas which they thought a part of the dead, forgotten past came up under hypnosis and seemed somehow to be affecting them in the present.

The Lovesick Patients

Dr. Breuer's approach was exactly what Freud wanted to try. He was eager to employ the newly discovered technique of hypnosis in exploring the ideas and memories people held below the level of their consciousness. Unlike the French medical psychologists who implanted ideas for experimental or therapeutic purposes during hypnosis, Freud wanted to use hypnosis to discover what ideas were *already present* in the dimmer recesses of a patient's mind—ideas which might be propelling a patient to behave symptomatically without his awareness of these deeper, inner reasons. In other words, to use the language familiar to us today, Freud wanted to probe the unconscious for the purpose of determining our major motivations. To his own surprise, although he set out to study the unconscious, he found himself studying love.

Freud summarized these early cases which led him to the study of love in his first book, a book done in collaboration with Breuer. It became clear to him, as he analyzed his and Breuer's cases for publication, that each one of these hysterical patients, without exception, was lovesick. Theirs was a lovesickness not in the springtime or romantic sense of the word, but in a far more penetrating and pervasive sense. They were sick because of their inability to love, or more properly, they were sick because of their inability to love *again*. Each of them had failed to survive some previous attachment. This failure, of course, was an emotional one; they never regained their freedom from the early attachment. The anguish they had suffered at the time of their emotional involvement had remained with them in the form of symptoms.

Breuer quit this work before long, but Freud pressed on. In every case, he continued to find that the more he uncovered, the more clearly did he see how the previous emotional attachments of people exerted power over their present behavior. Just as Bernheim's experimental subjects finally recognized *really* why they opened the umbrella, so did Freud's patients finally recognize *really* why they did many of the things which troubled them. Whereas Bernheim's subjects discovered that the reasons for their behavior had been implanted by the experimenter, Freud discovered that the reasons for his patients' behavior lay in their strong emotional experiences of the past.

Hypnosis helped Freud reveal that whatever had involved the individual's emotions in the past were still present in his unconscious memory. Freud said that the person must be still *attached* to whatever can influence him so strongly. He called this attachment love.

A Definition of Love

The question with which we began this inquiry was, What is love? Have we followed this labyrinthine path only to find that love is no more than an "attachment?" A discussion of love promises the expression of great emotions and grandiloquent feelings. Even the lackluster prose of a dictionary defines love as the "tender and passionate affection for one of the opposite sex" and further that love is a "strong liking, fondness and a feeling of strong personal attachment . . ."

But Freud says love is the attachment and not the feeling. Let us see where this idea leads us. Of course, there are feelings associated with our attachments but it is misleading to define them as always fond, pleasant ones. Love can surely be romantic and lofty, but love is also often narcissistic and selfish. Sometimes it is overwhelming and dominates our behavior; at other times it asks only for the most intermittent expression. Some of our loves make us happy and leave us with a rich sense of fulfillment; others keep us constantly striving, feeling inadequate and full of anguish. The *feelings* associated with love, then, are clearly not dependable, for they vary as much as the ways in which we express love.

At the pinnacle of his love, the lover tells us ecstatically how he feels about his love. It is the most glorious thing that ever happened to him, his beloved is the most wonderful creature, and he is the happiest man in the world. That is the way he feels today. No doubt it would be unkind to ask him how he will feel about this love three months or three years—or thirty years—from today. And yet this is, after all, a fair question. Our feelings of love transform our lives—for the moment. But we do not live for the moment. The question is not how we feel, for the moment, about our love. The question is how we act on that feeling.

To say this does not mean we are going to dismiss the feelings we have of love. Our feelings are what make our attachments important to us. But in order to explain why we act as we do and why we feel as we do when we are in love, we must uncover the origin and development of our attachments. The feelings involved in love are deeply interesting to us and we readily respond to their description; yet description, no matter how sensitive and how perceptive, is at best merely descriptive. It fails *to explain why* we have those feelings when we are in love.

Once we resolve to look upon love as an attachment influenced by previous and other attachments, we have a hypothesis which begins to help us understand how we come to feel and behave as we do when we love. The kinds of people we select, the kinds of things we do with these people, the kinds of feelings that move us, all tend to grow out of our previous attachments. This is not to say there are no differences from one experience to another, but rather that there are enough similarities to suggest patterns of conduct which make us reasonably predictable. Although the psychologist does not have a crystal ball, he does understand that to know how someone will behave tomorrow, he must find out what he did yesterday.

There are attachments that we develop out of desire and

choice and others that we develop out of need and experience. The former have a conscious, rational quality; the latter, an animal and accidental quality. We are not the sole masters of the directions we choose. Our bodies drive us and life itself bends us irrevocably in directions of its own. Attachments evolve and we pursue them only because we already have them. These attachments need not even be to people. We become attached to an idea, an object, a possession, a place, a fantasy, an ideal—to anything at all.

Love now begins to be something we can study and explore. It is not some rare, delicious, incomprehensible set of feelings growing out of some special attachment to some special person. Love is that attachment but also any and all other attachments as well, whether they be to things or people, pleasant or unpleasant, new or old, conscious or unconscious. Our loves are many. Many of them coexist; some nourish each other, and some conflict. The future of any one love depends upon its place in the complex pattern of all our loves.

Since we all have attachments, everyone, in this sense of the term, is "in love." And all these loves bear the stamp of the lover. We come to understand an individual best through a study of all these loves, all these attachments he has formed. And the best way to understand any particular attachment or love is to study the quality of his previous attachments or loves.

CHAPTER TWO

Where Love Begins

WHAT PREVIOUS ATTACHMENTS should we know about, in order to understand the love that we experience as adults? Obviously, any previous attachments that were strong, for attachments that were strong in the past may well be strong today. Most of us, for example, admit that we develop an attachment of some strength to our parents. We can hardly avoid becoming attached to those who care for us during infancy and childhood; although it may emerge as a negative attachment and therefore not very sweet or acceptable, it is undeniably an attachment, and a strong one. In many subtle ways, parts of this attachment remain with us, influencing our later relationships.

The ways in which we first expressed this and other early attachments must certainly change, and Freud realized that they must, but he insisted that we should not be deceived into believing that they no longer exist. He proposed that other attachments might arise even before our attachment to parents, and that their influence too might persist.

Indeed Freud saw that other efforts to explain love had failed because we had not gone far enough back in the life of the lover to understand him. Possibly the very first experience, which came long before love as we ordinarily know it, might in fact shape love as we eventually experience it. Some of our very early bodily needs, and the ways we come habitually to act on them, might determine the kind of people we will be, whether happy or sad, optimistic or pessimistic, hard or easy to please, clinging and dependent or grown-up and free. He suspected that what we come to feel about ourselves and others might grow out of these first, primitive, *physical* feelings of satisfaction and dissatisfaction, even before psychological and social awareness develop. And so he pushed his inquiry back to

17

the mute, misty experience with which we all begin life, the experience of infancy.

Back to the Source

Although the infant at birth is identifiable as a member of the human species, he is unquestionably more animal than human. He is as undisciplined, as uncivilized as any other little animal and considerably more helpless than most. He is demanding, irascible, impatient; like the fledgling birds in the nest with their mouths continually open, he wants, wants, wants. He is a bundle of physical wants; he suffers his greatest pain from these wants and enjoys his greatest pleasure from satisfying them. The needs of his body are in fact the whole world of this little animal. He is scarcely aware of anything beyond these bodily sensations of discomfort followed by comfort, of pain succeeded by relief.

The baby cries when he is hungry because hunger to him is an actual physical pain. By the time we are adult, we have forgotten how painful hunger is, since we are never acutely hungry. We eat routinely because it is mealtime. We may feel hungry sometimes but we scarcely ever wait until it hurts, certainly not under ordinary circumstances. We may say we are parched with thirst but most of us have never experienced genuine thirst, the thirst of a man crossing the desert, who will gulp even brackish, foul water. Our physical needs as adults are satisfied long before they become painful.

The small organism of a child does not have our reservoirs of stored nutrients and fluids to keep him in balance if lunch or dinner is late. The young child is at once thrown into a state of disequilibrium, unrest, and pain acute enough to make him cry. Now someone comes and gives him food or drink, and his pain and discomfort vanish. The food and the fluid actually bring him this relief, but he is aware of it only in terms of his own body and its sensations as the balance of his inner world is restored.

Love Is Born

Freud pushed his observations a step further: in these first pleasures that the child's own body gave him, Freud saw the beginnings of sex.

Now people had never thought of sex in these terms, as a normal and natural component of infant physical pleasure. Sex was something that sprang fullblown with the adolescent's beard, a phenomenon that appeared overnight with puberty. They had never observed and could not conceive that it might have early manifestations of some sort in childhood. Infantile sexuality was as foreign a combination of words as was water in a solid state to someone who lived in the tropics, or liquid gas to someone living a century ago.

Today we would find it odd that such a powerful function should spring into existence so suddenly, without preparation or development. So it appeared to Freud. He saw that the pleasures involved in satisfying the basic vegetative wants for food, drink, warmth, and so on, so closely resembled the touching and caressing pleasures, that they might as well be called one and the same. To the infant, limited to his small world of physical sensation, they *are* one and the same. They are all physical satisfactions, physical pleasures.

The earliest appearances of things frequently have this undifferentiated character. Seeds are seeds, saplings differ somewhat from each other, and by the time the grown trees bear flowers and fruit almost anybody can tell an apple tree from a cherry. The baby, it is true, has some specific sexual responses. Even during his first year, a baby boy will have an erection in response to being dried, powdered, or touched in the genital area. But certainly he has no desire for the elaborate sexual behavior which is later culminated in intercourse. Freud is saying only that all attachments initially have a bodily or physical basis. They all grow out of the sensation of satisfaction, comfort, pleasure. In pursuing them, the baby is using his body to obtain pleasure.

Freud recognized this as the same function of sex later on, for in addition to procreation, sex is essentially the use of the body for the purpose of pleasure. Ordinarily when we call any part of our behavior sexual, the bodily pleasure we seek involves our primary (genital) and secondary erogenous zones. But Freud saw the value of putting things together rather than treating them as separate and different. Physical satisfaction is physical satisfaction he contended, and of what importance is it whether it comes from being fed, having one's soiled wet diapers removed, or being rocked in a parent's arms?

At different stages of life, just as at different moments in life, our demands for certain satisfactions will be more urgent than for others. A child comes upon the pleasures of sucking, biting, eating, five or six years before he discovers the pleasures of masturbation, not to mention the many, many years before he discovers the enjoyments of sexual intercourse. Of course, these pleasures are all different from each other. But they are all part of a continuum of physical growth and development.

In other words, although we ordinarily use the term "sexual" to refer pre-eminently to genital pleasure, pre-genital physical satisfactions can also be called sexual since they are part and parcel of the same developmental pattern. It is important to recognize this link because, as we shall see in a moment, the child learns to love through these same bodily pleasures; that is, he develops attachments outside of himself to others by building on his own pre-genital but sexual behavior. Love and sex have a great deal to do with each other *at the start*. They actually begin together. How they remain connected with each other depends upon the satisfactions and dissatisfactions the individual enjoys during the whole of his sexual history. Various phases of his pre-genital or genital development may present problems which distort and change love he had begun to build on them.

Let us see now how Freud related these infant pleasures to the experience of love. Again, he traced the relationship in its simplest terms, in terms of the infant's own world of limited experience.

In obtaining these simple satisfactions, Freud said, the child learns to distinguish certain portions of his body, those which give him pleasure and satisfaction, and he strives to use those parts of his body more and more often. He develops attachments to them.

Since eating gives him satisfaction by relieving him of the pain of hunger, he soon loves to use his mouth because it represents the beginning of satisfaction. He likes the food itself, the hand that feeds him, and of course that to which the hand is attached, the mother. Her voice, her touch, every aspect of her presence and contact with him become part of his satisfaction or the promise of it. Thus, tracing love to its origins as Freud did, we see that it is through his body that the human being first learns to love. Here we see love in its simplest, most primitive state, its newborn state.

The Infant World of Sensation

Life does not, of course, remain that simple, and neither does love. What begins as an attachment to that which gives pleasure goes through many convolutions, and in the end it may be an attachment to that which gives pain. Presently we shall trace that course.

While we are still exploring the infant world of sensation, we observe that if the child's own body gives him his first experiences of pleasure, it also gives him his first experiences of pain. All his experiences are limited to body sensation. Initially he is aware of nothing else except his body. The physical and social worlds beyond do not yet exist for him.

We would imagine, then, that whatever attachments he develops at this point must take place within the narrow confines of this tiny world of his own body. And this is exactly what happens.

Infancy is the time when the little human animal entertains the most exclusive interest in his own body. He explores it as though it were a foreign continent. He discovers his hands and becomes fascinated with the way they end in the fringe we call fingers. He manipulates these fingers and he uses them to advantage in his exploration of other parts of his body. He discovers a hole in each side of his head and he may easily spend several days investigating this interesting oddity.

His first strong attachment, as we have noted, is to his mouth. Through it comes relief from his first, most deeply disturbing experiences, the experiences of hunger and thirst. He becomes so attached to this oral mechanism of satisfaction that soon he tries to use it for other purposes. He puts all sorts of things in his mouth, using it now for the recognition of objects. Some children go on to use the mouth for pleasure when they are not hungry, sucking a thumb for hours as though they were in fact enjoying a meal. It is as though sucking one's thumb were the next best thing. And as a matter of fact, if you are not hungry, it is even better.

At another stage the same innocent human animal discovers the pleasure his organs of elimination can give. Once his diapers are removed he comes upon still other portions of his body and he discovers his genitalia. They too become a source, a most important source, of physical pleasure. If you were to come upon a child four or five years old who is masturbating, a child who had never been scolded or stopped or had any attention called to this activity, and if you were to ask him what he is doing, the chances are that he would say, "I'm tickling myself." If you asked him why, he would answer, "Because it feels good."

In these early years a child has an unabashed, unashamed enjoyment of his own body. He comes by this naturally, unless he has been hampered in his enjoyment by adult interference. His own body is his first and, for a considerable period of time, his principal source of pleasure. Like the cat preening itself or the dog chasing its tail, the child uses his body to satisfy himself. At this stage he shares the mentality of dogs and cats; he has not yet discovered the pleasures beyond himself.

The Patterns Become Set

The intensity of these early pleasures and pains is powerful in fixing responses; that is to say, in making them habitual. The intensity of these experiences combined with repetition, constitutes the heart of the learning process.

That is why Freud felt it was important to dwell on the early life of the child. Infancy and childhood represent our introduction to life, and our subsequent participation in life continues to be influenced to some extent by the nature of this introduction. This becomes clearest in those who suffer hardship, especially emotional hardship, in these early years.

The things we learn in these early months and years are not in the realm of intellect; the things we learn involve our guts. As infants and babies we are not yet civilized enough to be responsive to ideas. It is our basic biological processes which dominate us. What we learn initially is learned by the body. The tiny infant does not *consciously* select or reject what he likes and does not like. He is helpless and without choice. His body merely responds with pleasure or displeasure to what happens to him.

This means that *his body* will select and fix many habits for him long before he develops any conscious, deliberate method of weighing and choosing. Even later in life, when we are quite capable of conscious choice, the habits of the body will frequently intervene and make the selection for us. If, for example, we have developed a strong attachment to the mouth or, more technically, an oral fixation. we may express this by habitual overeating. The most conscious and resolute decision to go on a diet gives way again to the sheer physical habit, growing out of the attachment that we formed early in life. We do not necessarily or easily do what we want; rather we tend to do what we have habitually done before.

The specific habits, fixations, or attachments we develop early in life largely depend upon the incidents of our biography. Freud proposed that the way parents manage these bodily or vegetative functions—the functions of eating, eliminating, sleeping—had a great deal to do with making us different from each other.

One six-months old child, for example, finishes his bottle so rapidly that his sucking needs, which exist independently of his need for food, remain unfulfilled. Although his mother is proud of him for being such a good eater, we all know what happens. He substitutes his thumb for the nipple and falls asleep again and again sucking on it. After a while his teeth begin to appear, piercing his tender gums, and sucking his thumb now offers him additional relief. He comes to associate sucking his thumb with satisfaction, with relief from pain, and after a while it helps comfort him from anything that troubles or frightens him.

At first his mother regards this as innocent enough, but as he becomes older she discourages him from sucking his thumb. Now he does it only surreptitiously. Yet when pressures mount, he is not even aware of how easily his thumb finds its way into his mouth.

The future of this attachment to his thumb depends, of course, upon many other aspects of his total experience. Yet once we develop a habit, we commonly enough reinforce it, finding new expressions for it. The infant who sucked his thumb may grow up to be the adult who is a chain smoker or who habitually keeps a pipe in his mouth, bites on pencils, or in some other way is continuing to express the attachment he initially had to his thumb.

Where Love Comes In

We may legitimately ask, "What has this to do with love, with the attachments we develop as adults?" The answer is that the kinds of attachments we develop as adults depend first of all on how adult we really are. If we continue to "suck our thumb" through life, we may well be responding to pressure as we did in childhood. We may not yet have outgrown our basic attachments to parts of our own body. If we are still infantile in some of our attachments, there is a good chance that on closer observation we may be infantile in others too.

This is inevitably a matter of degree. Human beings are so complex that their behavior cannot be reliably predicted from the study of only one aspect of it. We have had an illustration, not an explanation, of how one early attachment could very easily persist in our behavior and how it could possibly keep us trapped on an emotional level below our real age. Whether it would do so depends upon many other contributing factors.

On the face of it there is little reason to believe that thumb sucking, even if it persists in more adult forms, should have anything to do with the attachments we later call love. It would be hard to recognize the connection if it existed, for it is never simple and explicit. Predicting our behavior from any single dimension or set of experiences is fairly risky.

Few of us have the inclination or, even more important, the technical knowledge necessary to explain our attachments in such terms. More often than not we merely say, "John met Mary; she's an attractive girl; it's easy to understand why he fell in love and wants to marry her." We have no reason to see a clinical case in every social relationship.

On another level, however, we might observe that John has any number of infantile attachments which continue to possess him. He is attracted to Mary, not because she is pretty—he has gone out with many girls as pretty or even prettier—but because she seems to offer the promise of letting him continue to remain attached to himself; he feels in her a basic approval of the less adult aspects of his personality. He naturally does not put it this way when he talks about her. More likely he says, "I've never been more comfortable with a girl. She seems to know how to handle me." What he is saying is that an attachment to Mary is consistent with his other infantile attachments which still persist in his behavior.

It may seem a far cry from finishing one's bottle too quickly and sucking one's thumb, to the selection of a particular kind of girl to love some twenty-odd years later. And it is! But life has a continuity that must be recognized. The fact that something occurred twenty years ago does not diminish its importance. It may be even more important for precisely that reason. Furthermore the fact that something occurred in one area of life—in this case the vegetative—does not mean that it can bear no relationship to other areas, to the emotional and the social. In fact it may dominate other areas of behavior precisely because it is vegetative.

Our basic biological processes involve our strongest needs, our deepest fulfillments and deprivations, and therefore our most poignant satisfactions and frustrations. Our emotional life and its needs build on our bodily life and its needs, and the directions we take in our relationships with people are strongly influenced by this sequence of development.

The Saving Inconsistency

At this point it becomes necessary to warn the student of love that however important the vegetative activities may be, studying them exclusively will not entirely reveal to us the nature of love. Although we cannot dismiss the beginnings of our attachments, we must nevertheless get on with their subsequent developments.

The individual is not doomed by his infancy. He will not necessarily have to spend years on the psychoanalytic couch because of some vegetative mismanagement he suffered during his first year.

He will be permanently marked only if the same mistakes are made again and again. Suppose a mother has forced her child to sit on the potty long before it is biologically possible for him to have sphincter control, control of the muscles of the organ of elimination. The same mother may later keep her child on the toilet for two hours until he performs. She may lock her five-year-old out of the house for not scraping the mud off his shoes before entering. She may nag him about his toys which are not put away, about his table manners, his uncombed hair, the disorder of his room, his irresponsible friends.

With this kind of experience behind him, such a child frequently invites the same treatment from others even though he hates being treated in this way. His friends' parents find him untidy, his teachers are annoyed at his forgetfulness, and so inevitably the same experience he is having at home is reinforced everywhere else.

Fortunately our growth does not usually suffer this monolithic influence. The mother who changed her child's diapers the moment she discovered they were soiled, no matter how often this occurred, is frequently the same woman who later invites her child to play in the playground sandbox or the backyard dirt to his heart's content, no matter how filthy he gets. Her inconsistency is a saving grace.

Consistency is generally recommended in the management of children, but some people carry it to an abnormal degree, and we find them rigid and unrelenting. Others fuss about one aspect of their child's behavior and are willing to accept other forms of the same behavior. As a result of this mixed experience that most of us have in childhood, the vegetative attachments we develop tend to predispose us to related attachments in each succeeding phase of growth, but they are not so binding as to exclude other kinds of attachments entirely.

Sometimes, however, a child's early attachment is reinforced on the next level of experience, when he is forming his first relationship with another human being, usually his mother. We have seen how the infant, taking his food from his mother, becomes attached to the hand that feeds him, the arms that hold him, the mother herself. As his awareness of reality grows, he comes to realize how very little he can do for himself. His mother, who does everything for him, represents solace, satisfaction, security. If he now happens to fall ill, this is even more powerfully impressed upon him. Only she can take care of him. No one else will do. Add to this one more ingredient, the mother's emotional need for this relationship with her child, and we have an attachment with enormous power to control this child's later life and loves.

Biography in Terms of Love

The evolution of such an attachment is described with great sensitivity in D. H. Lawrence's novel, *Sons and Lovers*. The novel is largely autobiographical, and it is both a work of literary merit and a study of what Freud named the Oedipus complex; that is, the attachment of a boy for his mother.

The boy Paul is born late in the lives of his parents, who

have already suffered considerable disillusionment with each other. His father is a miner, a heavy drinker, a dour man who displays little affection. His mother, left to herself, transfers to this child all the love and attention she once gave to her husband. The boy is sickly to boot, giving her all the more reason to envelop him in love. For the boy she is everything and his attachment to her is complete.

In early manhood, seeking a girl, Paul meets Miriam. She lives in a home dominated by men; her brothers consider her useless because she is a girl and cannot work with them in the mine. She is a girl so hungry for love that she knows no limits; love for her means total possession.

Now Paul has been possessed all his life, and is still possessed by his mother. He is not free for another possessing and enveloping love; it is the only kind of love he can be attracted to at this point in his life, and yet it is the one kind of attachment he is not able to maintain. His attachment to his mother conflicts with his love for Miriam, leaving him more guilty than he can bear. And so after a brief affair he leaves Miriam.

In the city where he goes to find work he meets Clara. By this time his mother has died and Paul is feeling somewhat lost. To Clara, an older woman and an experienced one, Paul is a sweet and unspoiled boy. To Paul, Clara is a mother, one with whom he can enjoy the same kind of attachment he had for his mother. But this love, too, is flawed. She is not his mother, and if she were, he could not love her as a man.

Paul at the novel's close is wandering in the country, undecided whether to do away with himself or to turn back to the city and to life. His conflict is almost too much for him. His early and enduring attachment to his mother leaves him desperately in need of her, or of some other woman who will substitute for her, and yet his relationship to any other woman must be different; he himself wants to be different.

Paul is left with his attachments and desires in apparently irreconcilable conflict. D. H. Lawrence, of course, turned back to life, and faced it with the help of his great talents as an artist.

The Stages of Love

We have seen, now, how love begins in the early vegetative life of the child when he forms attachments to his own person and specifically to certain organs of his body, and to at least one other person, the one who cares for him. In one way or another these attachments persist as the child grows, and they continue to predispose him toward other attachments consistent with the demands of these early ones. By the time any of us is old enough to find a girl, fall in love, and marry, we already have a complex history of many loves.

These loves progress through recognizable stages. Thus the first group are typically narcissistic; they are varieties of self-love, growing out of quite literal attachments to parts of the child's own body. As an outgrowth of his own biological functioning he also develops an attachment to his parents, mainly his mother, and we have traced the course of this, his first experience of love for someone other than himself.

The next significant period comes between the ages of six and twelve. Now the open expression of the child's attachments to his own body are discouraged. Thumb sucking and masturbation are no longer permissible, bathroom functions become private, and if the child still wants to pursue these attachments he must do so surreptitiously. Even his attachment to his mother now must become subdued in its display; a frank expression of dependence or a physical show of affection is frowned upon in a boy and is only a little less tolerated in a girl.

This does not mean that the child's powerful early attachments are eliminated overnight. They merely go underground and remain latent within him—hence Freud's term for this stage as the latency period of development. The child has stepped out into a larger world and the world encourages him to form social attachments.

These new attachments are for the most part asexual; boys play with boys and girls with girls. A boy who shows an interest in girls is considered a sissy and a girl who wants to play with boys is a tomboy. It is a period when children are encouraged to develop and accept their sexual role in life by pursuing all the interests characteristic of masculinity or femininity, with one exception: an interest in each other.

Finally comes adolescence. The sex glands begin to function, immense and rapid physical changes take place, and the body once again assumes great importance. It is once more a focus of attention for the boy or girl; the world now encourages the young people to take notice of each other, and old attachments are reshuffled and re-aligned as the basis for new attachments, which for the first time now take on an overt sexual character.

At last we expect them—and they expect themselves—to fall in love.

We have watched the prospective lover grow from infancy, and now we see him experiencing what appears to be a brand new phenomenon, the phenomenon of heterosexual love. But now we know that except for its overt sexual expression it is not, in fact, new. The lover's capacity to give and receive love has not sprung up overnight. It has been growing in him since the day he was born. Even its sexual aspect is not wholly new, for the use of his body for pleasure was at the heart of the infant's experience, his first step in learning to love.

And so we know that the lover, on the brink of what he expects will be the most significant attachment of his life, brings into it all the attachments he has already formed, those he knows he has and those he is unaware of, those that harmonize and those that conflict with his new love, those that enhance and those that restrict his enjoyment of it. As he approaches that rare, delicious set of feelings growing out of some highly special attachment to another human being, he is not in the mood for understanding and research. But we know that the quality of this love as well as its future depends on its place in the complex pattern of all our loves.

To see how he will fare in this most important love, we must explore his many other loves.

CHAPTER THREE

Our Many Loves

WE ALL HAVE a greater capacity for love than we make use of, and we all have many more loves than we are aware of. Every one of us has many loves, even those who are, by all the evidence, lonely and emotionally impoverished.

Not all these are loves of other human beings. When we define love as an attachment, we begin to realize how many loves we have.

Some of these loves we call interests. When we speak of interests, it is easy to see that an individual may enjoy many attachments of this order and still not be in love in the ordinary sense of the word. A man may have an interest in mountain climbing, mushroom collecting, Tibetan dialects, higher mathematics, and about some of these interests he may be quite passionate, but he may not have any interest in people, much less be emotionally interested in one of them.

A Love By Any Other Name

Interests are conscious attachments; we know when we have them. There is another order of attachments of which we are quite unaware, which yet may possess us more completely than our conscious interests. This is the order of attachments that begin before we have much awareness of anything, in that infant world of sensation which we have already explored. The infant's attachment to his own body, through the sensations that form his first awareness, are the beginning of his capacity for love, any kind of love, as we have seen.

As he becomes interested in, attached to, various parts of his body, the developing human being finds ways of pursuing

30

these attachments, and these ways to which he becomes accustomed tend to reinforce his attachments. We have talked of thumb-sucking, a familiar example of the way some babies pursue their attachment to the mouth and the pleasure it gives them.

This kind of attachment we generally call a habit. We repeat the same act, the same way of pursuing an attachment, and after a while the habit itself acts as an attachment, as though the particular way of doing the thing were itself a need, a desire. The baby loves to suck his thumb, or loves to sleep on his stomach, or loves to dawdle over his food. The grown man loves his newspaper at breakfast, his drink before dinner, his seat behind home plate at the ball game. These apparently trivial attachments may be so strong that he is disturbed and irritable if anything interferes with them. Because of the power of these habit-attachments, many people are poor travelers, and some are poor lovers. The attachments we lightly dismiss as habits may do more damage to love and marriage than we realize.

These habit-attachments can have very deep roots. Calling them habits gives them too mechanistic a name. We can dismiss a habit as simply a mode of behavior like biting one's fingernails. Biting one's fingernails is a way of expressing an attachment, but it does not reveal what lies at the other end of the relationship, what it is that the nail-biter is attached to. A habit-attachment may well grow out of some infantile ideal, for example the desire to remain attached to the mother's breast. Such an early attachment, if in one way or another it has not been resolved, can exert lifelong power over the individual. Unknown to him, it may be the root of other attachments he is driven to form, attachments which are not in his interest as an adult. The early roots of some habit-attachments is what makes them so hard to break.

Whether we call them interests, habits, likings or even infatuations, the names we give our attachments may describe our attitudes toward them, and in a sense it describes the kind of hold each order of attachments has over us. Our interests, and the things or people we merely "like," largely give us conscious satisfactions, and we also feel that we can consciously put them aside, for a time or forever, if we choose. Our infatuations give us conscious pain as well as pleasure, and we recognize them as transitory. Our habits surely do not always give us conscious pleasure, and they are by all odds the most difficult attachments to break. When a man speaks of a woman to whom he is still attached although he no longer takes pleasure in the attachment, he may say, "I suppose she has become a habit with me."

Many of our attachments, even habit-attachments, are pleasurable, and we have positive feelings for them. A habitual smoker may say, "I love my first cigarette in the morning." He may smoke two packs a day and may not enjoy another, may not even be aware he is smoking all those subsequent cigarettes, but he consciously enjoys his first one; he loves it. Other attachments that we form may bring no pleasure at all; they may be distinctly disagreeable to us. Yet we are no less attached to them. They take their place among our many, various, and on the surface often inexplicable loves.

The Tree With Many Branches

Interests, likings, habits—these are all kinds of attachments, kinds of love. The lover, however romantic he may feel, is in fact a configuration of all these rather prosaic habits, interests, attachments that he has formed since birth. This is the true history of his love life. Its elements are more commonplace than romantic. Romantic love is also an element, but his romantic love is only one part of his history as a lover.

If we think of our development as a tree and our loves as its branches, our love of another human being is perhaps the highest branch on the tree. Or, if we like, it is the stoutest one, the one from which we can hang a swing and thus enjoy the tree best. But essentially this most important love is a branch like all the other branches, and it is not always the strongest and best developed of them.

For example, girls are generally assumed to be the overriding interest of young men at college, but some youths care more about playing football, some about becoming the big man on campus, and some few actually care most about their studies.

A fair number really care most about cars. Many a young man tends furnaces and baby-sits for the faculty, diligently saves his money, and buys a used sports car. Now he spends

Sunday afternoon driving in the country with the object of his love. He may have a girl in the seat beside him, but the object of his love is not the girl. The object of his love is the automobile. He tests it, sees how well it corners, watches for a stretch of road where he can push it to its top speed. Its responsiveness to his touch is his great joy, the roar of its exhaust his most beautiful music. He talks to the car, sings to it as he drives; he spends his spare time tinkering with it, polishing it, caressing it.

This love may well persist long after the youth has his college degree and is out in the world, working at his career, supporting a wife and children. An expert in motivational research not long ago persuaded automobile manufacturers that they should frankly advertise their product as a love object, and extol its sexiness. This may seem extreme, and yet there is a psychological truth to it, one which we already have stated. That is, that all loves are essentially variations of the same theme. All are expressions of attachments.

This is not to say that a man who loves cars cannot love women. A man may love his car and also his wife, his children, his house, his work, friends, politics, fishing, poker, a certain brand of whisky, a certain favorite vacation spot, a dozen or a score of other objects of attachment. He may also be attached to free speech, low tariff, the novels of Ernest Hemingway, progressive jazz and certain stocks on the stock market.

Our many loves co-exist, and they are not necessarily exclusive. An individual with many loves is one who is capable of many attachments. If they are on the whole good for him— if they are loves that bring him positive satisfactions and enhance his life and his productivity—then he is a happy man and probably a healthy and well adjusted one.

Some lovers are exclusive in their attachments. If you were to meet someone who is attached to ancient Sumerian writings, or fossils of a certain geological period, or sailboat racing or undersea exploration or what you will, you would say he has an absorbing special interest and probably he is a lucky man. But if you found that he has no relationships with people— that he never had a love affair, never married, has cut himself off from parents, family, friends—then you would certainly conclude that this man was out of the ordinary and perhaps abnormal. What is abnormal about him is not that he has an unusual interest, an unusual love, but that this is the only love he has. We expect people to have a variety of loves.

Our Loves Have a Family Resemblance

All our loves bear the stamp of the lover. They all show some similarity in our way of expressing them. A man's love of golf and his love for his wife sometimes show a striking resemblance. He looks forward to his game, sets off for the golf course in high anticipation. He is going to have a wonderful afternoon. But somehow everything conspires against him. The people ahead of him make him wait at each tee, those behind him make him rush at each green, his caddy is slow finding the ball. Even his clubs let him down; his driver seems off balance, his putter snags on the turf. He ends up with a disgraceful score and a thorough disgust with golf, the world, and himself.

The same man plans an evening out with his wife—he will take her to dinner and a movie and enjoy a good time together. And then she takes an endlessly long time to dress, she cannot seem to make up her mind where she would like to eat—and before he knows it he is having the same kind of time he had on the golf course.

These loves bear a powerful family resemblance, because the lover loves them both in the same way: he loves them only when they are ideal, when they offer not the slightest test of his patience or his capacity to persist against frustration and disappointment. He loves, not golf, but an ideal game of golf. He may play three such games out of a hundred in the course of the year, and the other ninety-seven times he behaves miserably on the golf course. His love for his wife has the same limitation. If she did not spoil his pleasure by keeping him waiting, the maitre d'hotel would spoil it by seating him at a table he did not like, or the waiter by serving him either too slowly or too quickly—it would hardly matter which. This is a man who finds it very hard to enjoy his loves, for he can enjoy them only when they are perfect according to his desire. And all his loves, great and small, are marked with this selfsame defect.

Two such separate loves may have another quality in common: they may not be the genuine loves they appear to be, but substitute loves for another, much deeper attachment that does not appear in its own guise. A man may love golf for what seem like the obvious reasons but his real reason may be quite unrelated to golf. He may have deep-seated feelings of insecurity which are assuaged only by driving the longest ball on the links. His score may be quite ordinary but he does drive the longest ball, and this improves his status among his fellows, or so he feels.

In the same way, he may want the most beautiful woman he can find as his wife. He may not trust her, he may feel she is constantly looking at other men or cannot run a household or has any number of defects, but nevertheless he would not be married to a woman who was not an outstanding beauty no matter what wifely virtues she might possess.

This man is using both his wife and his golf as substitute loves, and in both instances his love is narcissistic. He loves neither, even though he may spend considerable time with both. He is really still in love with himself, much as a two-year-old is in love with himself, because it is only himself that gives him reliable satisfaction. He values his wife only for her beauty, his golf only for his long drive, because these fragmentary attachments win him attention and feed his self-esteem, his self-love.

The Pyramid of Loves

We make new attachments, form new loves in such a complex way that it is not easy to trace the path of their development. One love leads to another, and our attachments tend to pyramid. This is easy to see in the case of food: some people are attached only to steak, but more often people who like food like many kinds of food, and on this attachment they may build a love of gourmet dining, of exotic dishes, of fine wines, or of cooking as an art.

Some people become attached to one sport, either as spectator or participant, but more people like to watch or play a variety of games. Or a single favorite may proliferate: people who like swimming may become skindivers; they also become travelers, seeking the warm seas where skindiving is best, and they come to love the tropical settings where they enjoy their favorite sport. Their social attachments tend to fit the same pattern: they are likely to find other skindivers to fall in love with.

We pyramid our more subtle attachments in the same way. A man's self-love may lead to an attachment to the status he gains in a group, and thence to an attachment to the group, to which he may show a passionate and indeed an irrational loyalty. A woman's interest in herself may generate an interest in jewelry, in clothes; coupled with some special aptitudes and opportunities, she may go on to a career in fashion designing.

These are simplified examples, for the sake of illustration. We rarely fall in love with activities, ideas, things or people in quite so transparent a fashion. Often what we want or need or what truly attracts us is elbowed away by what we are taught to think is right or good. An army of advertisers are constantly trying to persuade us that what they have to sell is good for us. Subtle cultural forces direct many of our attachments.

Some of these cultural forces early distinguish between the sexes. Every toy store has its separate departments; from the age of two or three, boys are given toy cars and trucks, trains and planes, and girls get dolls and doll clothes and stoves and dishes. We encourage a boy to become attached to his lucky baseball bat that has got him extra-base hits; we approve his efforts to put together a car out of spare parts from an automobile graveyard; we applaud him when he earns and saves to buy himself a real car or some other desirable possession. We strongly influence our boys in forming attachments to possessions, activities, achievement.

We guide our girls toward many of the same material attachments, but we also encourage them to more human loves. When little boys are playing good guys and bad guys, achieving hero status with toy guns, little girls are playing house and taking tender care of their dolls.

We might generalize from all this, and conclude that boys grow up to have material and occupational loves, and women to have human and domestic loves, and to some extent we would be right. But again, such generalizations become hollow when we are dealing with human beings, because the pressures cross and crisscross. Some reinforce and some conflict with our personal configurations of wants and needs.

The Culture-Stamped Lover

Thus, although we all conform to some extent to the culture in which we live, some of us develop powerful and indeed dominating attachments to the idols of the marketplace, the goals that society defines for us. The right kind of neighborhood to live in, the right kind of man to marry, the right number of children to have, the very goal of getting married and having children become for some the unquestioned, inevitable attachments by which they steer their lives, regardless of whether these goals satisfy their true wants and needs.

Consider, for example, a child who has been punished time and again for the smallest disarray or disorder in his appearance, his room, his behavior. His hands must be always clean, his hair always combed, his manners always correct. Such a boy can grow up with an inordinate attachment to having everything in his life just so. Out of this attachment may grow others that reinforce and build on this aspect of his personality, even to his choice of an occupation. He may become a management engineer, a specialist in putting other people's business in order and setting up routines to keep them in order.

Such a man may have a lifelong attachment to things that are new and clean. He will move into an apartment or house only if it is newly built; it would never occur to him to buy a second-hand car. He will be attracted to a woman not for her warmth and love but rather because she is irreproachable in manners and appearance, with never a hair out of place. If he marries her he may well be happy with his choice, because she too is attached to the same principles of order and efficiency. Together they may create an immaculate, indeed an antiseptic household, marred only by the occasional disturbing eruptions of other needs of their personalities, needs which neither of these people can deal with in themselves or each other.

On attachments which have already been so deeply etched, socially acceptable goals find a ready soil. Such people tend to conform to whatever is socially correct in their group; any departure strikes them as bizarre. They behave as though they had a dread of standing out in any way, of attracting attention. They find safety in the protective coloration of conformity.

Loves Bad and Good for Us

Driven by the steady trade winds of our social environment, many of us do indeed lose touch with our own wants and desires. Some part of our individuality remains forever unasserted, and some attachments that might be better suited to our needs go by default.

Surveying these many ways in which we form attachments, we do not ignore the fact that some of our loves grow out of our conscious desires. We do make choices, whether or not they are always rational. And usually there is little profit in the effort to look beneath our rational justification of an attachment and trace it back to its origin. It is far more to the point to consider whether this or that attachment is good for us. An attachment may be quite irrational and still be good, or at least not harmful.

Some loves are so obviously against an individual's best interests that no one needs to tell him so; he knows very well that an excessive attachment to food, alcohol, tobacco is not good for him. A woman who becomes attached to a man for the prodigal way he spends his money to entertain her may find this attachment unfortunate, once they are married and his generosity turns out to be financial irresponsibility.

A man may fall in love with charming women, one after another, but never form a permanent attachment to any one woman; these light-hearted loves may be delightful and may even seem good for him, for he is never deeply involved and hence never wounded. And yet, a more stable attachment may be good in ways that he ignores. The difference in values is somewhat like a difference in taste; for example, people who enjoy only pop tunes need a new hit every month, while those who appreciate Bach can enjoy their attachment to the same music forever. The lovers who form a lasting monogamous attachment find satisfactions for needs far deeper than a series of casual relationships can ever touch. Furthermore, they are spared the empty, restive intervals between one love and the next.

A love is good for us when it satisfies a need and does so

without harm and without interfering with other good and healthy loves. Such loves make us feel free, able to choose, able to make decisions. We can forget such loves now and then, set them aside while we are otherwise absorbed, and come back to them with a pleasure untainted by guilt.

We need no elaborate rules of recognition to identify such loves. By the way they enhance and enrich our lives without leaving a bitter aftertaste, we know them as loves that are good for us.

A love that is bad for us may satisfy some needs, but it conflicts with the satisfaction of others, and the needs that it satisfies are likely to be neurotic ones. Such loves tend to enslave us, to command, compel, and possess us; we live hedged about by the fear of breaking the rules they set for us, as though we were living under a fascist government.

Sometimes, loves that are bad for us are not even recognized as loves. Let us consider a girl whose mother was always worried because she did not eat enough as a baby. Her mother's image of a healthy baby was a plump dimpled butterball, rosy and smiling. But this child was a colicky baby and then a wiry but underweight little girl, not dimpled, never rosy, and rarely smiling. Her mother took out her disappointment in anxiously trying to force food on the child, and the child retorted, as children will, by shutting her mouth tight or vomiting up her meal. Then at the age of twelve or thirteen she turned the tables and began to eat compulsively. Now when her mother (and to be honest, she herself) dreamed of a nymphlike figure and a creamy complexion, the poor girl is fat and dumpy and has a muddy skin. Now the same mother who once said, "You must finish what's on your plate before you can leave the table," is saying, "You must stop eating so much—you must go on a diet."

This is of course a sample of angry, hostile behavior, a protest against the mother who was never satisfied with her as she was. She has carried on this protest through all her life up to womanhood, sacrificing her own best interests for a victory she could never win. She has honed her figure down to a more attractive size but inside she is the same little girl, carrying on the same fight.

Anyone who has maintained a fighting attitude all through childhood is rather like an old-fashioned knight in armor, riding across the countryside with a lance, looking for dragons to kill. Our young woman finds a young man and marries him but nothing in the marriage vows dissolves away the hostility she has built up through the years. Sooner or later it will find an outlet, and where else but in her marriage?

And so her husband becomes the victim of a hostility for which he was in no way to blame. He had nothing to do with the protest, the anger, the rage that grew in her as she grew. All he has to do is disagree with her about the most trivial matter, anything at all, and unless she finds some way to resolve her hostility it may ruin her marriage, even though it is totally unrelated to marriage, to sex, or to her husband whom she may in fact love.

Love as a Battle

For fighting, too, is a form of love. We cannot assume that because two people fight they do not love. Freud, we must remember, said that love is an attachment. He did not say it was an attachment made in heaven. He did not describe it as romantic, poetic, idyllic. He did not compare it to a symphony or a sunset, nor did he say that it involved happiness or fulfillment. He called it, simply, an attachment.

The fortunate ones, of course, find fulfillment in love. They have enjoyed good early experiences, or have resolved the effects of bad ones, or perhaps a little of both. They find fulfillment in love, and they find fulfillment in their work—which is an attachment to a set of ideas or occupations or skills, and therefore also a love. They find fulfillment in play, in friends, and all of these are attachments, are loves.

All these are examples of love. The love that results in marriage, and a commitment to spend a lifetime with another individual, is only another kind of love, a more difficult kind of love than these others. We make a greater investment of ourselves in this love, and when we are successful we draw from it greater rewards. Other loves are easier. Friendship, for example, is easier to develop and easier to sustain because it is not so many-sided as sexual love.

Much love is negative in quality. The love between parent and child is very often a battle. When a child is well behaved and doing what he is supposed to do, he generally gets no attention. His parents are not likely to stop and comment on every act of obedience with, "You're a very good boy, Johnny." Not at all. The good child is invisible, inaudible; he might just as well not be there.

But the moment he does something wrong, then the spotlight is on him, he is downstage center, he is the star of the show. His parents scold him, spank him; if he is too big to spank or they are not the spanking kind, they devise dramatic ways of punishing him such as taking away his allowance or his Saturday afternoon movie or his favorite television show. They work hard at teaching him a lesson that he will remember.

And he does remember. He remembers all the drama, all the excitement of which he is the center, all the attention he gets for being naughty. And this becomes a pleasure. Even the punishment becomes a pleasure, compared with no attention at all.

In show business there is a saying that even bad publicity is better than no publicity. Obviously children would prefer good and loving attention; they would really rather have their parents' approval. They would like to be hugged and kissed and played with and have nice things said to them. But when they have been good and have earned all this good attention, perversely their parents ignore them. And so the children settle for the opposite, for anger and scolding and spanking and punishment, in preference to nothing whatever.

In the eyes of the child, this too becomes an expression of love. Any emotional expression is love whether good or bad, so long as it is not indifferent. For a child in whose life this kind of love has been predominant, this is the kind of love he will also recognize as an adult. Love for him is a battle.

Even for lovers who prefer not to fight, love is often a battle. The course of true love never does run smooth. When people say of their marriage that they have never had a cross word, we are inclined to wonder. Are they telling the truth? Do they really love each other? If they cared enough about each other they must have quarreled sometimes. Never to be angry, never to disagree at all seems to most of us a sign not of love but of indifference.

For between a man and woman making a life together, sharing a household and raising children, managing money and going through troubles as well as happy times together, love is no simple relationship. It involves the needs and desires of both, many of which they are not aware of, many of which they do not understand. Some of these needs cannot be perfectly satisfied even within a very good marriage indeed.

As two personalities meet in all the many aspects of a love relationship, naturally they sometimes rub each other the wrong way. Sometimes friction is the only way in which some unsatisfied need of one or the other becomes evident. A quarrel may be a most effective catalyst for some undefined dissatisfaction.

There are times when a man simply wants to be assertive with his wife. He feels the need to assert himself; he wants to show her, and perhaps himself, that he does not always have to be reasonable and ready to compromise, that he can sometimes put his foot down and keep it down. And there are times when a woman feels the same way, times when she wants to be stubborn instead of yielding, when she simply wants her own way, right or wrong.

The mere fact that there is a good deal of negative expression, of opposition and hostility, within a marriage does not mean that the partners are not attached to each other. There are many couples who spend years in bickering, get a divorce, and marry each other again. Or they marry other partners, but somehow they manage to keep in touch and keep on fighting with each other, about alimony or the children or the lawyers or an unpaid bill that goes back to their first year of marriage. Whatever it may be, they will find a way to make an issue of it and fight on for the rest of their lives. They may be quite peaceable with their new spouses, but with each other love is still a battle and they refuse to let it end.

Love is all these things, positive and negative, good for us and bad for us. It should make us happy. In its first manifestations, in infancy, love does bring happiness, contentment, bliss. It is only to the things that bring him pleasure that the infant becomes attached. His infant loves are simple and they are all positive, all pleasurable. But as he grows out of the hothouse shelter of infancy, out into the world of which he is no longer the center and where his wishes are no longer all-powerful, his loves become tainted with non-pleasure and non-happiness. He loves his parents but he also hates them, if for no other reason than that they make demands on him that go counter to his childish wishes. He loves his brothers and sisters but he hates them, too, because he must share with them everything including the most important thing, his parents' love. He loves and hates teachers, best friends, school, games, vacation, jobs.

Despite these considerations, many people find it hard to accept love merely as an attachment. By sheer habit of thought we continue to want to use the word differently. We like to think of love as a favorable or pleasant attachment or even as an ideal attachment between a man and a woman. Many people use the word so exclusively in the ideal sense that at best most mortal love enjoys only the merest glimmerings of the "real" thing. Furthermore, our desire for happiness, approval, and acceptance and the rich warm feelings associated with all this prompt us to imagine that love is the answer or the solution to these needs.

The result is to narrow our interest in love to only one kind: the durable, deeply satisfying attachment men and women sometimes develop toward each other. But this is as sweetly unrealistic as the garden sundial which reads, "Count none but the sunny hours." More sober thought must remind us that we live through twenty-four hours each day, gray or sunny, and that we grow older even during the ones we sleep away. Some of our lives have the bright quality of sunny hours, but we understand love better if we count them all, from the dullest and the most painful attachments to our richest partnerships of feeling.

Realistic thinking, then, suggests we agree that no human experience is perfect; no human being grows up without a flaw. The ideal, perfectly adjusted human being is a fiction, something we strive for but never in fact achieve. In everyone there are certain infantile attachments which remain with us, which we never shed although we have grown in age, in experience, possibly in wisdom. These attachments find their way into the pattern of our adult love.

Fortunately for us there are forces which pull us together even despite our imperfections. We cannot afford to wait until we are ideally ready for each other. One of the most impelling of these attractions which promotes our human attachments is sexual awareness.

CHAPTER FOUR

Sex With and Without Love

THE VERY FIRST thing we notice about anybody is whether that person is male or female. And it is the one thing we never forget! Name, telephone number, profession, politics—all these details may slip from our memory, but never the individual's sex. This we know even if we know literally nothing else about a person. Right from the start, when a new baby is born, the first question we ask is, "Boy or girl?"

Anything so deeply rooted in our habits of perception and memory must be important. Yet until a few decades ago sex could not be discussed in public. Even today, although our attitudes have been considerably liberalized, a blanket of censorship still lies over many of the mass media in regard to sex.

The nature of this censorship varies from one society to another. Many motion picture films made in Europe are made in three versions: a standard version for Europe, a somewhat looser one for Latin America, a considerably stricter one for the United States. Within these differences there are still other differences. In foreign films, for example, there is much more bodily exposure than in American films but much less kissing.

Island Ways

The larger the gap between two cultures, the more conspicuous are the differences in attitudes toward sex. Until World War II made the Pacific Islands a major battlefield and drew them into the Western cultural orbit, the islands were an anthropologist's delight. They were still relatively uninfluenced by our society, and the sexual practices on some of the islands were strikingly different from our own. When Margaret Mead's book *Coming of Age in Samoa* first appeared, readers all over the United States discovered that adolescent boys and girls there were not deterred but actively encouraged to engage in sexual intercourse. In our own country, this is the time when parents turn gray, not with age but with anxiety over the possible sexual activity of their teen-age children.

People were either enchanted or appalled at this Samoan revelation, depending upon their own bias in the matter, but they were also full of questions. What happened to all the illegitimate babies? What kind of marriage, what kind of promiscuous infidelity must have resulted from such a custom? They were further surprised to learn that few illegitimate babies resulted from these early relationships, and that infidelity after marriage was virtually unknown in Samoa. Many primitive peoples find premarital sexual activity acceptable, for girls as well as boys, but they punish adultery by death, sometimes preceded by the most grisly torture. Some ancient peoples stoned the adultress to death. Every society tries to make its own peace with the potent sexual drive.

Our attitude toward illegitimacy reveals a specific taboo not shared even by some cultures very close to our own. One of the most shameful disasters that can befall any woman in our society is to be an unwed mother. Yet in nearby Puerto Rico until fairly recently and still in some sections of the island today, babies are often born out of wedlock and the society has an accepted sensible, and humane custom for dealing with the event.

Some years ago at St. Luke's hospital I was examining a baby whose care required a slight change, and I was confused as to which of the people around me were the parents. Two were very young, a boy and girl in their early teens, and the third was an older man. None of them clearly seemed to be the parents of the baby. Finally I asked, and the man said, "Well, I'm the grandfather. No, I'm not really the grandfather, I'm the father." This added to my confusion, until he explained: he had adopted the child, but the boy, his son, was the child's father. The girl was the child's mother but not the boy's wife.

"They are too young to get married," the father-grandfather told me serenely. "We will not let them get married but they live with us and we are taking care of the child."

There was no shame attached to any of this. Obviously the

boy and girl were too young for the responsibilities of marriage but yet they were biologically old enough to have a child. So the head of the family had taken over responsibility for all three, and presumably none of them would be the worse for what had happened. This was common practice in Puerto Rico, to such an extent that many children did not know who their biological parents were. Yet they had parental care and parental love. No stigma attached to them and no harm had come to them, nor to their too youthful parents.

Such an arrangement is easily managed in the large clan-like family, embracing several generations, of the Puerto Rican and other cultures. It is not so long since our own culture was built on large family groups, and yet we can scarcely remember a time when an illegitimate child was not a bitter disgrace.

What is this powerful force, with which every culture in the world and throughout history has had to come to terms? What is sex, that leads to so many and varied suppressions, censorships and taboos?

Of course we know it is not merely the definition of a word that we seek in these questions. A dictionary is no more helpful in determining the meaning of sex than such other words as beauty, truth, or love. These are not simple words. They are more in the nature of concepts and as such derive their meaning from the theoretical framework within which they are used.

What Is Sex?

Sigmund Freud defined sex as the use of the body for the purpose of pleasure. The framework of this definition involves his whole emphasis on the importance of the early physical life of the child. Freud saw in these infantile vegetative activities—eating, eliminating, sleeping, etc.—the child's first satisfactions.

These were bodily pleasures which pre-dated the later genital pleasures of sex, but so strongly resembled them that, for all practical purposes, they might be classified together. This is essentially a way of saying that *all* the sensory delights we enjoy are so similar to our distinctly sexual ones that we may as well call them by the same name.

This, of course, would mean that a woman trying on the first fur coat she ever owned, running her hand over its surface in a long lingering caress, savoring its texture with every tactile nerve in her fingertips, was enjoying a sexual response. A child coming to the end of a chocolate ice cream sundae, diving into the dish, sinking his whole face into it to get the very last little bit of sweetness, is luxuriating in purely physical and therefore sexual pleasure.

On a somewhat more sophisticated level, a connoisseur with a fine glass of wine holds it up to study its color with the light glinting through, passes the glass back and forth under his nose to sniff its fragrance, sips it, rolls it around his mouth, and over his tongue caressingly. He has enjoyed the wine with his sight, his sense of smell, his sense of taste. He is using his body—or parts of it—for the purpose of pleasure. Employing the same parts of the body in a more traditional expression of sex is the long soulful kiss of young lovers, expressed most delicately on their discovery of love or at their first anguished parting.

All these sensory experiences Freud called sexual. Sex, then, might be said to be the use of the body for the pleasure of enjoying an attachment, an affection, a love.

As we commonly use the word, sex has more limited connotations. We may mean simply exercising the procreative function, the purely biological side of sex; or the exploration of the primary and secondary sex organs for the purpose of pleasure, a purely sensual interpretation. Or we may mean acting *as though* we were expressing affection, but in fact only using this as a cover for a strictly solo physical satisfaction derived with the help of a partner.

All these uses of the word have one thing in common: they all describe a kind of behavior expressing an inner drive or desire for pleasure, and seeking the satisfaction of that desire. Furthermore, in all its forms this behavior makes use of the body for this pleasure.

In all its forms—and sexuality takes many forms with or without the specific sexual act—there is one more ingredient, one that dominates the entire range of the individual's sexual expressions. That ingredient in his personality.

We said earlier that we could not study love without the lover. It is equally impossible to separate sexual behavior from the individual. Some people enjoy a rich sexuality, using to the fullest all the intimate senses—the senses of touch, taste, and smell. Lovers also enhance their pleasure with the distance senses; they love the sight of the loved one, the sound of his or her voice, even footsteps.

Poets of the past gave eloquent voice to this total sexuality.

Their writings enthusiastically suggest that they really drank the loved one's breath, tasted her lips, smelled her hair and her skin; that they heard music in her voice, feasted their eyes on her body.

People have noted a decline of sensuality in our time. An automotive and automated age may be saving us the use of our bodies for work but it may also be distracting us from its uses for pleasure. As a people we are suffering an impoverishment of the senses, and with it an impoverishment of our sexuality and of our capacity for enjoying and expressing love. Even our speech lacks sensory adjectives—everything is exclusively "great" or "terrible."

We tend not to dwell on our purely sensory delights, savor them, enjoy their verbal proliferation, in short, value them among the basic goods in life. We are discouraged from being gluttons and yet a certain amount of gluttony is necessary for sexual satisfaction. The fullest sexual response occurs in people who are in fullest touch with themselves physically. They cannot be enthusiastic solely about ideas. They respect their feelings and they accept and enjoy the physical expression of them.

Love Without Sex

There are expressions of love, of course, that are not sexual, even between lovers. Any act of kindness or thoughtfulness is an expression of love, positive feelings. A man expresses his attachment to his wife sometimes most effectively by corroborating her opinion or asking for her judgment; his expressed regard for her intelligence and wisdom strengthens her self-esteem, makes her feel valued, and thus he has performed a loving act toward her.

There are kinds of love from which sexual expression is simply and naturally excluded, such as friendship, the attachment and respect of colleagues at work, the relationship of parents with grown children. Young children, of course, need and usually receive a great deal of physical love from their parents. The parents do not ordinarily think of this as a sexual expression of their love, but in the children's development it is precisely that, and a very important step in their sexual development.

Love without sex is very familiar; we can all think of numerous examples of it. Sex without love is also familiar.

Now love without sex has social sanction. We understand it, accept it, feel comfortable with it. But sex without love does not enjoy the same favorable position in the values of many people. At its most extreme, for example, prostitution or commercial sex is generally regarded as a social vice.

However, we can accept, or many of us can, the idea of a hedonistic roll in the hay. We accept and enjoy the robust Falstaffian kind of sex, the hearty 18th-century sex in *Tom Jones*. We accept this kind of sex because it is not really sex without love, although it may be very transient love, a brief, perhaps even momentary, physical attachment. It is sex with mutual and shared enjoyment, a direct and uncomplicated use of the body for pleasure. In such light-hearted sexual encounters there is equally light-hearted love. Society may not approve, cannot afford to approve, since society requires stability and responsibility which these encounters lack. But humanly we are not too deeply disturbed by this kind of sexual behavior, because it does imply a kind of love if only for the moment. It is not sex in cold blood.

Some kinds of sex without love are not cold-blooded, but are even less satisfying, and psychological investigation bears this out. There are many powerful unconscious forces that drive some men and women into sexual behavior which seeks satisfaction for needs created a long time ago, which remain unresolved. Initially they are not sexual needs but unconscious emotional needs which have found a channel of expression in sex.

For example, there are women whose driving need is to arouse a man. Whether they accept or reject him is not important—and the more men there are, the better. Every generation has had a name for this kind of woman—coquette, flirt, tease. We can speculate on what drives her to behave this way. It could be narcissism, the pleasure of being desired and exercising power in both the attracting and the rejecting. It could be a way of avenging herself on the first man who rejected her, perhaps her father. Another woman arouses a man not to reject him but to enslave him, drive him into submission; she wants to dominate men, psychologically castrate them, and like the tease she also is using sex as a weapon, an expression of hostility.

Still other women unconsciously offer themselves to be taken advantage of by men and thus prove that men are no good.

They have repeated pregnancies and abortions out of marriage, and each time they are abandoned by the man and must deal with the problem, pay the bill, suffer the miserable experience alone. To anyone who will listen they say over and over that men are no good, and over and over they become involved in the same compulsive demonstration of the theme.

Some women will do anything for affection or approval, and being desired and made love to is a show of affection, however illusory. These are usually people suffering from a deep sense of unworthiness, like the girl who can't say no. Some become involved in repeated sexual affairs in an effort to prove their womanhood, about which they are unconsciously in doubt.

Nor are men exempt from using sex for unconscious and unrelated purposes. There is the obvious Don Juan who is driven to prove his adequacy again and again. A proposition that has to be proved again and again is not being proved at all, and yet he is compelled to demonstrate his sexual prowess of which he is never quite sure.

Some men take an opposite road and avoid sex for fear it will reveal their inadequacy. Some avoid it out of fear of arousing strong emotions in a woman; such a man is likely to be afraid of a woman's love, afraid of being dominated by it as he was in childhood, probably by his mother.

Sexual aversions take odd forms and are yet not entirely uncommon. A man may develop an aversion for kissing a woman, even the woman he loves, with the explanation that when the woman is sexually aroused she smells different. A healthy lover reacts in just the opposite way. He enjoys every aspect of sex including the scent of a woman's body. Peculiarities in a man's sexual behavior strongly suggest obscure forces other than simple sexual desire.

Sex is used by both men and women, but perhaps more often by men, as an expression of hostility and aggression rather than love. This has been a socially accepted custom in the past. It was a right of conquering soldiers to rape the women of the defeated city. We will have more to say about aggression in sex.

Some Social Distortions

We have been talking about abberations in sexual behavior that are highly individual, highly personal. There are cther ways in which a healthy sexual expression of love is thwarted, distorted, and in these it is society that is responsible.

We have said that every human society has had to find some way of controlling the powerful sexual drive. Our way is to suppress it as long as we can. Even though we know that children are sexual beings from birth, that all of a child's early physical experiences are likely to have some bearing on his happiness in sex and love for the rest of his life, we still find ways of pretending that it is not so.

We behave this way despite the fact that nowadays we are all acutely aware of the importance of educating our children about sex. We want them to learn about sex openly and honestly. We want to avoid the secrecy and the association of sex with naughtiness, with something forbidden and dirty. We institute programs of sex education in the schools.

Parent-teacher organizations have become very militant about this. They hold meetings, collect films and other teaching materials, and urge their school boards to incorporate a course in sex education in the curriculum. These are all very worthy efforts and they do succeed in liberalizing the subject of sex somewhat, but unfortunately they accomplish little more. For the content of all this sex education is the *biology* of sex. The biology of sex is a proper scientific subject or it may be an interesting intellectual excursion but it is a long way from helping us to understand sex as something in which feelings and emotions are concerned, or to develop healthy and happy sex lives.

We do not approach an understanding of sex by way of biology. When we tried earlier in this chapter to answer the question, What Is Sex? we drew several word pictures and there was not a word about biology in any of them. Many children who have dutifully attended these sex education courses have told us that they come out of the course feeling cheated. They learn a little anatomy and physiology but they still have not learned what they want to know, what they need to know about this powerful function that will play such a large part in their adulthood. Biology does not give them the formula.

What is the formula, then, for a wholesome sex life? From one point of view it is very simple; from another, most difficult. We can state it, for example, this simply: all we need for a wholesome sex life is to have an unadulterated appreciation of sex.

This is what is difficult to come by. The fact is that few people do grow up in our culture with their appreciation of sex unadulterated, unspoiled, uncontaminated by other attitudes. We bring with us into maturity a burden of inhibitions, fears, notions that sex is sinful, dirty, low, even disgusting and bestial. Few people can escape some degree of this contamination.

It is one of the prices we pay for civilization. Civilized peoples cover the sexual characteristics of the body with clothes, avoid talk of sex before children, and conduct sex relations strictly in private. In our society, children are ideally kept from seeing and from knowing anything about sex except what we choose to tell them and when we choose to tell it. In practice, of course, it does not work that way. We cannot keep children from seeing, from wondering, from wanting to ask.

Wrong Questions, Wrong Answers

The books about how to bring up children tell parents how to answer children's questions about sex. They even put down the words to use. But the parents themselves were brought up by the hush-hush method, and their parents before them, and it is hard to break down these old barriers.

Parents do try. They make a really conscientious effort. There was the little girl who came dashing in one day when her mother was entertaining a friend, and asked, "Mommy, Mommy, where do I come from?" And the mother, liberated from old-fashioned attitudes, ignored the presence of her friend, and launched into a thorough-going explanation of how babies are born. After about ten minutes of polite listening the little girl finally interrupted with: "No, no, Mommy—Jane next door says she comes from Boston and I want to know, where do I come from?" Sometimes, in their anxiety to do the right thing, parents answer the wrong question.

Many times parents realize that they have missed opportunities to explain things to their children and they become anxious lest the children grow up knowing nothing about sex. By the time a child is six or seven or eight, it is not uncommon for parents to take him to the pediatrician and say, "Doctor, you tell him."

A prominent New York City pediatrician tells this story of

one such occasion with a boy of about seven. He got the boy comfortably settled in a chair, and set about explaining the so-called facts of life. Once again the child dutifully listened, and when the explanation was ended he exclaimed, "But doctor, when I grow up I want to be a businessman!"

Children usually find that their questions are simply ignored, not answered at all, or else they are answered all too thoroughly. Either their parents shy away from the subject or they are altogether too solemn about it. The children feel that the subject is too complicated and they are not that interested, or it is something wrong and they had better not ask.

Long before they have words with which to ask, long before they are capable of understanding the subject with their minds, they have already been taught certain attitudes. Civilization has already made its impression. Our civilized custom of privacy, our civilized habits of shame and modesty, and our civilized sanitary arrangements have their combined impact on the child while he is still very young. He associates this part of his body with dirt and shame, and he reveals this association later when he learns the sexual function. The first shocked response of many children is, "My parents never do that. My father would never do that to my mother." This is very sad, for it tells us that the child begins by responding to adult sexuality as something dreadful, something unthinkable, something that good people like his parents would never do.

Sexual Pleasure and Guilt

The feeling that there is something wrong about sex is, in large part, produced and maintained by the guilt generated by our experience with masturbation. There appears to be little doubt that all children, as they discover their genitalia and the sensations they yield, go through a period of manipulation we call masturbation. Parents, of course, vary considerably in how they treat such behavior in their children. Some are openly horrified and punitive, many attempt some subtle discouragement, but very few parents, if any, greet such behavior the way they did the child's first steps. The fact is that although the books on child care mince no words in their disapproval of punishment, none of them point out that through masturbation

the child is discovering the pleasurable use of a highly significant portion of the body which later, we hope, will be used for
one of the deepest and most valid expressions of love.

Parents have not really been strongly encouraged to be completely bland about masturbation. Children inevitably feel that
something is wrong, and yet they remain attracted to the pleasure of self-exploration. Many children come to feel that what
they did was so wrong, they push it out of consciousness completely. By the time they become adults, they never remember
having masturbated at all. Their parents' disapproving glances
have also been completely forgotten. But the subject of masturbation remains distasteful and they are uneasy about it.

This does not stop people from masturbating once they are
grown up. They may no longer physically employ their genitalia, but their thoughts may continue to have the same mas-
turbatory quality as ever. The newsstands are flooded with
magazines designed to encourage and to indulge such mastur-
batory fantasies. We leave ourselves, as a result, with guilt—
sexual guilt—which continues to contaminate our attitudes
toward the use of our bodies for the expression of love.

Attitudes are extremely hard to change. Knowledge is much
more flexible; facts can be quite easily altered. If tomorrow we
were told that hitherto unknown records of Columbus's voyage
had been found, which proved he had discovered America not
in 1492 but in 1490, the change would be accepted at once.
The school books would be revised, the teachers would teach
the new date, and all of us would comfortably say for the rest
of our lives that Columbus discovered America in 1490. But attitudes have deep roots. They are entwined with emotions and
feelings. They cling like vines to our everyday patterns of behavior. They are not arrived at by the paths of reason, and
reason has little effect on them.

In due time the child's situation changes. He reaches adolescence, new stimuli arise within himself, and he finds encouragement for some new kinds of behavior among his peers. This
is especially true of boys as they reach adolescence. A boy may
still feel that sex is wrong, but after a few bull sessions he too
wants to be in step. In fact he finds that his status in the group
depends upon how far he can get with a girl, and he feels
obliged to boast about his success whether or not it is true. For
teenage boys it is a kind of Dun and Bradstreet rating. Their
tales of sexual exploits represent their dreams and desires more

often than reality but they feel obliged to recount their supposed adventures in full detail.

Sex for Status

At this point in a boy's life sexuality has little or nothing to
do with love. Sexuality is a mark of personal adequacy. Feeling
the pressure of the group to perform sexually, he goes out to
prove not how much he can love but how manly he is in the
terms in which he and his peers have come to define man-
liness.

This is far from plain sailing for him, for the pressure of the
group runs directly counter to a boy's inhibitions at this age.
On the one hand he feels that faint heart ne'er won fair lady,
and on the other that fools rush in where angels fear to tread.
He is afraid that if he is too aggressive sexually, any girl he
goes with will reject him. Even though he is out looking for
sexual adventure, he is not free of the attitude he has long
since formed toward sex—that it is not right, not nice. And any
girl with whom he can "make out" is not a nice girl.

Consequently, even today when we believe ourselves relatively free, adolescent boys think in almost Victorian terms
about girls. Nothing in the average boy's childhood, or the
average girl's, for that matter, counteracts the cultural pressures toward shame and concealment of the body, the cultural
associations with naughtiness and filth, that begin at the age of
two. By the time a boy is adolescent, these associations are too
deeply buried for him to be aware of them. Yet they go with
him into his first sexual experiences, and they color his attitudes toward the girl he goes with.

He makes the discovery that there are different kinds of
girls. There are the nice girls who will not tolerate any sexually
aggressive behavior, and then there are the girls you can have
fun with. The girls whom he feels able to approach sexually,
and who share his newly blossoming sexual desires, come to be
the girls he thinks less of, the girls he does not respect. And
this is sad, not only for the girl but for the boy and his future
sexual behavior in marriage.

For of course the girl he marries will be one of the "nice"
girls. These attitudes do not always persist into married life but
when they do they make trouble. Many a man is an ardent
romantic lover during courtship, during the engagement, right

up to the altar. Once inside the conjugal chamber, his performance falters.

This man loves his wife, but he does not know how to express his love sexually. *Up to this point he has had little
experience with sex as an expression of love.* He has had sex
only with girls with whom he would be unlikely to fall in love,
since he does not really approve of them. Now that he has
found his true love, and married her, he is at a loss. The
inhibitions he grew up with about sex, which he was able to
put aside only with a different kind of girl, now rise up to
thwart him. He would never be able to admit it, even to himself, but he is acting out the feeling he had as a small boy,
when he recoiled in shock at learning the facts about sexual
intercourse and said that his parents would not behave that
way.

This is one reason why many good husbands are poor lovers,
and many otherwise good marriages founder.

The Wife's Story

What about the wife's side of this story? Her childhood experience of modesty and secrecy has more than likely been
identical with her husband's. As she becomes adolescent, she
too has sexual desires although they are not aroused quite so
readily as with boys. This is partly because the female genitalia
are less exposed to stimulation, but there are also cultural
reasons.

The girl in our society is encouraged from childhood to accept the domestic role. Her mother is her natural model and
most mothers do what mothers have always done—they take
care of the house and the children. Most mothers, even today,
are not career women; the proportion of professional women
has remained static for decades, and it is very small. Many
women have jobs, and many need their jobs and the income
from them, but if they are married and have children they are
wives and mothers first and job-holders only secondarily. We
give our little girls dolls to play with; we encourage them to
play at being little mothers; this is the way our girls grow up.

Thus, in so far as we can generalize, girls tend to be more
conforming. They tend to accept the culture they know best.
With boys it is quite the other way. Young boys at play turn
their backs on their home and run as far as they can from it.

They play cops and robbers, or sheriff and outlaw, or cowboys and Indians, or Superman against the Martians, whatever fantasy happens to be in vogue at the moment. They do not duplicate in their play exactly what exists around them. They transcend it with heroic adventures and boundless accomplishments.

Girls sometimes manage to get themselves accepted in this kind of play, because girls also like exciting and even scary adventures. But a girl who succeeds too well in playing with boys gets the reputation of a tomboy, and as she grows toward puberty she is more comfortable in any event with other girls.

Typically, as we have said, little girls in their play duplicate the conventional domestic scene. And as they approach adolescence they accept more readily than boys the social inhibitions against any unconventional expression of sexuality.

We must not assume that they find it easy to do this. They build defenses against their own impulses and the boys' sexual advances, and one of these defenses is an especially interesting one. We have observed that boys during adolescence easily disassociate sex from love, that sex for them represents altogether different things such as status, manhood, personal adequacy. Girls, however, take the opposite path. They surround sex with an elaborate framework of love, a highly romantic framework. It is not surprising that the fairy tale age for girls is most intense in the years of approaching puberty. Many boys and probably a good many girls nowadays skip fairy tales entirely, but girls who do read them do so at the ages of ten, eleven and twelve. For the girl, the princess imprisoned in the tower, with a high wall and a moat, is a perfect symbol of her defense against sex. Only the prince who loves her enough to slay monsters, swim moats, scale walls and dare every peril for her sake can finally win her.

In other words, she defends herself against sex by insisting on a setting of love. Naturally it is more difficult to stimulate feelings of love than feelings of sexuality. Her demand for love is her armor against the purely lascivious onslaughts of the young male, to say nothing of her own blossoming sexual desires.

Yet her relationships with boys are beset with practical difficulties. Boys will not date her if she refuses to neck a little, if she will not let them "make out." The very line that boys use may be transparent to her but it is stimulating all the same even if untrue. In our unchaperoned automotive age she may not be able to keep up her defenses for too long, and meanwhile her fears of becoming pregnant reinforce her need for the framework of love. And so we have many youngsters going steady through high school and—ready or not—getting married as soon as possible.

These are the social and psychological pressures on a girl. Besides these, as we have seen, there are the many kinds of individual needs and unconscious forces that come to be expressed in sexual behavior. Together these form a complex pattern, driving many men and women down sexual pathways which represent neither their rational wishes nor what is best for them. These unconscious compulsions find sexual expression, but with little resemblance to the wholesome and forthright sex that is an expression of love.

CHAPTER FIVE

The Sexual Expression of Love

THE LANGUAGE OF the body has a quality of unmatched validity. Words, on the contrary, lend themselves to easy corruption. Not only is it easy to say things we do not mean but it is even easier to say things the meaning of which we do not know. The body has a more primitive unsophisticated mode of expression.

There is an old story told about a duke of long ago who had the doctor come to his palace to deliver his wife's baby. He was an extraordinarily devoted husband and when he heard his wife in labor call out how great was her pain, he enjoined the doctor to see her at once. The doctor coolly continued the game of cards he had begun to play with the duke to pass the time. Despite repeated pleas from the woman and her husband, he merely went on with the game with the brief remark, "Not yet." He repeated "Not yet" for many long hours until finally he heard not a plea for help but an inarticulate animal cry. "Now!" exclaimed the doctor, dropping his cards, and proceeded at once to deliver the baby.

Strong feelings find their clumsiest expression in human speech. The language of the body comes to our rescue because of the utter simplicity of its expression. A man's and a woman's hands reach out and touch. Silently they eloquently speak of their mutual awareness. An all enveloping bear-hug more deeply proclaims one's affection than even the prettiest words. A first-rate actor can move an audience to tears merely reciting names from the telephone directory. What we say moves us far less than how we say it. Acting it out, using the body gives any message its most deeply felt meaning.

This is exactly why sex is necessary for the deepest expressions of love. The affection we feel in a relationship is strongest when we act it out, when we use our body. This use of the body by a man and woman for the purpose of seeking and expressing satisfaction in each other is what we mean by sex.

In the attachments people develop, sex can figure prominently in initially attracting them to each other and in subsequently cementing them to each other through the fulfillment and pleasure sex offers. Yet in many relationships, sex is a disruptive force as well. It may appear where it cannot, for moral or other reasons, be expressed. Or sex may be abused by being dominated by selfish and even hostile motives.

Although sex can be love's greatest ally, sex is often an expression of much that is not love. Sex without love is a phenomenon easy to uncover in our American folkways. There are men's magazines that guarantee their sale by making the major theme of each issue some aspect of the bachelor paradise. They maintain a fantasy of perpetual adolescence, a kind of Peter Pan with sex.

But the phenomenon of sex without love does have a more subtle and peculiarly American ingredient. Characteristically we do not use our bodies for the expression of feeling. In our relationships with people we literally keep our distance from each other.

People of other cultures are considerably freer in expressing a relationship by direct physical contact. In some societies men traditionally embrace and kiss when they meet; Frenchmen used to, Russians still do. When two Arabs meet, they shake hands and each man with his free hand takes the other's arm; they stand thus and talk, linked together physically. The men of many countries walk together down the street arm in arm.

Americans do none of these things. They are not even great hand-shakers. Young European lovers walk with their arms around each other; even young Londoners and their girls do this occasionally, but not often American young men and their girls. A European takes his lady's hand and draws it through his arm; a Parisienne almost automatically takes a man's arm when she is walking with him. But an American husband holds his wife's elbow as they step off the curb to cross the street, and hastily drops it as they reach the other side.

Travelers have noticed that in a railroad station in India, if there are only twenty or thirty people in a large area they somehow manage to sit on the floor in the smallest possible space in the center, huddled together and bodies touching even though they are strangers to each other. In an American railroad or air terminal, at an odd hour when it is not crowded, a small number of people may be sitting in the waiting room and they are sitting as far apart from one another as possible. Americans habitually sit down a seat or two away from a stranger at lunch counters, at motion picture theaters, on park benches.

Americans maintain their physical distance. People from other societies find it hard to talk and even hard to do business across this distance. Characteristically Americans do not seek physical closeness, do not want to touch other people, do not enjoy the contact of bodies.

We go farther, as our drug store counters and toiletries advertisements reveal. We do not like to smell other human beings and we take every precaution in order not to let others smell us. The normal healthy odor of a human body, even as well showered and scrubbed as we usually are, is supposed to be unpleasant and possibly offensive. Marriage manuals recognize this, hence inevitable hints on feminine "daintiness."

Even if this is merely a superficial kind of cultural fastidiousness, it is obviously not easy to make the transition to the intense intimacy of lovemaking and the sexual embrace.

But in a people of such diverse cultural origins and backgrounds as we are, a pattern so widespread and characteristic is not likely to be merely a superficial overlayer. We could easily have broken through our physical diffidence if it did not express some deeper restraints. One could speculate that we keep our physical distance because we are afraid not to. Or one might suggest historically that when our Pilgrim forefathers brought to these shores the notion that cleanliness is next to godliness, they did in fact succeed in launching a nation which 150 years later would have more tiled bathrooms than any other country in the world. Cleanliness and its corollary, privacy, are unquestionably dear to us, but the price we pay for them may well be the habit of physical separateness. Perhaps this is one reason why we choose our own park bench instead of sharing one already occupied.

One could also argue that our intense early training in covering the body, in controlling and concealing its natural functions, has left us with a deep distrust of so many of the body's uses and especially its uses for pleasure.

The Body as a Weapon

Yet here is a revealing contradiction: we have no hesitation in using the body for aggression. Little boys learn very early how to fight—and if they do not, their fathers or even their mothers soon teach them. "Hit him back!" we tell the toddler in the playground. We cultivate the body-contact sports. We make heroes of prize fighters and urge our boys to go out for football even in high school. To the child it is clear that the most approved use of his body is for the expression of hostility.

Sex, we also know, can become a channel for many unconscious forces that may have little connection or perhaps none at all with sex itself. We cannot be sure whether the aggressive impulse is an integral part of sexual behavior. Freud suggested that it is. Others have believed that it is not. A lively debate has gone on in some circles over whether the human infant is born loving and learns to hate, or whether he is born hating and learns to love. For our purposes the debate is interesting but academic. Whichever we are born with, or whether we are born with either, the human infant learns both love and hate at such a tender age that they might as well be inborn.

The aggressive element in sex thus has powerful support. We do have hostilities, we do accept the use of the body as an expression of hostility, and the link between aggression and sex is firmly forged.

It is not an accident that our language itself reveals this linkage. Consider, for example, the word "seduce." In its sexual usage it means to impose one's sexual will upon another person in some deceptive fashion. The word has the same connotation in its non-sexual usage. People are "seduced" by propaganda or by advertising into doing something they do not want to do or buying something they do not want to buy. Its literal meaning is simply "to lead astray," but the seducer is not presumed to be doing this innocently or inadvertently. He does not have his partner's interests in mind, only his own. In every sense a seduction is an aggression, and the partner is no partner but a victim.

In the language of the street the link between sex and aggression is still more candid; indeed it is aggressively bold and forthright. To screw another or to be screwed may mean simply to have sexual intercourse, but in another colloquial use it means to take advantage of another or be taken advantage of. And in still another use ("Screw you!") it is an angry and scornful rejection. We need not press our language inquiry any further to make our point.

We have talked of sex as a channel to release tensions, and we might include here its use as a release for the tensions of frustration and boredom. An Italian film, *La Dolce Vita*, ended its bitter investigation of boredom with a joyless orgy. The final scene was a reduction of everyone and everything to sex, a common descent into a kind of sexual inferno without heat, without passion, without pleasure and most certainly without love.

Sex as an Aspirin

Psychologists long ago developed the thesis that often when the individual suffers frustration the result is a kind of blind rage. We see it illustrated in the child's temper tantrum. As we become older, the temper tantrum is no longer an acceptable outlet even to ourselves, and either we find a socially approved way to release our rage or we bury it. Boredom, and depression, can also produce the rage of frustration and be even more directionless and paralyzing, preventing the individual from taking any action in his own behalf. Sex, powerful in itself, easily opens the valve and releases into its own store of energies the pent-up energies of this buried blind rage of tension, depression, boredom.

None of these unloving motivations for sex produce reliably happy sexual experiences. At best they are harmlessly negative; they achieve relief, like taking an aspirin for a headache. Like the aspirin, they are temporary anodynes; like the headache, if there is a continuing cause the symptom will return. The tensions will gather again, and again they will need release.

For some people, indeed for many, the use of sex in this fashion adds the further tension of guilt. If we do not feel guilty, we at least experience distaste—we hate ourselves in the morning. Not everybody does, of course. There are "happy" bachelors who apparently have no hangovers from their loveless use of sex.

The Sexually Happy Individual

Who, then, is sexually happy? What is a sexually happy person or as psychologists phrase it, a sexually well-adjusted individual?

To begin with, he or she is a person who does not feel sex is dirty, who does not have fears about it, who accepts it as part of nature and of human nature and a natural source of pleasure. It is a person who is interested in sex, appreciates it, enjoys it.

But this interest does not exclude all other interests. An exclusive interest in sex is a preoccupation with it, an obsession with it, and this as we well know is not happiness or good adjustment at all but something approaching sickness.

The sexually happy person is happy in other pursuits as well. He has other interests, other drives, other sources of pleasure. He has managed to develop a balance among all of his desires and needs, in which sex has its place and possibly even a large place, especially during early adulthood, but not by any means an exclusive and all absorbing place. It is the harmony of the whole that we call, again to use the deliberately uncolored psychologists' term, a good general adjustment. A harmonious life is what the ancient Chinese and the ancient Greeks in their wisdom called a happy life. The enjoyment of sex is obviously part of this harmonious happiness.

Next, he accepts his sexual role in life. Now we know that although the external physical characteristics of sex are explicitly of one sex or another, within the individual the separation is less precise. The body works by delicate balances. Every male glandular system produces a small component of female hormones, and every female system a proportion of male hormones. In the personality the shading is even more subtle, because here we have psychological refinements added to the physical. We have all the individual's own responses to his individual experience, his individual environment. And we have the influences of the culture in which he lives.

Yet the net sum of all these is either a male or a female. If one is born male, one is predominantly a man; if a female, one grows up to be predominantly a woman. Accepting one's sexual role in life means that a man accepts doing things as men do them, a woman as women do them.

We mentioned earlier that we recognize and remember maleness and femaleness no matter what else we recognize or remember about an individual. We can go further, and observe that virtually everything we do has either a masculine or a feminine quality in the way we do it. The way we walk, talk, sit and stand, the way we dress and undress, some even say the way we think is either male or female. When we see feminine mannerisms in a man or masculine ones in a woman, we become confused; we may wonder if the individual is a homosexual. And the chances are that such a person's confusion in life is even greater than ours in merely regarding him.

With a sexually happy individual there is no such confusion, either in external mannerisms or in inner feelings about himself. The sexually happy man would rather be a man and the sexually happy woman is happy to be a woman. Either of them may complain now and then about the advantages of the other's position or the disadvantages of his or her own. It is not long, as history goes, since women made a considerable protest and nullified a good many of their disadvantages in society. There are still many inequities, and both men and women are still often confused about which role they are playing, for example, in marriage and the rearing of children. Socially the male and female roles are less clearly defined today than is perhaps good for us.

Yet basically and in all the major essentials, sexually happy men and women are in no doubt about which is their role. What is more, they accept their role, and enjoy it to their utmost capacity.

Feelings Versus Behavior

We come now to the feelings of the sexually happy person. Despite the vast amount of information in Dr. Alfred Kinsey's two-volume work on the sexual behavior of the human male and female, our understanding of our sexual patterns is not greatly advanced without an equally comprehensive investigation of our feelings, attitudes, and thoughts about sex. What we do about sex represents only a fractional part of our total concern with it.

Even in biblical days, Jesus cautioned that "He who looketh upon a woman to lust after her, hath committed adultery with her already in his heart." In modern terms that is to say that the individual suffers conflict as a result of secret desires even if he merely glances at the object of them. Since he has done nothing overt, he does not have to account to anyone; he has not injured anyone. In the eyes of the world he is guiltless. In his own eyes he may not be so.

The law, which is an authorized arm of society, takes the social view. If you were walking down Pennsylvania Avenue, angry with the government and thinking you would like to burn down the White House, no one would molest you, no one would threaten to lock you up. But if you were walking down the same street and idly threw a lighted match on the lawn, at once a plainclothes policeman or secret service man would confront you and demand, "What are you trying to do? Burn down the White House?" You would protest your innocence but he would point to the fact; you threw a lighted match over the White House wall. He might not lock you up, but he would certainly rebuke you and caution you not to do it again.

The law punishes us not for our thoughts or feelings but for expressing them, for our behavior. We can be punished for expressing hostility in threatening letters even though we may never carry out the threat, because writing the letter is a performed deed. We may think murder, wish murder, even plan murder in our minds, but as long as we perform no act the law has no interest in us. Society does not punish us for wishing.

We are much harsher with ourselves. We punish ourselves not only for what we do but for what we think, what we feel, what we want to do but never actually do. In our lives we are subjected to great sexual inhibition, and at the same time great sexual stimulation, and the combination of these contrary elements acts like mutually activating chemicals. Like fumes rising out of the test tube, the mixture sends up clouds of sexual wishing and desiring which are not and often cannot be acted upon.

Thus it is important to examine the sexual feelings of an individual. His sexual behavior is significant but his sexual feelings are also significant because they register his satisfactions or dissatisfactions. Feelings set the tone and atmosphere of every act. Two people making love may engage in the same kind of lovemaking behavior, but their feelings may be at opposite poles, and thus to each one the sexual act has opposite significance, opposite values. Even seduction—aggressive acts, as we have seen—can be performed tenderly, considerately, apparently lovingly. In fact it usually is, to be successful. But in the seducer's heart it is not an act of love. It is an act of deception, of hostility.

What are the feelings of the sexually happy lover? They are feelings of love, of the acceptance of his attachment to the sexual object. Sex, the use of the body for pleasure, began with our earliest infant experiences, the sensory experiences of the satisfaction of our bodily needs. And love began at the same early, primitive stage as an attachment to that which gave pleasure. Sex is linked to love, not for moral reasons, not as an excuse to indulge in physical pleasure, not out of guilt because society disapproves otherwise, but because they were linked together in their very origins. Thus in physically expressing his attachment to the woman he loves, the lover is tapping the deepest sources of his being.

The very forms of sexual expression echo those profound origins of love as an attachment to the source of physical pleasure. When we tried to define sex in the previous chapter, we sought simpler expressions in other sensory experiences— in the pleasure of a woman stroking her first fine fur coat, of a child diving into a chocolate sundae. These sensory pleasures are sexual in the large sense, even though they do not involve the primary erogenous zones. The pleasures of a warm tub, a splendid dinner, a fast downhill ski run, a massage, a ride in a roller coaster, are sexual in this sense.

In the act of making love, many sensory pleasures contribute which also do not involve the primary erogenous zones. Lovers who are rich in the physical expression of their love develop a wide range of sensory pleasure in each other, and the longer and closer their attachment, the freer and more deeply satisfying are these physical endearments.

When people laughingly say that sex is here to stay, they are acknowledging its power over us, not only because of the strong desires it generates but also because of the profound satisfactions it can deliver. An attachment to a human being of the opposite sex potentially offers the maximum physical pleasure; no comparably satisfying way of using the body has yet been discovered. The sexual expression of love brings satisfaction to the loved one, to the self, and to the strongest feelings of attachment that we know.

People who are attached to each other express this attachment by winding their arms around each other, by getting as close as possible to each other, by exploring each other with all their senses. They want to be with each other exclusively; they want to shut out the world and fill their consciousness solely with each other. The complexities of adult life, of living together and managing household, children, money, of sharing intellectual and social enjoyments, all these aspects of life that have bound them to each other are for the moment transcended in the total physical satisfaction of the sexual embrace.

The sexually happy person is in harmony with himself here, as he is in other respects. For him, sex and love go together. His sexual feelings are loving feelings.

This does not mean that sex is the only way in which he expresses his love. Love is a much broader word than sex. Love has many forms of expression beside the physical. Two music lovers may sit for hours, not listening to a bar of music, merely talking about music, but they are enjoying their love of music all the same. Similarly, we express love a thousand times, in many different ways, for every time we express it through sex. But when we do engage in sex, then we engage in it as an act of love. That is, we do so if we are sexually happy individuals.

The Sexual Ways of Love

The sexual expression of love is not easy to study. We see the failure of many marriages and we often jump to the conclusion that the failure is probably sexual, but we may be wrong. In many marriages it is the love that is weak. Many a couple remain married, and live and work together in apparent harmony, but they may not accept their love together to the same degree. Theirs is a kind of domestic arrangement rather than a strong attachment to each other which they enjoy. In many marriages, sex occurs as a demand and an obligation rather than as a continued desire to express the attachment they have for each other.

If we remember that sex is the body's way of expressing love, then we can trace its forms of expression. We can trace them in our own and others' experience; the artists and poets have given us most eloquent evidence of them.

Lovers have an awareness of each other, a *physical* awareness, and by the same token a heightened awareness of themselves experiencing this awareness of the other. Two people walking down an empty, lonely beach together may be just two people, enjoying the sea, the sky, the wind, the sand under their toes. If they are lovers, they may be enjoying all this but what they are most intensely aware of is that they are enjoying it together. They are enjoying each other's enjoyment as well as their own.

In a room full of people this may not be so easy. They may not even see each other through the smoke. Yet lovers may be aware of each other, even in a crowded room, as Ezio Pinza told us so convincingly when he sang "Some Enchanted Evening" in *South Pacific*. If we have not been so fortunate as to experience it ourselves, we have observed others who did. Some husbands and wives are always somewhat aware of each other at a party, even without realizing that they are.

Some, of course, watch each other like hawks, out of jealousy, hostility, possessiveness, competitiveness. There is love in their relationship in the sense that they feel and endure some kind of a strong attachment to each other. But there is little pleasure in it for them. Physically, they remain leaden, their sensitivity dulled. On the other hand, people who find pleasure in their attachment to each other, enjoy an increased awareness of each other, an increased enjoyment of the other's enjoyment, a greater concern for the other's comfort and wellbeing. Frequently each one knows when the other is ready to leave a party, without any signal or overt sign.

This heightened physical awareness of another is a sexual phenomenon. It is one of the body's ways, by sense and perception, of expressing love.

This physical awareness seeks communication. They speak to each other, share their thoughts, share their plans and dreams. And they touch each other. They stroke, they caress, they kiss.

In this physical communication of love, the lovers are restating their ideal of acceptance and satisfaction in the most personally valid form. This is what they knew from the start, what they first experienced as babies; this is what they have continually longed for at each age and at each new level of maturity. They recognize in this a language they learned long before they could speak, one that is far more powerful in expression than any spoken language with all its benefits of syntax and grammar. This is the ancient, unchanging physical language of love.

In this language they come to feel free. They are able to express a whole range of moods and feelings. Their sexual behavior does not always follow the same pattern. Like any true language, it has a vocabulary for its expression. Sometimes one of them feels like loving, the other like being loved; sometimes one takes the active role, sometimes the other. Sometimes they are frolicsome, imaginative, serious, playful, tender, stormily passionate. In their sexual love they develop the same freedom of expression together that people ideally enjoy in what we call freedom of speech.

The love of man and woman is incomplete without this sexual expression. Some of the most eloquently expressed loves in history and literature were never physically consummated; we may well suspect that for this very reason they were not the most profound loves. They were loves of hope, promise, loves of an idea or fantasy of the loved one but not loves in reality.

When Sexual Expression Falters

A man who says "I love you," but draws away from the loved one's touch, may want to love but be unable to, because other loves or attachments conflict. Or he may simply be lying. In either case he does not actually love, or he would love with his body as well as with words. The body is as much a part of the individual as the mind, the emotions; the personality expresses itself through all its elements. We may fool ourselves with words but the body does not easily deceive. The physical language of love may well be its most honest and valid expression.

Unfortunately our social customs are so powerfully repressive in this area that many of us grow up scarred and invalided and find it difficult to free ourselves for the sexual expression of love in adulthood. The young husband who has known sex only with girls he did not respect finds it hard to give full expression to his love for his wife, whom he does respect. The young wife, who has spent her girlhood years keeping sexually aggressive youths within the bounds of propriety, finds it hard to discard her fears and inhibitions automatically with the acquisition of a wedding ring. When both approach their sexual relationship with such hesitation, the probability is that the wife, at least, will not achieve much satisfaction.

Women today expect to enjoy complete sexual satisfaction, and many are deeply disturbed when they do not experience orgasm. This is of course a comparatively new development in sexual attitudes; earlier generations of women had no such expectations. Nowadays a failure to reach climax with her husband raises in a wife's mind the spectre of frigidity, of neurosis. She may think her husband is to blame, but if he is loving and attentive she is left with no one to blame but herself. The more anxious she becomes, the less chance she has of reaching the peak of satisfaction.

A good deal of confusion surrounds the subject of orgasm, or physiological climax in intercourse. The fact that the physically healthy male reaches climax and ejaculation does not necessarily mean that he always enjoys a sense of fulfillment. Sexual fulfillment is more than merely physiological climax. A man may feel as restless, searching, and unsatisfied a few minutes afterward as he did before. Or he may feel detached, indifferent, with little of the deep, glowing sense of satisfaction and tranquility that we mean by fulfillment. He may even be sunk in guilt, shame, loathing for the experience.

A woman, too, may experience these feelings which are very far from fulfillment, even though she has reached the physiological climax in orgasm. And the reverse is equally true: a woman may not reach orgasm and yet feel happy, satisfied, deeply content in the closeness of physical attachment to the man she loves.

A woman's disturbed feelings about her failure to reach orgasm may actually be the result of other disturbing factors. She may be troubled by something in her marriage not related in any way to the sexual relationship. She may be self-conscious or discontented with some aspect of her husband's lovemaking, and be unable to tell him so. Almost anything that troubles her is easily channeled into her dissatisfaction with her sexual experience, and so her failure to achieve orgasm absorbs and is intensified by all her other dissatisfactions.

Honesty and Sexual Fulfillment

A full and mature sexual relationship is many-sided; it expresses many aspects of the personalities, the moods and feelings of the lovers, many nuances of their attachment. The sexual expression of their love cannot be performed by rules. We cannot write an etiquette of sex as we can of social behavior. Books that describe a variety of sexual acts or positions of intercourse have value only in that the authority of the printed word helps to liberate our attitudes toward sex. But ideally people in love feel entirely liberated with each other. They have no urgent need for diagramming their sexual life together. They act as they feel with each other and generally their feelings are of positive attraction and desire for each other.

A rich and mutually satisfying sexual relationship involves a willingness to shed reserves and be completely oneself; this obviously requires a feeling of freedom with one's love, a sense of being accepted. If either of the partners does not enjoy this confidence in other aspects of the relationship, it is extremely difficult to enjoy it in sex.

Sometimes people find themselves joined together in a marriage having little to do with romantic love. They may learn to accept each other and live together in reasonable comfort, but their sexual relationship may not have much to express in terms of positive attachment; it may be a mere dutiful routine and release of tension. When two people have a positive attachment, a satisfying love for each other, they try to enjoy each other in every possible way. They help each other, take care of each other, laugh together, sit together, walk together. They dance and play and roll up into a ball together; they delight in being together. Husbands and wives who habitually take separate vacations obviously do not delight in each other very much, or they would hoard their vacation as a time of special pleasure to enjoy together.

When people reach adulthood with many negative attachments, they may not know how to cultivate positive ones. They may begin a particular love positively enough, but eventually they succeed in grinding it down to the kind they are most familiar with, the negative kind of love. Spoiled though it is, they may continue their relationship for many social and psychological reasons, but they can no longer take much delight in each other, and under such circumstances they are not likely to maintain much of a sexual relationship.

Sex may falter even when there is a positive attachment, but the difficulties then are likely to be transient. With young lovers the obstacle may be merely a lack of experience. Also, the role of sex in our lives changes with age, with experience, with events. During a time of intense absorption with other things we can be almost oblivious of sex. We can put aside sex entirely, or many of us can, during a period of separation from the one individual whom we love and to whom we have deeply committed ourselves.

The sexual expression of an attachment varies with the incidents of a lifetime, and these are sometimes happy, sometimes not so. So long as the attachment remains strong and positive, its sexual expression can always be renewed and refreshed. A purely physical, sexual attachment cannot substitute for the many-sided love in which the whole personalities of both partners are engaged. A rich sexual expression of love is worth nurturing for the depths of its satisfactions, and for its power to weld a positive relationship ever more strongly together.

CHAPTER SIX

Our Basic Love: Self-Love

THE WORD LOVE has a fine sound. It glows with warmth and beauty and even heroism; if it brings grief rather than joy, at least its grief has grandeur. Love honors the lover and on occasion it may glorify him. Even on a modest scale, love has agreeable overtones. It need not suggest the grand passion of literature nor the devotion and sacrifice of a parent for a child; it may be no more than a love of strawberries out of season. Yet it is a pleasing word—until we slip a prefix ahead of it and call it self-love.

Instantly the whole tone of the word changes. All our pleasant associations with love vanish in the blink of an eye, and an ugly troup marches across our minds: selfishness, vanity, coquetry, egocentricity, greed, avarice—the list is long and all of it is disagreeable.

In this chapter we hope to dismiss these unpleasant associations and explore the idea that self-love has another side. Perhaps we need the love of self; perhaps we cannot do without it. We may even discover that it is our basic and essential love.

Intellectual Sleight-of-Hand

Now the philosophers have bandied about many interpretations of self-love, and on a dull weekend any good logician can entertain himself with the argument that there is no other kind of love. He can prove that every fine human endeavor is in the last analysis only another expression of self-love—the patriot who serves his country, the humanitarian who wants to improve man's lot, the prudent father planning for his children's future, all can be shown to be expressions of self-love. The lover enjoying the company of his loved one is a prime example.

To reduce love to these terms is to commit the same fallacy as the wit who says, after hearing a fine violin concerto, "A mere scraping of horsehair on catgut." Or the viewer of a beautiful painting who comments, "Nothing but a collection of chemical pigments." Elsewhere in the study of logic, we are reminded that this is fallacious explanation by reduction. The cathedral at Chartres and the Parthenon of Athens can also be described—very inadequately described—as mere stones piled one upon the other.

The subject of logic reminds us of still another thought common among dialecticians. In their very meticulous analyses, they make a distinction between necessary and sufficient conditions. Air is necessary for life, but not sufficient to live on. It is necessary that charity begin at home, but by no means sufficient if it ends there. The same is true about love. It does in fact begin at home with the love of the self. This much is inevitable. But unless we come to accept and enjoy this primary attachment, all other subsequent loves suffer. When our emotional growth is unhappy and impaired, we become enslaved by the demands of self and enjoy neither being by ourselves nor being with others. A more favorable attitude toward the self, then, becomes a necessary condition for the enjoyment of the love of others. We build all our other loves on the love we have for ourselves, and the quality of all our other loves depends upon the quality of this initial love.

The Unloved Self

Let us glance once again at how love begins. It is, as we have seen, the infant's first attachment, an attachment to himself, his own sensations and his own body. This is inescapable because he himself is his whole world; there is nothing else. Everything of which he is aware is at first part of himself. His mother's breast, his mother's hand—at first these also are part of himself. He cannot distinguish the boundaries of his own person.

Weeks pass before the baby can make the simple physical distinction between himself and not himself, before he knows his fingers and toes as his own, and his mother's hand as not his own. And to develop an image of his whole self, a sense of his own identity as an individual, takes several years. During this time he not only discovers his identity; he discovers it already colored by the values his parents have given it. He discovers not merely a self separate from others but a good or bad self, a self that wins smiles or frowns, friendly voices or angry ones.

In other words, we begin to think well or poorly of ourselves at the same time that we learn to recognize the very existence of ourselves. Our initial attachment to ourselves begins tinged with positive or negative feelings.

This is a most significant development, so significant that if an individual goes into therapy many years later much of the time spent in his therapy is concerned with this same matter, namely his self-image. Many therapists' offices have two doors, one by which the patient enters and a second by which he leaves. There might well be a sign over each of these doors; over the entrance door the sign could read, "Through this door pass the people who think too little of themselves," and over the other, "Through *this* door pass the people who think better of themselves." There is no therapy without an increase in the value that one places on oneself. It is the cornerstone of what we call good adjustment.

This improvement in one's self-opinion may of course be an artifact, a superficial product and not a genuine development from within. Sometimes after a month or two or, unfortunately, a year or two of analytic treatment, a patient talks egotistically, boastfully, as though he were the most important individual in the world. He displays his improved self-opinion like a banner; he parades it with a brass band.

Obviously, if he must shout his importance in everyone's ear, he does not believe in it very much himself. This kind of demonstration is much like what therapists call a "flight into health," in which the patient's symptoms sometimes disappear almost as soon as he steps into the doctor's office. We all recognize that this improvement is illusory and transient. So is a loudly proclaimed self-importance.

On the other hand, the undervalued self is revealed in a huge variety of ways, ranging from the most ordinary to the most striking. A beautiful woman may think of herself as plain, even ugly. She shows it by dressing dowdily; in her own eyes she is not worth the expense of dressing well, and so she wears only the most drab, commonplace clothes.

A highly capable man may remain unconvinced of his abilities although he has made a fortune. He may remain in constant fear of losing all his money, his credit and standing, and wind up a pauper. Performers of many kinds, especially opera singers, often live in terror of suddenly being deserted by their gifts.

There are many other people whose fears are even more intense, specific, and less rational. Although these phobias are familiar enough by name, their origins are generally clouded in a long complex etiology. Yet a person dominated by one of these fears is in essence someone who cannot manage some particular situation unless he is taken by the hand and conducted safely through it. This kind of situation uncovers a truer image of himself: he sees himself almost as no more capable than a baby. His terror at finding himself in this special set of circumstances strips him of all his adult defenses and shows the quivering, helpless child he deeply feels himself to be.

Also revealing of a poor self-image is daydreaming. The habitual daydreamer likes himself so little that he would rather be someone else, and when left to himself for a moment he quickly becomes someone else. Although few people dream so splendidly as the fictional Walter Mitty, many people reading about some celebrity will say to themselves or even aloud, "Wouldn't it be great to be that person!"

These are merely a few of the many ways in which negative feelings toward the self are expressed. Such behavior falls roughly into two major categories. The first is underperformance or the inability to live up to one's potential. Faint heart never won fair lady not because of a lack of personal attractiveness but because of a lack of personal conviction. The person who thinks poorly of himself shrinks his aspirations to a level below his ability and even his ability is frequently impaired by the distraction and discouragement of his intense self-concern.

The second major category of responses characteristic of the under-valued self might be labeled a sense of unworthiness. This is more than modesty or humility; it is downright self-deprecation. Deep down inside, Cyrano believed his nose made him unworthy of a beautiful lady. He could express his love for Roxanne only when concealed in the shadows of the night and mostly through the more elegant looking young

Christian. If "many a flower is born to blush unseen," it is largely because anyone who does not like himself is apt to retreat in advance from his own fear of rejection.

The self we live with is our own, and how we live with others is no better or worse than how we live with that self. We may blame others for the disappointments we suffer, but we would be just about as happy or unhappy without the people we blame. Certainly we hate to admit all this about ourselves, but if we did not have these people to blame, we would find others. The tone of our daily life is set not by our stars nor by most external influences, but by the attitude we have toward ourselves.

This attitude colors our relationships with people, and the more important the relationships, the more marked the coloration. When we are romantically attracted to someone, our relationship is initially dominated by desire and longing. But as the attachment develops and we invest more of ourselves in it, then the feelings we have about ourselves inescapably come to dominate the relationship.

It is natural at first to idealize a woman but if a man thinks poorly enough of himself, this very idealization may be enough to frighten him away. In his own eyes he is not worthy of such a desirable woman, and he may not be aggressive enough to capture her.

Another man, because of his poor self-image, may be pleadingly seductive enough to win the girl. But his impoverishment of self will become the major binding force of the relationship. The only kind of love he seeks is a love that will look after him and take care of him. The only kind of love he can offer is dependent love.

Dependent love may be strong; sometimes it is strong enough to strangle the loved one. But its strength is no measure of its richness. It is love within a single dimension: one leans and the other is leaned upon. But other needs are left wanting. There is no many-sided exchange, no genuine sharing in this kind of love; one is forever taking, the other forever giving.

The Grammar of Love

Every sentence must have a subject, and in the grammar of love the subject is the lover. We promised in our first chapter that, unlike the Cheshire cat who vanished, leaving nothing but his smile, the lover would not be allowed to disappear from our study of love. We do not intend to let him slip away. He is the subject. But in the sentence that begins, "He loves," there is also an object.

What or who that object will be depends upon the lover's age and experience. At first, as we know, the object is himself. And this object—this idea of himself—remains the primary one through his years of development to maturity.

Through all these years—infancy, childhood, adolescence— the lover is developing his self-image, creating an identity for himself. He tries on a variety of identities as he goes along; hence the daydreaming of which we spoke earlier. He looks for models in history, story books, and in the world around him. He develops crushes on teachers, athletic coaches, older friends, school heroes and heroines. His first heterosexual attachment is still primarily an expression of his attachment to himself. As we shall see in our exploration of romantic love, the lover at first loves his own image of the beloved, not the beloved herself.

The child takes his first self-image from the way he is mirrored to himself by parents, by family. We noted in an earlier chapter how a child can develop a poor self-image, how he can come to see himself as unlovable, and thus fail to develop a pleasant attachment to himself. How does he develop a good self-image, a self that he can love?

The Attitude Toward the Self

As parents we are urged to give our young child all possible encouragement. He is so often inept, so often frustrated by his own inadequacy, and in addition so much of our function as parents lies in restraining, admonishing, civilizing the little animal, that we must seek and even manufacture occasions to praise and approve him. He needs an abundance of praise and approval if he is to build up a healthy valuation of himself as a person.

We give our young child opportunities for self-expression, in order to serve that same end. We exaggerate his achievements; we celebrate his first shaky steps, repeat his first tentative words. We praise his crayon scrawls and poster-paint pictures. We tell him how good he is, how remarkable; he will be president of the United States, president of the whole world. While he is still only marginally in the real world, still encircled in our protective embrace, we can afford to be unrealistic with him. He thrives on it.

As the child's world grows larger, these unrealistic elements begin to filter out of his image. He goes to school, and although until this point he has been told how remarkable he is, he finds now that many boys and girls are brighter at studies, more skillful at games. He discovers that after all he is not remarkable but merely an average child, in the middle of his class.

Does this discovery shatter him? Not at all, if his parents are wise. They no longer tell him he is the brightest student, and then drive him to prove it by standing over him while he does his homework or scolding him when he brings home something less than straight A's on his report. They love him and think he is doing fine when he is in the middle of his class. There are many boys and girls in the middle of the class, lovable boys and girls; he is in good company. His parents encourage him to enjoy himself at school and with his friends.

School is of course competitive, an early experience of the competitive society in which the child is going to live. But his parents have been his first and most constant interpreters of that society, and their attitudes remain a powerful influence. The image of him that they convey is the one he is most inclined to accept. He goes out into the world feeling that it is nice to be himself, the world is a nice place to be, and life is likely to be nice on the whole.

With such an attitude toward himself and the world, even the competitive school life into which he is suddenly plunged cannot shake him too severely. We noted earlier how the child who is under constant criticism from a perfectionist mother unwittingly invites similar criticism outside the home, how his teachers, his friends' parents also find him sloppy, unreliable, irresponsible. Although he hates to be treated this way, his behavior makes such treatment almost inevitable, and his unfortunate home experience is repeatedly reinforced outside the home. In modern learning theory, psychologists would call this "conditioning"; folk wisdom says tersely, "Give a dog a bad name."

A Sunny Climate

The same holds true with the child who has had a sunnier climate in which to discover himself, a climate that was more approving than disapproving, more encouraging than critical. He too will find reinforcement for his developing image of himself. He may be only average in his school grades, but because he has a sunny face his teachers tend to smile and encourage him instead of frowning and reproving. He may not be the best player but his classmates welcome him in games because he is a good teammate and likely to be a good sport. Even if he strikes out or misses the pass, he takes kidding and criticism well because essentially he is at ease about himself. He does not need to be perfect and above reproach in order to feel accepted and loved.

If he discovers that there are limits to his abilities in one or another direction, he also discovers that he has certain skills. He may be a poor batter but a good enough base runner; he may be slow in reading but quick in arithmetic. He may be such a dependable and cooperative lad that his classmates elect him to committees, and may even elect him class president. Or he may be so lively and imaginative that he gets parts in all the school plays.

Thus even from the tough, realistic society outside the home such a child can draw reinforcement for his good image of himself. This is not to say that all his experiences are happy— quite the contrary. He suffers as many disappointments as any other child, as many frustrations and setbacks. He goes through hard times that may shake his belief in himself for short or long periods. Like every boy and girl, he has to learn that the world is not his oyster.

But he is not likely to be overwhelmed by his disappointments. Unlike the child who begins with a poor opinion of himself and sees in every misfortune a confirmation of it, such a youth is buoyed up through stormy seas by the confidence that he can somehow make it safely to shore. For him the sun is sure to shine again. He will survive and that is confirmation of his feeling of strength.

In a word, he feels adequate. And with this sense of his own adequacy he can forget himself and enjoy the world, people, things.

Riches to Share

Anyone who has a reasonable feeling of adequacy about himself is a pleasant person to be with. He is not given to complaining about his lot and the way the world treats him. He does not assume in advance that people will be unkind or untrustworthy, that they will try to take advantage of him. Why should they want to take advantage of him? He is, after all, a nice fellow and he lets it go at that. He then proceeds to forget himself and become interested in others. He is one of those nice people we remember as good listeners.

It is easy for people to like such a person because he begins by liking people. It is easy for them to be interested in him because he is interested in them. He is a person whom it is easy to love.

And not only does he win love easily—he also gives it. Liking what he has, he wants to share it. He shares his pleasure in this food, that book, one or another friend. He does not try to steal his enjoyment of life when no one is around; on the contrary, he says, "Come on in, the water's fine."

When he falls in love, he brings to his love all his other loves, all his other attachments. He is rich in enjoyments and he says to his love, "Here, enjoy this! Share this with me, and this, and this." He brings to the love of his life a wealth of things to share.

What he is sharing is essentially himself. Finding himself good, he has elaborated this good feeling about himself through his maturing years, to include in it friends, interests, tastes, ideas, activities. He draws a wealth of enjoyable attachments to himself, and builds and expands his identity, enriches his individuality with them. He has a rich self to share with his loved one.

No Bed of Roses

Again we must remember that life sets limitations to his enjoyments. His life is no more a bed of roses than any other man's. He is not immune to unhappiness, to discontent. Even the sunniest lands have their bleak and stormy seasons. Although the inner climate of the self-accepting individual is more often sunny than not, he has his times of darkness and dissatisfaction. He may well be dissatisfied with many aspects of life; we are not living in the best of all possible worlds, and we are all aware of inequities, of poverty, disease, the hazards of nature and man's inhumanity to man. His healthy self-love does not blind him to all this; it does not make him a fool living in a fool's paradise.

Self-acceptance does not mean passive acceptance of any status quo, whether within or outside the self. It does not exclude protest and action against unacceptable conditions of life. It does not exclude dissatisfaction with many aspects of oneself. The most self-accepting people are often the ones most active in self-improvement as well as in the improvement of their lot and the lot of others. They may reach constantly for new knowledge and new skills, new understanding and insights, not because they expect perfection of themselves, but because they like and want the best for themselves. Their dissatisfactions are realistic and specific, not a projection of a general dissatisfaction with themselves focused on some momentarily conspicuous defect in themselves or the world.

Suppose we have two individuals, both expressing discontent. Let us say they are two colleagues in the same office, both complaining about the job. How can we tell how much of each one's discontent is specific and realistic, and how much stems from a general dissatisfaction with himself that he is projecting?

For this we have many signs. One, at least, is subjective: how does each of these men feel about his life generally? Are most aspects of his life satisfactory, or does he feel that nothing ever goes well with him and is his discontent with his work part of a generally unsatisfactory world? Other signs are external and easy for anyone to see. How well does each man function in his work, despite his discontent? Does either of them do anything to cure the source of the trouble, to reach a better understanding with their superior, to develop a better system on the job, or perhaps to change the job?

We are all familiar with the floater, the man who is constantly changing jobs, who is not happy for long in any job because in fact he is not happy with himself. A man who is happy with himself can also be unhappy with his job and change it, perhaps even change jobs a number of times, but sooner or later he will find the job that suits him and he will stay with it. His discontent is not with himself but with a situation, and he takes action to change the situation.

And there is a further point. In the course of taking action, he gains experience, and possibly he changes his attitudes as well as his job. Having a good opinion of himself does not mean that he cannot grow and learn. His image of himself is good but it is not finite. One of the nicest things he knows about himself is that he can always add to the picture; he can always grow and learn, and probably he will continue to grow and learn as long as he lives.

The man whose discontent is basically with himself may be all too willing to change jobs, and change and change ad infinitum, for he will never find one that suits him. Or he may take the opposite tack, and be fearful of relinquishing even a really unsatisfactory job, because he has no confidence that he can get another, let alone a better one. He is fearful of approaching his employer for an improvement in his salary or his working conditions, because in his heart he does not really believe that he is worth such consideration. And when he does screw up his courage to confront the boss, he will be likely to present his case badly, either understating it so that he fails to get what he wants, or overstating it so that the boss has no alternative but to humiliate him or fire him. Whatever the outcome, it is likely to be of the kind that reinforces his poor self-image.

We can see the difference sharply in the way two men face genuine disaster, for example a bankruptcy. Both men suffer, but one is sustained through his ordeal by already planning how he will dust himself off and begin again, while the other can see only that it is in the end of the world. He is a man who thinks so poorly of himself that when he is stripped of his fortifications, his wealth and business status, he is truly naked; he has nothing. During the stock market crash of 1929, such men jumped out of their skyscraper office windows.

And what if an unsatisfactory situation cannot be changed? Life presents us with many problems that cannot be resolved. Many a man does dull or uncongenial work all week, without too much complaint, because he lives a rich leisure life. He enjoys his family, a hobby, a dozen varied weekend interests. There is no law of nature that says every man must derive satisfaction from the work he does for a living. For centuries men lived by the sweat of their brow and never asked to enjoy it, only to survive by it. Today we wish that all men and women could enjoy the work they do, but that is an ideal and not easy to realize. We work because we must, and a healthy self-love will lead us to find our joys on our own if not on the company's time. Earning a living is in its way satisfaction enough to make the job endurable for many men and women, and many find pleasure in the companionship of their fellow workers to brighten even a hard or monotonous day's work.

Everyone His Albatross

It is all very well, one might say, to talk about developing this good self-image, but suppose a boy grows up to be only five feet two inches tall, in a world where the average height is five feet eight or ten? What image can he have of himself in that case? Napoleon had to conquer the world and place the whole of Europe, kings and all, beneath him so that he could look down on them.

No doubt it is harder to have a good self-image when one has obvious handicaps. People born with a grave physical defect, or who have suffered an accident or crippling disease, surely have an extra burden to bear. Yet therapists who have worked with handicapped people have noted that whatever feeling of inadequacy they may have, it does not necessarily prevent them from developing more courage and confidence than many who have no visible handicap at all.

Each of us carries some kind of albatross; a crutch or a brace is only a more evident one. The question is not what disability we suffer, but how we deal with it. Sometimes the handicap is itself a powerful motivation to create a good image of oneself, not only to the world but in one's own eyes. A man who lost his sight in a childhood accident became one of the best-read men in his town; he was so witty and delightful a companion that his friends competed to spend hours reading to him.

The grain of sand in the oyster's shell is frequently the irritant necessary for the birth of the pearl. Out of his puny size Chaplin created a character that made the world laugh. The great Yale football star of years ago, Albie Booth, was a small man among the gridiron giants. When Yale defeated Harvard 21 to zero, he made all the points himself. He did not have size and brawn but he developed speed and a variety of skills with which to overturn the giants. David matched his shepherd boy experience with a slingshot against Goliath's mighty sword; Jack matched his quick wits against the giant he found at the top of the beanstalk.

Of the world's most fascinating women, scarcely one was a beauty: Cleopatra had a longish nose, Queen Elizabeth I had a scrawny neck, Madame de Staël was a frowzy fat woman. Great beauties do not exert themselves to be interesting; Helen of Troy did indeed have the face and probably the figure to launch a thousand ships, but none of the legends suggests that she was charming, kind, or even bright, and historians believe that the fight was not over her at all but over a shipping route.

The Uses of Hardship

We all grow up with feelings of inferiority, if only—as Alfred Adler pointed out—because we are born young. Life offers us opportunities both to reinforce these feelings and to overcome them. Just as life damages and wounds us, so it also nourishes and heals us.

Even a damaging experience can have its positive results. A friend suffers an automobile breakdown and we exclaim sympathetically, "Oh, too bad!" And then he goes on to tell us that because of it he spent some of the pleasantest hours he had known in years: he walked on a quiet country road, discovered a charming village off the superhighway which he had never known was there, found friendly and helpful people— in fact he enjoyed his mishap so much that he makes us wish it had happened to us. Many Americans traveling abroad have had their most delightful adventures as a result of travel plans going awry.

People have said, of genuinely trying or even dangerous experiences, "I wouldn't want to live through it again but I wouldn't want to have missed it, either." As a result of losing a job, men have found more rewarding directions for their abilities. Many who suffer an early failure in marriage go on to make a wise and durable second marriage.

Physicians know that serious illness in childhood may build great hardihood and resistance to later illness. During the 1918 influenza epidemic, the tall, brawny young men from the farms succumbed by the thousands in the American Army camps, while scrawny youths from city slums showed a far better rate of survival. These young men had suffered so much illness and physical hardship during their underprivileged childhood that, having survived at all, they had great toughness in fighting off new disease.

In the same way, emotionally traumatic experiences early in life may develop strength, sensitivity, insight. For example, we used to believe that divorce was inevitably damaging to children. Today we recognize that divorce must have a strong effect on a child, and it may be hurtful, but it is not inevitably so. The separation of parents or the loss of a parent through illness or death is a grave hardship, but it has also been known to have a maturing and strengthening effect on a child.

Hardship can actually become a favorable part of one's record. A business organization never suffered a loss in its Dun and Bradstreet rating for having to borrow money. As a matter of fact, the more money a firm has borrowed and fastidiously paid back, the better its credit rating.

We cannot plan what is best for us in every detail of our lives, and even if we knew what was best we could not always bring it to pass in the way we dream. Life gives us many chances, and sometimes those that seem most unpromising turn out best of all. No one has only good luck, and no one only bad. Some people do seem to suffer a string of misfortunes, it is true. But the individual who complains too often about how badly the world treats him is really complaining about how badly he treats himself.

Guiding Fictions

Whether or not we have visible handicaps—short stature, a plain face, hair straight as sticks or curly as corkscrews—we all have invisible ones, and the invisible ones are the ones that give most of us the greatest trouble. These are our neuroticisms—and we all have them. Also, we all have some strivings that cannot realistically be fulfilled. We must all settle for less of something than we dream of—less talent, less recognition, less money, less power, less beauty, less virtue, perhaps less love. All of us, in some area of life, must suffer some disappointment, some frustration. No matter how much we have, there is always something we desire, of which we have too little or none at all.

How can we accept this self with all its shortcomings and disappointments?

Yet, we do. We learn to soften the rough edges, shade the hard truths about ourselves—to ourselves as well as to others. A man likes to think that his best round of golf is more truly representative of his skill at the game than all those days when he "was not really trying." A woman, buying a dress, sometimes asks for a size smaller than she takes, and when she tries it on and it fits too snugly, she says something about having put on a pound or two recently that will have to come off. Actually she may not have worn that size for years, but she likes to think she still can.

These pleasant, if unrealistic, beliefs about ourselves might be called guiding fictions. And what is the harm in them? A man who pretends that he is an expert on the stock market could lose every cent he owns, or if he boasts of being a great mountain climber and then tries to prove it, he may lose his life. In any practical aspect of living where facts have real importance, we cannot afford to deceive ourselves. But in the little things, there is no harm in touching up our image here and there, the way a man straightens his tie or a woman touches up her makeup or her hair.

There is, on the contrary, good sound sense in it. The fisherman is expected to boast about the size of his catch. Paul Bunyan and John Henry, those doughty heroes, reflect an essential folk wisdom that gives us all leave to boast a little where it will do no harm to ourselves or others. Legend is full of men who accomplished wonders of strength or skill or cunning, women as beautiful as the dawn who could spin gold out of straw or tame the wild beasts with their gentleness.

Because we like ourselves, we adorn ourselves a little in our mind's eye. We give ourselves little compliments, as we give compliments to other people we like. No one was ever hurt by a compliment.

The more kindly we judge ourselves, the more kindly we are in judging others. The more we accept ourselves, with all our defects and shortcomings, the more acceptance we can offer to those we love. Anyone unhappy with himself is easily sullen and irritable with others.

Helpful and Unhelpful Self-Love

We have been describing self-love in its adult flowering, the healthy self-love that is the basis of love for other human beings. The love of self can of course be stunted in its growth, and remain narrow and infantile. Twenty years later the child within the grown man may still be crying for the extra attention, still be demanding the satisfaction of his needs at no matter what expense to others, still be exploding in temper tantrums when his wishes are not met.

We have said that a woman who does not have an adequate image of herself may show it by dressing herself poorly, as though she were not worth the money and trouble of dressing well. When human behavior goes to extremes it may go to either end of the scale. Instead of adorning herself too little, the same mechanism may drive another woman to adorn herself too much, to become preoccupied and even obsessed with her wardrobe, her coiffure, her complexion. She may spend endless time and much more money than she can afford in the dress shops and beauty salons. And no matter how long she sits preening before her dressing table, she is still preening all evening. She has little mind to give to her dinner partner, the conversation, the play, the music. She is far too taken up with her dress, her face, her hair. Her relationship with others is largely in terms of what they will think of her and of how she looks.

It is not narcissism when a woman dresses and grooms herself with care, looks to every detail and checks the total effect one last time in the mirror before she goes out. She may even fuss a bit, and go back for a different pair of earrings or gloves. When she looks at herself for the last time, she may not see the outstanding beauty of the age—nor did she expect to—but she is content. She has put herself nicely together. And now she can forget about herself and her appearance and go out and enjoy herself. This is not narcissism, but an acceptance of herself, a wholesome self-love that in fact frees her from further attention to herself.

Infantile self-love is not liberating, but limiting and enslaving. The narcissist cannot enjoy another's pleasure or happiness, and most surely he cannot sympathize with another's pain. No one's toothache hurts as his hurts, no one's problems are as difficult to solve, no one works as hard or sacrifices as much as he. And no one understands him.

He can be selfish, self-centered, inconsiderate, even cruel, and never know that he is hurting others. He is like the child who took to pinching all the other little children in the playground, until his mother despaired of stopping him with words and decided to show him in deeds. She pinched him, hard enough to make him cry. And from then on he understood why he must not pinch others.

The adult whose self-love remains infantile does not necessarily express it in obviously infantile ways. Society itself encourages a man to cover himself with glory in a fashion that frequently denies the value of any love other than self-love. The powerful competitive forces around us harshly dictate that "we do them or be done by them." Anyone caught up in such a struggle can develop a drive for wealth, power, status at any cost to his other relationships. There are undeniable satisfactions in financial success and there are dangers to the rest of ones love life. Both are worthy of a deeper look.

CHAPTER SEVEN

Love and Status

WE ALL LOVE things—material things that cost money. We love them so much they actually become a significant part of our love life. All we have to do is listen to people to hear them assert this love again and again. "I'd love to have a new car." "I'd love a fur coat." "We love our new home." Are they using the word "love" differently when they speak this way? The answer is an emphatic "no." We may commonly link love with romance, sex, marriage. But love is an attachment and it does not limit itself to an involvement exclusively with people.

In these materialistic reveries, people not only reveal their desires but, because these desires are strong and recurrent, they simultaneously suggest how absorbed they are and how much they might do to obtain these things. This absorption may occupy even more of their time, thought, and energy than their love of a particular person. No one ever says so outright but acquisitiveness and the status many seek to derive from it could become their major love.

We like to think of ourselves as capable of great love in the romantic sense as opposed to this crass acquisitive addiction. And it is true that we are eminently capable of dreams, desires, and even some of the most tender feelings for someone who "walks in beauty like the night." But few of us enjoy enough freedom from nagging forces within us and potent social forces around us not to respond strongly to the attraction of ownership. We see this early in the life of the child when, by the age of 4 or 5, he begins every other sentence with the same phrase, namely, "I want" or "Give me." Many of us never get over this.

What Things Do for Us

The culture of our Western world has, of course, placed a high value on acquisition. Nor is this a recent development. It has been going on for centuries. Possessions held in abundance give us status. And this does something for us psychologically. Most people find it a lot easier to feel secure at the wheel of a gleaming new expensive automobile than they feel in a battered old one. Many a man spends more time on a Sunday polishing and caressing the automobile of which he is so proud than he spends with his wife. Possessions and position do help blunt the sting of anxiety from which we all suffer in varying degree. They even give the illusion of unconditional love, or if not love, at least approval for which we all unconsciously yearn from early childhood.

To put it simply and directly, things satisfy us and in this satisfaction the largest component is generally self-love. Our first step in learning to love is self-love, and that self-love is the love we know best for the first years of life. We never relinquish our infantile self-love entirely, although we learn to transform it, to sublimate it, in ways that bring us more adult satisfactions.

The drive for wealth and status and the consequent public approval offer direct satisfaction for infantile self-love. It creates no complications, makes no demands on us to consider the needs and wants of another human being. We do not have to consider anybody to win this general approval. We need only to consider ourselves and acquire things. After awhile, our acquisitions become part of us—an indistinguishable part of us—so that we come to feel bigger, more important as a result of them.

Things have a tangibility that makes the ethereal quality of love seem pale and elusive. We are taught to believe that "he who steals my purse steals trash," but we take good care not to be robbed. We use locks and burglar alarms and we take out insurance besides. And we become suspicious of love itself. Many a person wonders whether he is loved for himself or his money.

Love may be inconstant, unreliable. We discovered that as children, and some of us rediscover it as adults. Possessions, on the other hand, are reliable, barring a stock market crash or a business failure. They do not return our love, but neither do they give us harsh words, or run off with someone else.

They also lend themselves to mathematical enumeration. They can be counted, catalogued, and their value added up in cold cash. How do you count or measure love? Elizabeth Barrett tried, in a sonnet that she wrote to Robert Browning:

"How do I love thee? Let me count the ways.
I love thee to the depth and breadth and height
My soul can reach . . ."

She went on in this vein, and it is a beautiful sonnet, but at the end all we know is that she was very much in love.

We are told, and only half in jest, that we all have problems and money will not cure them, but if we must have problems it is better to worry about them in the back of a Cadillac. They will be much less painful. We are also told that since we must work anyway we may as well do a good job of it and make as much money out of it as we can. There is just enough hard practical sense in all this to be persuasive.

Back to the Lover

In order to understand love, it is the lover as we have stated earlier who must be understood. The lover himself is easily shaped by many influences, creating many attachments, which crowd out the love he believes is primary in his life. For many people, the love between a man and a woman gets to be like the book they have been promising themselves to read or the letter they have been meaning to write. Somehow, despite the genuineness of their desires, the goodness of their intentions, things get in the way.

The reasons for this are many. In the first place as members of society it behooves us to act like others. And we do. We spend the greater part of our waking hours engaged in the mechanics of living. This consists of earning a living or cooking, cleaning, saving, and purchasing the things we require for our everyday life. So little time is left for love, entertainment, self-education, or play that we easily become more proficient at work.

Secondly, although we may become attracted to someone for a variety of reasons, the love we develop is one of the ways we reduce the feelings of anxiety we all have. Other ways of anxiety reduction are even more available. Many things which serve as a buffer and protection from what we dread can simply be bought. All we need is the money. And there are countless ways we are spurred on to make money.

The Timeless Conflict

These two ways of allaying anxiety have been in conflict from time immemorial. By Jesus' time the conflict was already old, for it was he who emphasized that we love our neighbor as ourselves and that a camel could go through the eye of a needle sooner than a rich man could enter heaven. And Jesus followed his own precept. According to St. Matthew, when Satan led him to a high mountain and promised him the world and all its glories, Jesus turned from it and answered, "Get thee hence, Satan."

Although Jesus succeeded in gaining our confidence on the importance of loving one another, he was less successful in teaching us to abstain from loving material things. John Calvin, a religious leader of far less note, fifteen hundred years later taught a different doctrine. Seeking to strip religion of its panoply and ritual, and simplify it to its essentials, he preached that industry and thrift made a man acceptable in the eyes of the Lord.

In the wealthy city of Geneva where Calvin preached, this was a most appealing precept, and events of the following centuries strengthened its influence. Inherited nobility and power perished in the American and French revolutions, and with the industrial revolution of the next century, wealth and status came within reach of everyone. A man could be born a nobody, but if he followed Calvin's teachings, worked hard, and used his earnings prudently, one day he would be rich and respected. He would have the status of an honorable man.

The word "status" is often on our lips today but it is not new. The man who introduced it into American thinking was Thorstein Veblen, a highly original economist of the first quarter of the century. His book, *The Theory of the Leisure Class,* was a searching critique of the drive to acquisition and status, which until then had been respectable beyond question.

He examined the behavior of people who subscribed to the doctrine of working hard and spending prudently; and he discovered that they were not nearly so rational as they believed.

They believed that they bought what they needed and what they liked; that is, that the consumption of goods was rationally motivated by physical and aesthetic wants. A man might think he bought an overcoat to keep him warm, thus satisfying a physical want, and that he bought one coat rather than another because it looked better on him, satisfying an aesthetic want. Not so, said Veblen. A man bought his coat and also his house, furniture, horse, carriage, not out of these rational wants but out of the motive of emulation. He was seeking to win the same attention and respect that was accorded to men who already had such possessions.

This pattern of social behavior was not born in the United States, but it was especially easy to trace in a land where many men had begun side by side with an equal lack of resources. Out of a number of men who settled, for example, at the same period on the same rich land in Indiana, one man after a decade might have a flourishing farm, many head of cattle, a fine house and barns, while his neighbors were still only moderately well off and some remained poor and struggling. Naturally the man who had done so well won the respect of the community. People saw in him superior ability. They went to him for advice, listened respectfully to his opinions at the town meeting, voted for him as a church elder and a school trustee. His possessions proved his superiority and he was honored for it.

Once possessions became the basis for popular esteem, by a psychological transition they also became the basis for self-esteem. So far the pattern seems logical and rational. But then Veblen observed a most irrational reversal. Instead of saving thriftily what they had worked so hard to gain so that they could have many possessions and hence much popular and self-esteem, people tended to spend their money in a most reckless fashion.

Money: A Showcase for the Self

Yet this was not so irrational as it seemed. To win attention and esteem, people had *to display* their wealth. If a man lived shabbily and at his death a half million dollars was found stuffed in his mattress, he would not have enjoyed anybody's respect. But if he spent his half million on a palatial mansion and a yacht, even if he went into debt to keep them, people would respect him. The chances are that the business community would not only grant him generous credit but would put him in the way of earning still more millions.

Having great wealth is not enough, said Veblen. It must be displayed. For this he invented the phrase, "conspicuous consumption," and the companion phrase, "conspicuous leisure."

By conspicuous consumption, Veblen meant a blatant display of wealth. The principle involved is just the opposite of what goes into a search for bargains. Instead of trying to stretch a dollar and get the most for it, the idea is to give the impression that one's dollars are limitless. There was a time during the wild prosperous 1920s when a man who was anxious to establish his social position following the accumulation of wealth would become an art collector. What he bought was not nearly so important as the price he paid for it—because it made news, front page news. If an old bathtub of Louis XIV was expensive enough, it was worth buying.

This becomes a way of saying, "I am so able, so ingenious, and consequently so wealthy that I can afford to indulge my every whim without in the least threatening the substantiality of my wealth." Wealth so huge certainly commands notice, envy, respect and its possessor becomes the inevitable subject of our attention. Additionally, if what he collects shows good taste, he grows in stature and, to some degree, this is bound to happen merely as a result of the facilities available to help him choose. Something has to rub off; even people who fall asleep regularly at the opera cannot escape becoming somewhat familiar with a libretto or aria or two.

Despite the Depression at the end of the twenties, the practice continues. In fact there has lately been a resurgence of interest in the purchase of art. This is not to doubt that many art collectors like the paintings they buy, but the monetary value of a painting frequently usurps their thought and discussion of it.

Although our democratic society is abandoning more and more of the ritual and formality it inherited from its monarchical forbears, many occasions remain to display wealth. The first night at the opera is one of these, not only in New York but in Paris, London, Rome. The choice seats are not those from which one can best see the opera but from which one can best be seen by the audience. The newspapers the next morning publish photographs and descriptions of what each celebrated lady wore. This consists of two things straight out of what Veblen called the man's "unremitting demonstration of the ability to pay": jewels and a dress by a famous couturier. Like a painting, she is signed with the artist's name.

Women are constantly used, perhaps not altogether reluctantly, by men to put their wealth in evidence. Even as a girl approaches womanhood, the process begins. Even today, the father of a debutante would think nothing of spending many thousands of dollars just on the flowers to decorate the ballroom for her coming-out party, flowers that would have faded by the last waltz of the evening. This conspicuous consumption is frequently matched later on, as these girls marry, by the conspicuous leisure their husbands make possible for them. These women are seen and photographed at social events, on shipboard, at expensive resorts, always magnificently dressed and magnificently doing nothing.

Aside from a merely decorative and deliberately unproductive wife, a man can collect many other things of status value for himself. The longest or most expensive automobile, membership in costly even if seldom used clubs, fine homes, servants, the best seats and first nights at theaters, dinners at fine restaurants, prominently placed tables at such restaurants and night-clubs, costly recreations such as polo, yachting, fox hunting—all these things confer position in society worthy of emulation. The quest for status along these lines occasionally reaches such humorous extremes as the need to have an indoor dog and an outdoor dog.

For most of us, who cannot afford such extravagance, Veblen described the imitative elements in our own behavior as consumers. "Pecuniary emulation" was the phrase he used to mark the nonrational purchase of goods for the purpose of satisfying not our physical wants but rather our desire to be thought well of by others.

We buy a new coat not because the old one is frayed or no longer warm but because the style has changed and we feel poor and sorry for ourselves if we do not keep up with others. The purchase may be a modest one and yet it bears the stamp of emulation. The mass-produced clothes most women have to settle for are generally copied down versions of costly designers' clothes worn in their original form by the wealthy. Similarly, girls who cultivate long, polished fingernails are generally unaware that this high-style manicure originated as a symbol of wealth, for obviously such hands did not have to do housework.

Although we are cautioned that "clothes do not make the man," we are just as often and realistically reminded of the importance of the impression we make. And this, in turn, leaves us impressionable. Advertisements sell us again and again by associating things with the wealthy. The implication is that their product is either popular with rich people or that it is indistinguishable from the real thing. In either case, such a purchase will allow us to enjoy the status conferred by wealth.

No doubt an unsympathetic exaggeration of Veblen's thesis can easily reduce it to absurdity. On the other hand, it is true that many of our dreams have a material, monetary quality. And dreaming is little more than an extension of everyday thinking. It is naïve to believe that we do not act on our dreams. We do, perhaps more often than we like to admit. And, as Veblen helps us to recognize, there are strong social forces which aid and abet the process.

The Trouble with People

From a purely psychological point of view, our love of things is frequently easier to satisfy than our love of people. Our individual shortcomings give us much less trouble in making money than they do in achieving satisfying relationships with others.

There are many men who believe that the only sane part of their day is the time they spend in the office. They say, "It's impossible at home—everybody is always in a state. I can't get along with my wife, nobody can control the children, nothing makes any sense. In my office, even if things do not go the way you expect them, you can work them out. There are procedures, forms, principles by which we abide most of the time. At home we all love each other but things get out of hand, nothing goes the way you expect it to go. It's a mess."

So the man says. And from his point of view he is quite right. The vicissitudes of business and the stock market are more predictable to him than people. Many men feel that women anyway are hopelessly unpredictable, that they are full of moods, as variable as the weather.

We might note that the men who feel this most strongly are

usually the very men who give all or most of their time and attention to business and the acquisition of things, and have little to spare for becoming familiar with the needs or wants of wives. They study market reports and business news letters and keep well informed so that the twists and turns of high finance do not surprise them. But it does not occur to them that if they took equal trouble to learn about people they might find the study of human behavior equally valuable.

For many people, not being sure how others will act and feel from one moment to the next is far more threatening than they realize. Even surprises are not so agreeable for many as we tend to think. For most of us a real surprise, one which catches us truly unprepared, can be more disturbing than pleasurable even though it may be a happy piece of news. Remember how you felt the last time you were given a real surprise; remember the behavior of someone to whom you told an important and genuinely unexpected piece of news. The first response is not pleasure but shock. One has to sit down, catch one's breath, get used to the new idea. Some people burst out laughing but it is likely to be shaky laughter. A woman is likely to burst into tears. She may muster a smile but it is a tremulous one.

The fact is, we really do not like surprises as much as we think we do. As children, we certainly did not like them. The reason surprises are more disagreeable than otherwise to children is that a child has a small "apperceptive mass," as psychologists call it, a small backlog or body of experience, to which to relate the new experience. Anything totally new is frightening; it can please only when they have become used to it. Young children generally hang back from even the kindest and gentlest stranger until they have looked him over thoroughly. Every spring, some of the children who have been anticipating their first visit to the circus for weeks go home after the show and have nightmares for months. Many children have the same reaction after their first trip to the zoo, their first movie or children's play.

Children do not feel safe with the unfamiliar, because it is unpredictable. If a young child is to be exposed to a new experience, it is wise to prepare him for what he is going to see. The child needs to know in advance, so that he can enjoy the fun of the surprise without the shock of strangeness and its accompanying fear.

We do not get over this entirely when we grow up. Even as our apperceptive mass, our background of experience, grows with living, we are still wary of surprises. Experience makes fewer events totally surprising, but experience may also reinforce our basic anxiety, our basic feelings of insecurity about life. A really unexpected turn of events stirs up ripples in this unconscious pool of anxiety; a major surprise can cause a tidal wave. Our first response is one of disturbance. Only secondarily can we assess the meaning of the event and feel pleasure in it.

Yet, we like and seek some new experience. There are those of us who are more adventurous, others less so. Most of us have no desire to see what surprises may be in store at the top of Mt. Everest or under the Arctic ice cap. We will settle for lesser adventures. We like novelty, within reason. We mostly prefer predictability. And people, in a general way, give the impression of being unpredictable. The fear of unpredictability in a relationship with another human being is strong with some people. It may be so strong that it blocks them from the experience of love.

These may be people whose parents displayed extreme swings of mood and behavior. Or the parents may simply have been inconsistent in their handling of the child. The pattern is familiar: a parent is inattentive, perhaps reading the paper or talking to a friend, while the child forages around for something to do. The child finds something, but it is the wrong thing—he is dismantling the new coffee table lighter, perhaps—and the parent pounces on him, furious. "Haven't I told you not to touch things! Why must you take everything apart!"

To a young child, this is unpredictable and very upsetting behavior. One moment all was serene, mother was pleasant or at least indifferent, and the child was permitted to wander about unmolested. The next moment he is seized, shouted at, possibly spanked, and the all-important adult in his life has become hostile and menacing. If this happens often enough, he has good reason to mistrust the behavior of people for the rest of his life. And for the rest of his life, such a person may always feel safer with things than with people.

Lovers Are Predictable

Predictability may seem difficult to develop in a relationship between people, but it is very far from impossible. All of us have at least one friend whom we know well, and whose behavior is reasonably easy to foresee. We all take the trouble to know an employer or colleague whose reactions are likely to be important to us, and we can say in advance, "He isn't going to like that," or "She won't see it that way." We do not expect to be right every time in our prediction of how the boss will react. But neither do we expect to be right every time about the stock market or the sales figures. Our prediction is a guess, but an educated guess.

We can make the same kind of guess about a human being's behavior, if we take the trouble to become educated about that human being. People are not unpredictable; far from it. One might justly complain that they are too predictable, that they fall into habits and patterns of behavior too readily and too inflexibly. We only need to know an individual well enough.

Lovers are not unpredictable to each other. Lovers face few surprises in each other, once they have progressed from romantic love to a relationship based on real knowledge of each other. Some lovers arrive at this relationship before they marry, some not until after several or many years of marriage. There is a peak in the divorce rate at about five years of marriage. These are lovers who either never succeeded in coming to know each other, or else did not accept the reality when they discovered it.

Lovers who succeed in replacing the romantic image of the loved one with the real person are no longer afraid of what they may discover in each other. They learn that they can trust each other. They find security in each other and enjoy their interaction. Social status may remain important to them, but not nearly to the degree of their personal status with each other.

The Vulnerable Male

Since so many more men than women seem to turn to a love of things rather than people, we might ask whether men are in fact more susceptible to this type of love. We must recognize, to begin with, that a man's role in our society is traditionally that of the provider for his family. He is the one who goes out to make a living. His position in the community is a barometer of how well he is performing his role. His status reflects favorably or otherwise on his wife and children. In a very real sense, his public position is part of the provision he succeeds in making for their welfare.

A man is thus more vulnerable to the enticements of wealth and status than a woman, simply because of this traditional role. But there are also deeper psychological forces driving him to these goals.

Early in childhood a boy has the experience of feeling displaced by his father. He is at home with his mother, playing with her or perhaps being fed his supper by her. He has her whole attention, when suddenly his father comes home and the entire household changes. Mother gets up, greets father, talks to him, goes to check the state of father's dinner that she is preparing. Even if she returns, even if father sits down and the child is again made the center of attention, the constellation has altered. Until that moment the little boy possessed his mother entirely; he had her all to himself. Now he no longer has full possession of her, or of his father either. Each of them also has a share in the other.

Little girls have the same experience, of course. But later the experiences of boys and girls begin to diverge. The boy becomes inextricably involved in a kind of competition with his father. Yet his angry feelings make him uneasy, for he also loves his father and wants the love of this strong protector. So he succeeds in gradually converting his resentful rivalry into emulation, which is both more comfortable and more profitable. He sets out to equal his father and if possible outdo him.

Psychoanalysts make the further point that the boy is sensitive to the difference in size between himself and his father, and that this awareness of size tends to be carried over into other pursuits as the child grows. He soon discovers that in his world of school and sports, physical prowess is a great advantage, and this again involves size as well as physical skill. The heroes of his world are the ones who can run fastest, hit the ball farthest, get on the team, win the game. Being first, making records—these are the standards of excellence for the boy when he thinks about what kind of person he is or would like to be.

By this time the experience of boys and girls has diverged considerably, as a father discovers when his children are old enough to get their drivers' licenses. His insurance rates go up at once when his son begins to drive, for the accident rate for teen-age boys is the highest for any drivers. Characteristically, boys drive much faster than girls. They race their cars on the road, make a point of darting away first when the light changes from red to green, and take all sorts of risks to get there first and fastest.

Youths of every era have been preoccupied with being out in front, from the games in ancient Greece to the playing fields of Eton. The first rule of every game is to try to win. Rewards are not equally distributed. They are distributed only among the winners. Similarly, the satisfaction to be derived from one's performance depends on whether or not one wins. The admiration of others and the admiration one has for oneself both follow the quality of one's performance. This may not be love in its purest or best form, but is certainly a common substitute.

Women are not entirely exempt. A little girl competes with and then emulates her mother, and later she is competitive about her school grades, about the college that accepts her, about the man she marries. She wants to love her husband, to be sure, but she also wants to make a good marriage, and that means marrying a man of some importance, some distinction, perhaps some wealth and position.

A Conspiracy Against Love

All this adds up to a considerable psychological force of competitiveness and ambition in each one of us, male and female. Men are still more driven by this force in our society than women, but our society is changing, and women are finding or perhaps seeking increasing opportunities to express their competitive drive. We have talked elsewhere about the part parents play in instilling these drives in their children, and we have seen, too, how the family by its very relationships stimulates competitive feelings and competitive behavior. There is competition with one parent for the other's love, competition with brothers and sisters for parents' love and even for parents' non-love in the form of punitive attention. Competition is encouraged in the playground, in school, on the athletic field. The drive for achievement and honors is an inevitable and often an exaggerated force throughout the growing years, and none of us is entirely free of it.

Everything conspires to enhance the power of this drive in our adult lives. Behind it are not only history, tradition, and to some extent the religious influences of Calvinism, but also the most obvious appurtenances of our affluent culture. Advertising plays on our acquisitive desires and uses them to sell products to us. Our newspapers tell us about plain John Doe only if he killed or robbed someone or was killed or robbed, but we read every event in the lives of people of wealth and status the day after it occurs, and when they die we read it all over again at full length in their obituaries. In this respect, our newspapers are like our history books. Of all the people who crossed the Rubicon, only Caesar's crossing is recorded.

We learn business and professional skills to develop our ability to acquire wealth and status, but there are no courses in the ability to love. There is a Harvard School of Business Administration, but so far no Harvard School of Love, and if some eccentric millionaire alumnus were to endow such a school in his will it would put the trustees of the university in a pretty quandary.

The world does not accord us much honor for achievement in loving. When a man is unusually happy in his love, his friends say, "Wasn't he lucky!" When two people achieve noteworthy happiness in their marriage, people say, "How lucky they are!" and "Weren't they lucky to have found each other!" We look upon making good in worldly achievement as a mark of extraordinary ability. But making good in love is an accident of two people's blindly stumbling upon one another and haphazardly coming out all right. There is no notion that perhaps we may choose wisely and well, and that having chosen each other, we invest considerable effort and art in shaping our love to meet our mutual desire for harmony, happiness, and fulfillment with each other.

With so much pressure to turn us the other way, it is remarkable that the love of people, rather than of things, is still one of our major ideals. It might be that things, the acquisition of them and the status they bring, do not really satisfy our loneliness, our anxiety, our need for one another and our desire to find happiness with one another.

It is extremely difficult to avoid a primary attachment to the accumulation of things in a world where they figure so prominently. Success is important to us and its most common hallmark is financial achievement. Most everything has a price and people come to feel that money is the easiest and most universal measure of value. They see in their store of worldly goods satisfaction, security, status, an enlargement of self, a basic confirmation of their adequacy and worthwhileness. Like little Jack Horner, having gotten the plum, they now think, "What a good boy am I."

Things Are Not Enough

All this would be fine except for two considerations. First, there is an unabated lingering concern with self which more closely resembles infantile self-love than some of its more mature expressions. Why should someone so secure continue to watch the stock market ticker so feverishly? Why should someone with such status continue to wheel and deal even on week-ends and vacations? Security and satisfaction should bring freedom from the recurrent need to prove oneself; it should bring self-assurance and tranquility.

The second consideration is that we live in a world of people. No matter how much we do for ourselves in the successful accumulation of property, the emotional overtones of our life remain primarily influenced by the people closest to us and how we react to them. True, others may confer honor and status upon us, but our position in our own home is of greater ultimate value in the most deeply personal sense. The members of our family do not respond to us according to sociological principle. Their hair is down and they see us similarly unadorned by our rich socio-economic achievements. The millionaire and the ordinary man face their six-year-old child—and, for that matter, anyone else close to them—with the same naked ability to love. Sooner or later, the truth emerges. Not everything can be bought. There is no substitute for people.

The love of material goods and the love of people often conflict. Yet there is no law of human nature or society which makes this necessarily so. We all inescapably have many loves and one of the major challenges of life is to make them compatible. The ideal solution does not demand the sacrifice of one for the other. Enough people have combined the benefits of both loves to encourage the conviction that they can exist harmoniously together. Acquisition and achievement need not necessarily be at others' expense. Cooperative effort is not a mere dream. People have been known to achieve more as a result of working with others than against them. Even a business relationship leaves room for dignity, respect, for love. The more our daily behavior manifests this, the more consistent do work and love become. Our relationships with others yield greater satisfaction, we get to be less guarded, and the material symbols of status attract us less than the deeper values we realize people are willing to share with us.

This kind of achievement or success with people enriches the lives of many; others are less fortunate. They have difficulty freeing themselves from their self-attachment or the extension of this self-love, represented in their material possessions. They develop an inability to attach themselves to people with the same lasting vigor. This inability to promote durable human relationships deserves closer study.

CHAPTER EIGHT

The Inability to Love

VERY FEW, IF any of us, ever see ourselves as non-loving. No matter what the facts of our behavior may be, we generally credit ourselves with just, noble, and loving intentions. Not everyone always shares the generous view we take of ourselves, but then we feel misunderstood and harshly regarded. Yet we easily enough recognize in others and even deplore their inability to love. A more dispassionate view of the matter strongly suggests that non-loving behavior can be found in all of us. Granted this exists more in some than others but it is not negligible in anyone.

According to our definition of love merely as an attachment, we all inescapably develop many loves. Earlier chapters enumerated them. But some of us develop deeper attachments and more attachments to other human beings. The early experiences of many people leave them unsure, withdrawn and capable only of thin, superficial relationships later on. Still others, like Freud's first love-sick patients, have such strongly unpleasant experiences with love that they cannot fall in love again. And, of course there are many others who come to love things other than people and this attachment to status, wealth, or achievement may actually dilute the energy they devote to their distinctly human relationships. Worst of all, we inevitably—all of us—brush up against hostility often enough during our formative years to learn a great deal of non-loving feelings and non-loving behavior.

On the face of it, the early life of the child would seem to be innocent enough to be free of the imperfections of love which might later haunt us. After all, do not parents love their children? They certainly do a great deal for them. What are these imperfections? How do they develop in a child's experience of love?

Love Without Pleasure

In order to understand the emotional climate into which our babies are born willy-nilly, some self-examination is necessary. Let us start with a quick look at the assumption that as parents we all love our children. We all know that many people do not plan the coming of their children. They may not even want them, or they may want them at some other, future time but not at the time that they come. This is not necessarily a fault in parents. Life is full of surprises, and a child may come at a time that is inconvenient, perhaps actually difficult. The difficulty may be financial, emotional; it may result from circumstances out of the parents' control. Yet it can hardly help affecting their behavior toward the child if they are tense, strained, anxious.

It is also true that not everybody wants to be a parent, and some people who have children really do not want them. They have children because they are expected to have them. People badger them: when are they really going to settle down? It is almost as though being married were merely a hoax, requiring children to make it legitimate, or at best a sort of halfway house on the road to full marital status.

Many fathers resent the child even before it is born. They would never admit it, even to themselves, but they do, and often they have good reason. The moment the wife announces her pregnancy, the world turns its attention from the relationship between husband and wife to the relationship between the young woman and her yet unborn child. No one pays any notice to the prospective father. He is simply not there; he is the invisible man for the next nine months.

Even his wife tends to forget about him. Unfortunately for the husband, the wife's experience of pregnancy is a deeply absorbing one, especially the first pregnancy. If it is an uncomfortable one, beginning with morning sickness and going on to heartburn and overweight and aching feet, the woman can hardly escape being the center of her own attention. If it is a happy pregnancy it can be absorbing in another way. A pregnant woman can be so blissful, so inward in her enjoyment of her own creation that she forgets to share the experience with her husband, forgets that he is not enjoying the same extraordinary awareness of developing life. She forgets that his life is going on in the same old way, and he might like a little attention for himself.

If he has not resented the baby before, he is almost bound to resent it once it arrives. His sleep is broken, his life is disrupted, his comforts and recreations are curtailed, even his companionship with his wife is interfered with. His satisfactions are more in the wish than in the fact. He acts out a sort of charade of being interested in the baby because it is expected of him, but he is not really involved. His is a sort of ceremonial role, like that of royalty in a constitutional monarchy.

How much pleasure does a father actually derive from his new baby? He feels like a clumsy oaf, too awkward to handle this fragile little creature, or if he does not think of himself this way someone is bound to point it out to him. It is a very bold father indeed who can push his way to the bassinet through the assembled female relatives, and put out a finger to the baby, just to get acquainted—let alone pick the baby up for a hug and a chat.

On the other hand, the chores that do fall to his lot are not the most encouraging to fatherly love. A man getting up to give the night feeding in the small hours of a wintry morning may well wonder about the quality of his love.

Loving and Not-Loving

It is easy to caricature the father's role in the baby's life. In these early stages the father's role is not actually very crucial. As the baby books say, his principal job is to keep the mother happy. The mother is another matter.

If it is her first baby she can feel deeply threatened by this child. She soon finds that her status in the community depends upon how she handles the child. And since it is her first baby, everything she does is without precedent. She really does not know how to care for this mysterious, incomprehensible little creature, does not know what it means when it cries, does not trust her own judgment. Handbooks of child care tell her what to do, but no book can answer the many anxious questions that come up so very often. And the pediatrician's phone is often busy!

These trying first months do not last too long, it is true. Babies survive—for actually they are very hardy—and mothers gain confidence and fathers are reconciled and begin to take genuine pride, as compared with ceremonial pride, in their fatherhood.

But for the baby this is only the beginning of hard times. He takes his first steps, and is greeted like a conquering Roman hero returning from Gaul. Almost immediately afterward he is being caught and held and restrained and told, No, no! For now he is much more difficult to manage. Now the whole apartment, the whole house is his domain. He was much easier to love when he was lying in his crib.

And so it goes, through stool training and feeding new foods and reluctant naps and rebellious bedtimes and sibling rivalry, through crying when you leave him in kindergarten and not doing his homework and having chickenpox and mumps and many, many colds.

It is not easy to be a child and it is not easy to be a parent. It never was and probably never will be. It was not easy for our parents to raise us, nor for their parents to raise them. Some cynic once said, "The first half of our lives is ruined by our parents and second half by our children." Long ago parents did have an advantage, when children were an economic asset. It did not make them more lovable, but at least it was worth the trouble of bringing them up, because each child represented another pair of hands on the farm or in the workshop.

Even then, as we note from the more grisly episodes in the history of the human race, infanticide was an accepted custom among people and in many eras. Sometimes they killed all their babies but one, sometimes they killed only the weak ones or only the girl babies.

We no longer tolerate such a callous evaluation of children, of human life. To us, every human being has a right to life and to the best that we can give him. Our children are a solemn obligation, and we do our utmost to fulfill that obligation as we see it. We work hard and save money for their education. We worry about their health, their environment, the kind of playmates they have, the kind of schools they go to. We suffer agonies over whether they will be accepted by the right college, whether they will choose the right profession, whether they will marry the right girl or boy.

We also accept the obligation to love our children. And this obligation we also fulfill as best we can. But with all our efforts, we cannot be loving *all the time*.

And so, as surely as one birthday follows another and brings new problems and new anxieties, new frictions and irritations, there are many times in a child's life when his parents are not loving. And this experience, too, leaves its imprint.

Thus we begin to learn non-love even before we are out of the crib. We encounter it when our parents make their first demands on us. Parents may love and tend and care for the child and express their delight at having him, but after a very short while they make it clear that they do not want him just as he is. They want him to sit up, feed himself, dress himself, deposit his feces in the right place. They want him to smile for Aunt Jane, kiss Uncle John, behave well in the supermarket. They do not want him to pull things off shelves, wander off and get lost, throw temper tantrums in public. They want him to be able to do certain things and not do other things.

The Hard Climb

This is difficult for the child, even when the demands are reasonable. It means that he must constantly be giving up some familiar way of doing things and learn a new way. Often he is not prepared to do this. The child himself is not always ready to climb to the next level of growth.

Being a child with parents to do his bidding is like having a car and chauffeur. You do not have to worry about parking, lights, traffic, the best way to go. You get into the car and the chauffeur drives you. So it is with the child. He gives the sign that he is hungry or wet or sleepy or not feeling well and the good mother takes care of him.

Parents know that a child cannot be allowed to go on in this way indefinitely. The world is not made for people who demand to have everything done for them and can do nothing for themselves. It is part of the task of parents to teach their children to be self-sufficient.

Sometimes parents encourage a child to take the next step a little too soon. It is not always easy to know when a child is ready. Often a child resists even though he may be reasonably ready, simply because he needs to assert himself. He is discovering himself as a person, discovering the remarkable power to say "No!" This stage is also a part of his development, but unfortunately it comes just during a period when his parents are making a great many demands on him, asking him to give up a great many comfortable ways of babyhood.

A child feels his parents do not love him when they make these demands upon him. He does not see the value of what they want him to learn. All he sees is that his parents deprive him of the satisfaction of his desires, and he thinks they are mean and harsh and cruel—in a word, unloving. Once children learn to talk, they say so. Let a child ask for something out of turn, an ice cream cone before dinner. His mother refuses him. She refuses him, gently and even with a most reasonable explanation. The gentleness and the explanation do not, however, alter the fact of his deprivation. He cries. He says, "You are a mean mommy." If he is angry enough he may add, "And I hate you and I wish you were dead." He says this not to hurt his mother but because it is the way he feels. It is part of childhood to want a pleasure now, not later. When his mother makes the rational demand that he wait until after dinner for his ice cream cone, she is mean to him, she does not love him. He genuinely feels unloved. And he learns to unlove in return.

The Dragon-Slayers

Parents make demands not merely to please themselves but because the world makes demands and they represent the world to the child. The child begins to learn this even from his fairy tales, those highly instructive lessons in the ways of the world especially designed for children. In a fairy tale, what usually happens? The young man goes out and slays the dragon and then as a reward for slaying the dragon, he wins the hand of the princess in marriage. It does not say anywhere that he is going to be a good husband. It only says he is a good dragon-slayer! But he gets the princess anyway. Of course they live happily ever after, so the story says, and it ends there.

If it went on to tell what really happened to this oddly mated couple, the moral of the story would be lost. For the point of the tale, of all these tales in all lands and languages, is that the world makes you this promise: if you achieve enough, then love and a happy marriage will come as a reward.

The world makes this promise to the child in his childhood literature, but he grows up to find that life is not like that. He can become a millionaire or write a Nobel Prize novel or invent a better atom-smasher, but none of these accomplishments guarantees him love and a good marriage. As a matter of fact, many of these achievements have been the work of men who are neither good lovers nor good husbands.

Achievement has nothing to do with love. Rather, it has nothing to do with love of another person. There is love involved when a man achieves greatly, but it may be one of several other kinds of love. It may be self-love, an unslaked thirst for recognition of himself that drives him. It may be a love for power, another kind of self-love. The man who spends all his energies on making a million may be motivated by this power drive that serves his self-love.

Or it may be a genuine, absorbing, profoundly satisfying love for the work itself. A great actor may be something of an exhibitionist, something of a narcissist, but he is also an artist and he lives, thinks, and breathes theater; it is his first and sometimes his only love. This can be true of painters, composers, writers, or research scientists and physicians and astronauts and even businessmen.

Many a businessman is in love with his business, first, and his wife and children second. Many a working mother loves her work, many a non-working mother loves her bridge game or shopping or good works in the community, to the extent that she is annoyed when the children's needs interfere. This does not mean that these women do not love their children, or that they are not good mothers when they are with their children. It means only that they are happier doing these other things, that they derive more pleasure from their non-mother activities than from motherhood.

We do not have to achieve greatly to be in love with our work. But it is clear that great achievement that comes from an intense love of the work has nothing to do with the love of a wife or husband or children.

This love of work and the love of another human being frequently conflict. But the conflict is not inevitable. Some men and a few women of great achievement have had good marriages. One thinks of Professor Einstein, the Curies, and a great love of the romantic 19th century, the love of Robert and Elizabeth Barrett Browning. History suggests these people as exceptions rather than the rule. This is why many men and women whose names are famous had only one abiding love, the love of their work. The love that leads to happiness in marriage was not theirs, no matter what the fairy tales say. They were good dragon-slayers, and dragon-slaying was what they really loved.

Go in and Fight

The world has a further lesson in non-love for the child, and this one is no fairy tale. It is the straight command: get in there and fight. Here we encounter some contradiction. We are taught, "Do as you would be done by" and also "Do or you will be done by." Yet the contradiction does not trouble us. We profess the Golden Rule but we practice the rule of aggression, or non-love. We are after all a practical people.

A child comes home from the playground and reports to his father that Jimmy who lives around the corner took his shovel away from him in the sandbox. His father asks, "And what did you do?" The child answers, "Nothing. I cried." The father then counsels his child: "I'll get you another shovel, but this is the last time. Now I'll tell you how to hold onto your shovel. The next child who tries to take your shovel away, you know what you do? You hit him! And you say 'Now let that be a lesson to you!' "

The child, greatly impressed, does not think to ask, "But what if he hits me back, and takes my shovel anyway?" He does not think of that problem until it is pointed out to him by a clout on the head, and with his own shovel, in the sandbox the next day. And when that happens, his father begins looking around for a jiujitsu instructor, even if the child is only four and a half years old.

Of course the world is not made for fragile people. We must learn to defend ourselves. But in learning how to defend ourselves, we are also learning how not to love. It is not very loving to say, "You take this shovel and I'll punch you in the nose." It would be much more loving to say, "If you really want the shovel that badly, help yourself."

But that may well be an impractical approach to life. We lock our car and double-check it before we leave it. We lock our house and apartment doors, we put our money in the bank and our valuables in the vault. We have lawyers read our business contracts to make sure we are not being taken advantage of.

This is the kind of society in which we live. If we are going to bring children up to live in it, we must teach them that there are people who might try to take things away from them. Our children must learn to defend themselves against such people, just as we learned to defend ourselves. Granted that it is necessary. But we must also be aware that such teachings are teachings of non-love, not of love.

We were also taught, and we duly teach our children, that it is necessary to get ahead if we are to amount to anything. "Getting ahead" must of course mean getting ahead of something, or more usually someone. We learn that we must race other people for the things we want, for whatever we want is also wanted by many others. The good seats at the theater, the good table in the restaurant, the good buys in the semi-annual store sales—we have to hurry, we have to get ahead of others who also want them. And then there are the good colleges, the good graduate fellowships, the good jobs, the good business opportunities. Everywhere we turn, for everything we want, we must beat out other people to get them.

We implore our children, as our parents implored us, to make good grades, try out for the team, win attention, win honors, outshine others. This is not necessary in all cultures. Just as it is impolite to monopolize the conversation at a dinner party, so was it bad manners among certain Indian tribes to win more than one foot race in a day of field contests. But to win is part and parcel of the culture in which we live. The qualities involved are all non-loving qualities.

It is no easy task to be aggressive and competitive, and loving and giving, all at the same time. Many a father, who spends all day fighting the competitive business battle, finds it hard to be tender and soft with his wife and children in the evening. We cannot turn these opposing emotions on and off like hot and cold running water. Some of the fighting mood is bound to seep across into the loving mood. The instruction we get in being ambitious and competitive and aggressive may be a necessary part of our preparation for life, but it is no help in learning to love.

The Distrust of Sex

The relationship between sex and love is another area of our development which often abounds with negative qualities. In our society we grow up distrustful of sex, and the reasons for this are not far to seek. As a people we suffer from an uneasiness with the subject that is handed down unknowingly from generation to generation.

It is astonishing how ingeniously parents manage to avoid the subject with their children, and all unconsciously. At some point in every child's life, and usually at several stages and in several forms, he becomes curious and wants to know. He may begin by merely wondering why his body is different from his sister's. He may want to know where his baby sister came from. Later, as he hears various garbled bits of information from his playmates, he would like to ask whether what he has heard is true, or what is the truth anyway about all this.

We know beyond a doubt that all children have this curiosity. They are curious about anything and everything, and they can hardly avoid being curious about this as well. Yet many parents tell us that their children never ask any questions at all.

This is a way of saying that they, the parents, managed to avoid hearing the questions when they were asked, or to avoid understanding what the questions were about.

Children very quickly learn that this is a subject their parents do not want to discuss. There are a few other subjects that children learn are taboo. One of these, for many parents, is death. But nothing suffers as widespread a conspiracy of silence as sex.

Since it cannot be discussed, a child soon comes to feel that there is something wrong about sex. As if to confirm this impression, most parents are reserved in showing even the most public aspects of physical affection. There are many children who never see their parents hug and kiss each other. A kiss, though sexual, is surely permissible before others, and yet there are children who do not see even this small sexual act.

We build still further confusions in our attitudes toward the body, especially those parts of it that are involved in sex. The genitalia becomes the focus of all sorts of difficulty for the child. While we are trying to stool-train him, we urge him to be sure and tell us when he wants to go to the bathroom. We show our displeasure when he forgets; we may even scold or punish him. Then suddenly one day he finds that he is not to do this. Possibly he has embarrassed his mother by trumpeting the announcement in the bus. She hushes him promptly, perhaps a bit roughly. People around smile a funny smile; his mother looks funny too; she may even be blushing. She tells him, "We don't talk about those things in front of people." Even if she does not say a word, he gets the idea. We do not talk about going to the bathroom in front of people. If he happens to come running from the bathroom with his pants down, they are quickly yanked up. We do not show those parts of our bodies.

Our attitudes toward masturbation have been somewhat liberalized in recent years. Parents who read books about bringing up children no longer punish their children or frighten them with stories of what will happen to them if they masturbate. And yet it is extremely difficult for a parent who discovers a child masturbating to refrain from giving some sign of displeasure or disapproval. Again, the child gets the idea. We do not touch this part of our bodies.

Once a part of the body has become stigmatized in our emotional life, it is extremely difficult to free it again for a gratifying sex life. The records tell us in no uncertain terms what a struggle it is for many to overcome these prohibitions when the use of the body as an expression of love is important to their happiness in marriage.

When children reach the age for dating, parental anxiety takes a new form. Daughters are especially the target of this anxiety. Mothers, and sometimes fathers even more intensely, hover over a daughter, keep a hawklike watch on her comings and goings, lie awake until she comes in at night. Worst of all, in some families not a word is said. A girl is not given an opportunity to talk about her problems with dates who may be a shade too aggressive even for her taste. She might want very much to have a bit of counsel from her mother on how to manage this sensitive matter, how to control a young man's ardor without offending him. She might like to talk things over even with her father. He is a man, after all, with a man's point of view. He was a young man once himself. He might be able to give her useful and sensible advice. But no. The subject is still taboo. The atmosphere is thick with anxiety on both sides, but no one says or does anything to clear the air.

Thus, right up to the age of marriage, the experience of childhood is reaffirmed. Sex is not an expression of love. At best it is something that love might permit, within marriage.

It is not a good thing, never a good thing, never a fine and healthy pleasure shared with the loved one. It is always surreptitious, secret, a personal self-indulgence, not a giving but a taking of forbidden pleasure. This is sad, because ideally sex can be one of the deepest expressions of love.

Unworthy of Love

A most subtle and pervasive ingredient in the inability to love is the sense of unworthiness and guilt. This, too, is built on childhood experience. There are times when parents, even loving parents, bluntly reject a child. They are too busy, too tired, or they have been pushed beyond their patience. There are times when parents are frankly punitive, in the heat of anger or, perhaps more damagingly, with cold and calculated hostility. Out of their own inner tensions and unresolved dissatisfactions, parents can unconsciously lay a cloak of disapproval over a child that he will wear the rest of his life.

If you tell a child often enough that he is naughty, he comes to believe it. If you notice him only when he gets out of line, and then only to scold or punish him, he eventually gives up expecting approval. His parents do not approve of him, do not love him; hence he is unworthy of love, undeserving of it. He gives up trying to win their love, since obviously he can never succeed. But he still needs and wants repeated confirmation of the attachment he feels to his parents. The only way left for him to get this is to arouse his mother and father out of their pleasant indifference. He becomes naughty. They become disapproving and punitive. Their relationship is an active one again. Unfortunately, after a while, he begins to accept what his parents say about him as really descriptive. He begins to think he was born to be bad, born to be guilty, born to be punished.

With this poor image of himself, he unwittingly goes out into life seeking not love but punishment. This is all unconscious, but still a most powerful motivating force. Such a person goes looking for an argument, looking for someone to fight. He is looking for non-love.

Some marriages endure only because the partners can fight with each other. That is really what they want. They want someone who says or implies, "You're not worth the pair of eggs I boiled for you for breakfast." This is the climate in which they lived at home, the climate of unlove in which they spent their childhood. Their deep sense of guilt and unworthiness demands attention in the form of disapproval and punishment, and the need can be satisfied only in an unhappy marriage.

The Signs of Non-Love

There are telltale signs of the inability to love. Of course they vary from one individual to another. Also there are always exceptions. Yet it is worth our while to consider some of the clearest of these signs as questions to ask ourselves about our own ability to love, as well as about the lovingness of those we love or would like to love.

The first such question is about an individual who has no friends or very few. People give many reasons for this: a sick mother with whom they must stay at home every night, a job that is very demanding, or the fact that they have moved often from one place to another, or have simply had bad luck. The reasons for not having friends are almost endlessly varied and many of these reasons are true. There is still another reason: they may not be very loving persons.

Such an individual may truly love one person. He may be devoted to someone. But in general he has not been loving. Rather he has been critical. He discovers what is wrong with people before he sees anything good in them. He tends to hold himself aloof, not to become too interested or involved. He may make an exception of you, and pour out all his love in your direction. You come to feel that he was a victim of his environment and that he really has a great capacity for love. So he may. But the chances are small. One who has a great capacity for love spreads it over many people. He is loving in general. He finds almost everybody interesting. One who has few or no friends, who finds few people or only one person interesting, is not likely to have a well-developed ability to love.

Our second sign is the feeling that "nobody loves me." A variation of this is, "nobody understands me." An individual who feels unloved is generally one who is not loving and is not giving love. An individual who feels misunderstood is one who generally does not understand or does not try to understand others.

The psychological mechanisms involved in this are fairly complex, but we can clarify this individual's difficulty with a glance at the mechanism called *projection.* We frequently suspect in ourselves unpleasant characteristics which we hate to face. Unconsciously we save ourselves this disagreeable experience by seeing these traits in others, of whom we can then comfortably disapprove. We *project* the trait. How often, in an argument, the man who feels rage rising in him shouts at his adversary, "What are you getting so angry about?" When one member of a group is doing all the talking and someone else tries to get a word in, how often have we seen the talker accuse the other of monopolizing the conversation? Or accuse someone else of being dogmatic when he himself has offered more opinions with greater certainty and less documentation than anyone present? These are all familiar instances of projection. If I feel that nobody loves me, the probabilities are that I am not being very loving toward anybody.

Another danger signal that there may be an inability to love is excessive ambition. An individual who is possessed by a drive to get on in the world is already in love. We know this from our definition of love as an attachment to anything, an idea no less than a person. The man who is ambitious to make a million dollars is in love with that idea, that goal. Another man is in love with fame, with recognition. Some people are socially ambitious and use rather than love people to further their aims. Another man locks himself in with his piano and works on his concerto—he is in love with the concerto. It would be very difficult to break into that love and compete with the concerto. Ambition can exist in any field, and it may be admirable, but if it is excessive, it is a fair guess that that individual is not loving of other people. The love he already has is all-absorbing, and he has no love to spare for anything or anyone else.

This sign may be a surprise: it is the inability to say "no." It is a surprise because people who can't say no frequently look very loving; the girl in *Oklahoma* who just couldn't say no seemed to love everybody. The truth is that such a person may really love nobody; she is unable to carry on a stable relationship. All she can do is please everybody. She is compulsively driven to please, mostly because underneath she does not believe people will love her if she refuses. She is forever buying love, everybody's love. This is one form of the sense of unworthiness we spoke of earlier, which is so damaging to the ability to love.

Finally we come to the perfectionist. This individual can give only conditional love. He will love you if . . . If you do this and this and that, exactly as he prescribes it, because he knows the right way and he cannot tolerate the wrong way— then he will love you. He is likely to be inflexible, humorless, and extremely demanding. He cannot tolerate people's foibles and, in short, he cannot tolerate people. A female perfectionist makes a very fine secretary; she will do an entire letter over rather than erase one comma. She may also make a good housekeeper, but she can be a hard woman to live with as wife or mother. The emotional cost of living this way is very high, and the perfectionist frequently explodes with impatience and hostility, neither of which is very loving.

Love Has Strings Attached

The conditional love of the perfectionist is more common than adults like to admit. As children we all learn this fact about love. It has strings attached. Nowadays we are sternly admonished about this. We are told that we must not say to our two-year-old, suffering his first bitter taste of competition for love, "Now you stop hitting the baby or I won't love you." And we are careful not to say it. But our actions say it far more effectively than words.

For we really and truly do not feel love for that two-year-old who is showing the very antithesis of love for his baby sister. He is full of hate; in his heart there is nothing less than murder. Automatically his antagonism calls forth antagonism from us. Automatically we spring to defend the helpless baby and to counterattack the attacker.

Thus the child begins to learn very early that we will love him only under certain conditions. We will love him if he obeys, if he keeps out of mischief, if he gets good grades in school, if he washes his hands before meals and behaves nicely in public. Our conditions are of two general categories: the child must give his parents as little trouble as possible and reflect as much credit on them as possible.

In other words, the child learns that he must *earn love*. It is not freely given. It is not part of the furniture of the house or a natural product of his growth or something built into himself or his parents. It is an award of merit. It can be won or lost.

A spirited child will risk this loss of love; sometimes he may seem to invite it by his persistently unlovable behavior. A more vulnerable child will watch his step, will be docile and even fawning, for fear of losing love. Most children do not go to either extreme. But they do gamble—they play now, pay later. They take chances with having their pleasure and risking their parents' displeasure, or non-love.

It is not such a dangerous game, for most children. But inevitably it leaves its mark on their later ability to love. For they do not learn to love unconditionally. From their earliest days, even if they avoid the development of the inability to love, they fail to develop the ability for total love. Love remains conditional, partial, variable.

Love Is Unreliable

The child also learns that love cannot be relied upon. The child begins his learning of love, as we have said, by loving himself. He loves his mother as an extension of himself, a part of the pleasure he enjoys in his own body when she feeds him and makes him comfortable. He does not, at first, need his parents' love. He only needs their care.

But quite soon his parents' love does become necessary to him. This happens when it dawns on him that the world around is separate from himself, that it is big and frightening and he is small and helpless. Then his parents' love becomes essential, because it is a guarantee that they will continue to care for him and protect him. They will continue to satisfy his needs, to comfort him when he is upset, to shelter him from harm—if they love him.

Love is thus something of secondary value to the child. It is not a value in itself. Like credit at the bank, it is a value only for what it can get him. What it gets him is everything—comfort, safety, life itself. It is a promise of the satisfaction of all his needs, and in these early months and years they are literally all his needs. He can do nothing for himself, except as his parents provide him with the means. Their love is his guarantee of everything. Is it any wonder that love should remain so important to him for the rest of his life?

But he finds that this guarantee is unreliable. It is given and withheld unpredictably. Sometimes when he cries he wins smiles, caresses, comforting words, comforting food or a dry diaper or just the comfort of friendly company. Sometimes the same cry brings him a frowning face, impatient words, hurried hands, and a hasty departure of the pleasant company he had every reason to expect. This love from parents is far less dependable than the love he has for himself.

The child's experience of the unreliability of other people's love begins very early. Later he sees some connection. The smiles and pleasant words come when he performs well on the potty or eats all his food without fussing. He does not always feel like doing these things in just the way that will bring approval, or at just the time when it is demanded of him. Sometimes he is simply unable to meet the demands made on him. And sometimes, he discovers, no matter what he does is wrong. He cannot know that his mother has a headache, or is behind with her housework, or has quarreled with her husband or perhaps her own mother, or she has people coming to dinner and is worried about some course on her menu. All he knows is that she is being unloving.

The unreliability of love is not learned in one lesson or one experience. It is repeated throughout the child's early years on a thousand occasions, in a thousand incidents too small for parents to notice and too trivial for them to remember. Even the child does not remember them as separate incidents or separate occasions. The unreliability of love becomes simply a fact of life, one of the more painful facts but indisputably a fact.

The Happy Newlyweds

This fact can explain many things that happen later. Consider a pair of newlyweds. They profess that they love each other forever and ever; eternity itself is not long enough. This highly romantic expression of love is a way of saying that this love I have for you is something you can count on. It is reliable. It is not like the love you had as a baby. That was a guarantee that you would be taken care of but you had to pay a price for it, and even then you could not count on it. You got love and you also got non-love, resentment, and sometimes open rejection.

This love is different. When I say that I love you forever, that nothing in this world is good enough for you, that I will do anything to make you happy, that is a way of saying that this is reliable love.

That is what they say to each other, that is what they believe, and they are very happy. Three days after the wedding, the husband happens to be watching a crucial football game on television when his wife unthinkably walks in front of the set just as a forward pass is thrown. He has missed the big moment; he has not seen whether the pass was completed.

In his excitement and frustration, does he say to his wife, "Darling, there is never a time when I'm not happy to have you fill my entire visual world?" He does not say that. Most likely he belts out some ungentlemanly expletive, and at once she goes into a depression, feeling utterly unloved.

He is not even aware of this because he is now interested in the next play of the game. Hours later he perceives that she is not talking to him. He cannot understand it; inwardly he shrugs it off—that's how women are. Finally, expressing her hurt feelings more and more obviously, she wins his attention and manages to let him know that he does not love her. He says he does love her. There ensues an argument over whether or not they love each other, in the course of which he becomes baffled and angry, she bursts into tears, and neither understands why this trivial incident has had the power to evoke so much emotion.

It was not, of course, his sudden and momentary explosion as she obscured his view of the game. She might have brushed that off with a laugh, an apology, or an equally lively response—if it had not struck an old wound. It is a wound that never heals for any of us, that wound made by the unreliability of our early love. The slightest drop in the emotional barometer sets it to twinging.

During the many months of courtship and the three days of their marriage, he has assured her repeatedly that nothing could ever come between them. Then a television set got between them. A football game got between them. All this has happened before, many times before. He is saying, as her parents said to her in childhood, I love you—provided you do the right thing. And walking in front of the television set just as a forward pass is being thrown is not the right thing.

Promissory Love

This incident also tells us that their love, which they honestly professed and believed in, was more promissory than real. The moment it became real they did not like it. So long as their promise of undying love was not tested against reality they thoroughly enjoyed each other, but the moment something happens, something that shows them what their love really is, they are shaken. What shakes them is the discovery that this love is not different, this love is no better than the love they had years ago as infants and children.

It is the same love she experienced as a child when she was sitting on her father's lap, looking at her father's watch, listening to it tick-tock. She and her father are having a wonderful time together. Her father is holding the watch for her to look at, holding it to her ear to listen to, watching her face for the smile of delight as she hears it. Then her father puts the watch into her hand, she drops it, and on that instant her father turns from a loving person to an enraged and unloving one. Why? The child has no idea. She only knows that for her, love is unreliable; the course of true love does not run smooth.

Some people grow up to fall in love, marry, quarrel, and make up; the course of true love does not run smoothly for them, either, but they manage. Other people always remain wary and fearful of love and some of them never marry. They may come to the brink of marriage but they never cross it. A permanent love, with all its unreliability, all its painful untrustworthiness, is just too scary for them.

For such people, the imperfect loves of childhood have resulted in an imperfect ability to love. Non-love, conditional love, unreliable love have left too much scar tissue to make it worth their while to try loving again.

Most people are not this adversely affected. We may fall short of developing an ideal capacity to love, but we do learn to develop some capacity. We put this into evidence again and again by innumerable loving acts. We offer apologies and we offer forgiveness. Kindness and charity have not lost their meaning in modern life. Our aggressiveness has not totally crowded out our cooperativeness. We live in a world in which love and non-love co-exist and it would be equally fallacious and unrealistic to claim that one or the other is gone.

An Obstacle Course?

This examination of the inability to love can easily look discouraging. We cannot deny that the loves of our maturity are influenced by the earlier loves of our childhood. Love is frequently imperfect for adults because it was imperfect earlier. There appear to be so many points at which learning to love may take a wrong turning. And all in the normal process of growing up!

Yet no one who is honest would ever pretend that growing up is not an obstacle course full of normal and natural hazards. We might define our growth as learning to deal with these hazards. Even a plant, even a vegetable has many difficulties to overcome before it reaches the maturity of fruit and seed. It takes no great effort to imagine how much more challenging must be the maturing of a human life. And if we regard love as at the very core of our life, then we must expect to find that learning to love is also beset with stumbling blocks along the way.

Surely a serious reader should want to know all he can about these hindrances. The more familiar he becomes with them, the better his chances for satisfying his desires for love. A most important category of emotional obstacles consists of the neurotic elements in our love.

CHAPTER NINE

Neurotic Love: Its Sources

IN ORDER TO explore with any profit the subject of neurotic love, we must first determine what we mean by "neurotic." It once was a word we used with the greatest of ease—about others. We would dismiss another's puzzling or unpleasing behavior with the phrase, "Oh, he's neurotic," or "She's neurotic." But we almost never said, "You're neurotic," unless we were prepared to lose a friend. And it was rare indeed that anyone would say of himself, "I'm neurotic," except to his analyst. To paraphrase the Quaker's remark to his wife, "All the world's neurotic save thee and me," we might add to ourselves, *sotto voce,* "And thee's a little neurotic too."

Today the situation has become worse. We even call *ourselves* neurotic, but not with the diagnostic candor that prefaces some effort to help ourselves. People use the term like a password establishing their membership in the chic, sophisticated group now in vogue. It becomes simultaneously a boast of their honesty about themselves and a sneaking acceptance of their own helplessness.

In the interests of politeness, we might begin with the social disclaimer that when we discuss neurotic people, present company is excepted. But we will not do that, because we are about to discuss precisely thee and me. We may not be able to recognize ourselves easily in these pages because each of us mixes and hides his neurotic tendencies from himself so that none of us is accurately reflected in any case history.

But we all have neurotic tendencies. Just as none of us enjoys perfect physical health, so none of us enjoys perfect emotional health. We have no diffidence about discussing our physical shortcomings. People take a certain pleasure in telling each other about their headaches, backaches, their bouts with intestinal viruses, and especially about their operations. People even enjoy listening, provided they have equal time to detail their own fascinating physical complaints. Rarely, however, does any of us recount his emotional shortcomings with the same relish. We discuss the things which irritate us, the people who annoy us, the situations which depress us, but we rarely if ever see them as possibly revealing emotional difficulties in ourselves. We are presently learning so much psychology that future generations might recognize and talk about personal shortcomings with greater candor.

This is not to say that we should wallow in our emotional difficulties. They are nothing to be ashamed of, but neither are they anything to be proud of. They simply are; they exist. Some years ago there was a popular book entitled, *Be Glad You're Neurotic,* written by a psychiatrist. In his preface, the author said, in effect, "See, I'm neurotic, and I'm writing this book, so obviously neurosis can be profitable." The book was in fact a best seller and to that extent the author was proved correct. Many people longed to find something good about their neuroticism, and they bought the book probably for that purpose. But to be glad you're neurotic is to be glad you are unhappy. It is to be glad you are paying an excessively high emotional price for everything you get out of life.

We should make a distinction between being neurotic and having neurotic tendencies. We all have the tendencies. We are all vulnerable in some area, just as physically we are vulnerable to certain kinds of illnesses. Some people have frequent headaches, some catch cold easily, some get indigestion from certain foods. The neurotic, on the other hand, is not merely vulnerable. He is already ill. The neurotic is not merely a person who has a neurosis—the neurosis has him. He is possessed by it.

The Elusive "Normal"

It is normal to have neurotic tendencies, but it is not normal to be neurotic. "Normal" is another word that we use with great facility, and yet it is not easy to be precise about what we mean by it. When I was a student I thought it might be a good idea to determine what the psychiatrists and psychologists understood by the word. I looked it up in the index of every textbook on abnormal psychology and related subjects that I could lay my hands on and, to my astonishment, the word never appeared. Unbelieving, I thought it was perhaps an oversight, since the index of a book is often prepared by the editorial staff rather than the writer. Yet, reading many of these books and thumbing through the pages of others, I still found that the word "normal" was absent.

This seemed illogical, for these writers were discussing the abnormal, and the meaning of "abnormal" is derived in large measure from what you mean by "normal." I was prompted then to look up "abnormal" and "neurotic." Here I found enough and more than enough references, but there appeared to be so little agreement among the experts that I was thrown into confusion and gave up my private little research project.

More recently efforts have been made in the literature to clarify the meanings of "abnormal" and "normal" with the introduction of the concept of adjustment. By adjustment we do not mean a philosophical reconciliation to the inevitable, a kind of stoical acceptance of the ills that the flesh is heir to.

In clinical psychology we use the term much as engineers use it. A structure is adjusted when it can meet all the stresses of its function and still stand, still perform. By a well-adjusted person, a normal person, we mean one who has achieved a reasonable relationship between his needs and abilities on the one hand and his social opportunities and the existing sanctions of his society on the other. A good adjustment is a workable or efficient or fairly happy balance between what the man presents to the world and what the world expects of him. If the two can blend in such a way that the individual gains some gratification out of his life and society need not take much if any trouble with him, we look upon this individual as "normal" or "well-adjusted."

The normal person is free to propose and pursue rational goals. By "rational" in this context we mean goals that are the product of thought. A normal person has thought about his goals enough to know that they are probably good for him. Experience has something to do with this, of course. A young person might set an unrealistic goal, such as winning a tournament for which he barely qualifies, and we would think nothing of it. He is not being irrational; he is simply lacking in experience. But if at the age of thirty or forty he is still setting for himself the same kind of goals, we tend to look askance. By that age, we think, he should have learned what is good for him. The fact that a pre-school child wants to be a cowboy or a fireman does not dismay us, that a teenager romantically yearns to travel around the world on a tramp steamer, that the successful business man speaks of being a beachcomber. The aspirations of children and the dreams of adults are one thing; their decisions are another matter.

There is nothing derelict about dreaming. The goals of such idle thoughts do not really activate us. In fact our failure to reach such goals is often better for us than our success might be; our failure actually saves us from the disaster of some kinds of success. How often have we dreamed, "If only I didn't have to work for a living, if I had a million dollars and could retire, then I wouldn't have any problems. My only problem is never having enough money." Surprisingly often, such a man does achieve his wish and within a short time he begins to crumble and go to pieces, simply because he is no longer working, no longer aspiring, no longer attaching himself to goals that have some meaning and importance for him.

The normal person, we have said, is relatively free to pursue his goals. A neurotic person is precisely the opposite. He is not free. Being possessed, he is driven by inner forces that are beyond his control, forces which prevent him from reaching or working rationally to reach his goals, forces which in many cases prevent even a rational choice of goals.

The Test of Reality

We need to make a further distinction, the distinction between "neurotic" and "psychotic." "Psychotic" is the professional term for what we popularly know as insanity, and the distinguishing sign of the psychotic is that he has lost touch with reality. He sees or hears as real what is going on only in his imagination, and we call this hallucination. Or he misjudges or misinterprets what is actually going on around him, to such a degree that he not only suffers intensely but can get into serious trouble. He may see two people talking together and conclude that they are plotting to kill him, and he may run and hide in actual terror. Or he may attack his supposed enemies, believing that he must do this to save his own life. This is of course dangerously psychotic behavior, and it proceeds from a gross misinterpretation of what is going on around him, a complete break with reality.

The neurotic, on the other hand, suffers no such break with reality. His behavior is not generally odd or unusual in any way. He is more often than not indistinguishable from the normal people around him, because he develops defenses by which he tries to keep his emotional difficulties largely to himself. We actually help the neurotic maintain his secrecy. In our daily relationships we do not diagnose, but rather we pass judgment on people, according to how we feel toward them. Of someone we like or who is close to us we say, he has the courage of his convictions, he sticks by his guns. But if we dislike him or he is in a position to make difficulties for us we call the same behavior obstinate, stubborn, mulish. In both instances the diagnostic picture is basically the same, namely that of emotional rigidity. This can be acceptable or not to us depending on our more general affection or disaffection for the individual involved.

Thus the neurotic's behavior may be favorably regarded although it may be irritating or even unbearable to others. In the ordinary course of things this does not strike us as abnormal. None of us expects to be liked by everybody—that in itself would be an irrational expectation.

The neurotic, then, is adjusted to reality. He has come to some sort of working arrangement with it. The emotional price he pays is higher and, in this sense, his adjustment is strained. It is not easy to determine what the price is that he pays in loss of freedom. We can observe it only when his neurotic demands take an obvious form.

Such an instance is a man who is compelled to wash his hands every time he touches something. If he washes his hands dozens or hundreds of times a day, obviously he has little time for anything else. He would make a very poor lover, if for no other reason than lack of time.

This is of course an extreme example, and because it is so extreme the limitations on this man's freedom are glaringly obvious. He is quite literally driven by his neurosis. Each time he touches something his hands are rendered unusable, and he must at once do something about it to right himself with his peculiarly distorted world. He himself may well recognize these tyrannical inner forces which drive him as irrational.

He may make some feeble attempts to rationalize his behavior, he may try to justify it with, "Well, you know, a person can easily get infected." But even so he is likely to recognize his excuses as mere excuses, and admit that he cannot help himself, that he is driven by these forces.

Compulsive hand washers are not exactly common, although they are not so very rare, either, except in this extreme form. Yet although most of us are not dominated by our neurotic tendencies to this degree, none of us is entirely free to pursue happiness, despite what it says even in the fine print of the Constitution of the United States. Everyone has some neurotic elements in his personality.

Since we are not at the moment interested in neurotic people—that is, people with neuroses, who are by our criteria abnormal—but with normal people like thee and me, we need not go into the vast subject of the neuroses. We want to know about our own neurotic tendencies, how we can perhaps recognize them in ourselves. And then we want to know how these tendencies affect our freedom to pursue happiness, specifically to pursue it in the form of love.

We can narrow down the common signs of neuroticism to these four: anxiety, a poor image of oneself, immaturity, and unconscious fixations. Let us look at them one by one.

The Commonest Sign: Anxiety

The neurotic tendency that most of us share in some degree is anxiety. It is a form of fear but not so sharp as real fear; it is fear blunted, diffused, a pervasive feeling of uncertainty or insecurity. Suppose you were walking in the park and, on turning a corner, suddenly came upon a lion, a real honest-to-goodness live lion confronting you on the path. Now if the lion were not in a cage, you would experience real, honest-to-goodness fear, as who would not? But if he were in a cage in the zoo, and you still felt uneasy, if you wondered whether the cage were really strong and what would happen if he escaped from it, then you would be experiencing anxiety.

Anxiety is fear somewhat detached from reality; it is like a low-grade fever. You may walk around with such a fever, go to work, forget that you have it for hours at a time; yet its presence predisposes you to more extreme reactions, more disproportionate reactions than you would normally experience.

In the same way, anxiety makes us prone to excessive reactions. It is a chronic anticipatory fear that underlines and emphasizes the possibly threatening aspect of any situation we encounter. It makes us feel an element of danger where little or no actual danger exists, as with the lion in the cage. It is our major mark of insecurity.

Where does anxiety come from? There are a great many theories, some of them quite fanciful. For example, there was a psychologist of considerable prominence named Otto Rank, who said in effect that merely being born is enough to make anybody anxious. He developed what has come to be known as the birth trauma theory. Reduced to its barest terms, this theory holds that we are all initially so comfortable in the womb, with all our needs cared for, that the experience of being dumped unceremoniously into the cold, cold world is a traumatic experience, a shock from which we never entirely recover. We tell the world how we feel about it with our first vocal expression, a wail of protest. From then on we may not literally try to crawl back into the womb, but we do literally seek ways to reduce and eliminate the anxiety of having been born. According to this theory, anxiety would be absolutely universal. No human being could entirely escape it.

Alfred Adler, another distinguished psychologist who was a contemporary and for a time an associate of Freud, proposed that a certain amount of anxiety is inevitable simply because we are all born young. We are initially helpless, dependent, unable to do anything for ourselves. Our first years are spent in a world of giants peering down upon us who are sometimes kind and sometimes not and in any case do not always understand us. It takes us several years to be able to reach up to a door knob and then we find we do not have the strength to turn the knob and push open the door. The first years are full of such crushing experiences, and they leave us feeling anxious and threatened for the rest of our lives. This anxiety is intensified or diluted according to the way we are treated during the early years, and so the degree of anxiety with which we are left is variable. But according to Adler's theory, too, anxiety in some measure is virtually inevitable for all of us.

Sigmund Freud had a more complex theory, stemming from his assumption, with which we are already familiar, that we are all members of the animal kingdom and at birth are simply little animals, little bundles of physical needs and desires. These basic animal desires he grouped together as part of the human personality and named it the "id." Initially, as he described it, the infant human being is dominated by these clamorous physical desires, this seething id. But within the first few years of life the child finds that he does not live alone and he does not live in a jungle. He lives in a complicated world, surrounded by others like himself who are older and farther away from the animal stage than he, more humanized or civilized, and they make demands upon him to learn their more civilized ways. They command him to do certain things and restrain him from doing other things, and the child feels obliged to accept their ways in order to continue to have his needs met.

In this way, each of us joins the civilized human community. We identify ourselves or join with these older members who have power over us, and we develop a conscience, that is we accept their rules, so that even when they are not around to tell us what we may or may not do, we tell ourselves. We ourselves undertake to control our desires, to govern the id within us. This conscience is what Freud named the superego.

The superego, then, comes to exert a certain measure of control over the id, but it never eliminates these seething animal forces. And so we are left with a continuing conflict between the two, between the forces of the id and the forces of the superego. This lifelong battle within us sends up a good deal of smoke, and the smoke is our anxiety. In a battle there is always the threat that one of the contestants might win, that one side might dominate the other—either that the superego would deprive us of satisfaction for our deepest desires, or that the id would drive us in directions that would leave us with guilt, since from our first years we have learned that these desires of the id are mostly not acceptable in the human community to which we belong.

And so, according to Freud, again we have no way of avoiding the early experiences that generate anxiety.

Many of the ordinary experiences of childhood may heighten that initial anxiety. A kind of hostility-guilt-anxiety complex is a familiar component of the growing years. We love our parents but when they deprive us we become angry with them and we feel or may even express great hostility toward them. Then, loving them or fearing to lose their love, we experience a backwash of guilt, which in turn leaves us with a need for punishment—to wipe out the guilt—and then we are afraid of how we are going to be punished. Parents may pressure us, or even if they do not, life itself and our own growth pressure us into new situations such as school and friends. We are steadily pushed out of the safe and comfortable—because familiar—present stage of growth into the next one, in which we have to confront situations and people for the first time, make decisions, take increasing responsibility for ourselves.

And there are the sheer accidents of life, of getting locked in a closet or lost in a supermarket or encountering a growling dog. We see someone else get hurt, or a parent or playmate falls ill, or someone in the family dies. All these chance experiences leave scars in the form of a proneness to fear, to anxiety.

The wonder is that we are not all of us more anxious than we are. To be alive is to be insecure; living at all is fairly hazardous. We learn about its hazards when we are too young to counter them or to be philosophical about them.

One reason we are not all overwhelmed by our anxiety is that we have evolved ways of dealing with it. We band together in social groups of various kinds, whether organized or by geographical accident; we identify ourselves with our fellows and feel an expansion of our individual ego in the group. We also enjoy the protection of the group; whatever happens, we will not have to face it alone. The family is such a group; so is the teenage gang, the country club, the neighborhood, the nation. Groups come in all sizes, to suit all needs.

We also reduce our anxiety by gathering around us not people but possessions; wealth, success, status all buttress us against the threat of unnamed disaster that may befall us. Much rarer, and requiring very special gifts, is to achieve a great creative expression. For the artist, the production of a work of art is a catharsis, a release in the disciplined and acceptable form of art, and such a release has very often the effect of dissipating anxiety, at least for a time. In this solution for anxiety not only the artist but all of us can participate, for when we see his play or his painting or hear his symphony or read his novel or poem, part of our aesthetic response is the release of some of our own anxiety. Part of the enduring greatness of the great Greek tragedies and of

Shakespeare's tragedies is their power to bring us this catharsis of the spirit.

Finally, we allay our anxiety by seeking out love. How we
bring our anxiety into love and how we succeed or fail in
using love to allay it we will consider more fully below.

The Self-Image and the Cultivation of Failure

In the course of growing up we develop an awareness of
our own identity and an image of that identity, a self-image.
We form an idea not only of who we are but also of what we
are like. This development goes on through the same years
and through much the same experiences that contribute to
our anxiety. Being small, dependent, incompetent and often
in the wrong, finding ourselves apparently unloved much of
the time, and much of the time inadequate to do what is expected of us, we begin to believe that we are, in fact, rather
poor specimens. We tend to accept what seems to be our
parents' and the world's opinion of us as inadequate and unworthy. We develop a poor self-image. This is a second, common neurotic tendency.

One way that we express this poor opinion of ourselves is by
making sure that it is confirmed: in other words, by cultivating failure. If this seems contradictory, we must remember
that if failure was the pattern that seemed to be our lot
through our growing years, then we had to make an adjustment to it, and our adjustment has been to accept it. Failure
is our norm; it is familiar, and hence comfortable. Anything
else is strange and tends to be frightening.

And so we see many people who, with success within their
grasp, "deliberately" seem to avoid it, throw it away, turn it
into failure. I remember a youth in his senior year in high
school, who won two major prizes in the school but could
not pass the language requirement. He was a brilliant student
who was making high grades in all his subjects and failing in
Spanish. Now at that level one can pass a language course
simply on rote memory, and memory of any kind was one of
his strong points. It was incredible that he could not pass his
Spanish course, unless he "wanted" to fail. If we examine his
performance in terms of a self-image that was comfortable
only with failure, then we have our explanation of this boy's

behavior. He f·iled because he "wanted" to fail, because he had to fail despite his abilities.

The more obvious expression of a sense of unworthiness is the opposite one, the drive to disprove one's poor self-image, the drive to win success. We have all known people who seem to be driven repeatedly, compulsively, to win. They must have success; they must prove themselves over and over again. They have no time or interest for anything else; they do not even derive much joy from their successes. That deep sense of unworthiness can be only momentarily allayed. It is voracious; "as if increase of appetite had grown by what it fed on." No amount of success can ever satisfy it.

Still another way of dealing with it is to withdraw from the battle entirely, to withdraw from people and their demands and all the kinds of demands to which one feels oneself unequal. A fairly common form of this withdrawal is illness. For many who suffer chronic illness of a psychosomatic variety, this is the deeply unconscious reason. They are indeed ill; they do not invent or imagine the illness. They are physically ill, and they suffer real pain and real disability. But it serves their unconscious need. Illness excuses them from trying to do what they deeply feel themselves inadequate to do. It also wins kindness and sympathy, instead of disapproval for the failure which constantly menaces them.

Such a disabling manifestation of a sense of unworthiness is not, of course, the average. In international affairs there is the "diplomatic illness," the convenient illness which excuses one from attending a meeting or an event which it would be more diplomatic to avoid. No doubt we all have our diplomatic illnesses from time to time. If they are too frequent, we may have reason to wonder about the quality of our self-image.

The Persistence of Childhood Ways

We use the word "immature" often, but usually as a criticism rather than as a diagnosis. When immaturities of one kind or another persist into adulthood we do not generally notice them unless they are irritating, or they interfere with relationships and the serious business of living. We all retain some of our childish ways, and there are some that we should not give up even if we could. We need our childhood love of fun and games, of nonsense and fantasy; we need to be able to kick over the traces and be foolish now and then, so long as nothing suffers but our own dignity.

But some forms of immaturity are troublesome and they are neurotic signs, signs of unconscious forces restricting our freedom to be adult and to pursue happiness.

A familiar one, and one that is very disruptive to marriage if not to love, is the childish inability to look ahead, to see and pursue long-term goals. In childhood this is natural. Learning to save some of this week's allowance for next week's pleasure is hard even for a teen-ager. A young child can hardly accept his mother's rule that he must save the lollypop someone gave him until after lunch. Learning to postpone pleasure is part of growing up. Much of our adult life is concerned with planning and working for something we want; much of our thought and energy is invested now for satisfactions later. A partner in love and marriage who cannot collaborate on this adult level can cause havoc to the relationship.

A blanket description of immature behavior is *wanting* rather than *giving*. A child knows very little of giving. We ask a child to share his toy or his candy with a playmate, and he may refuse outright, or he may do it reluctantly, only because we ask him to and he wants to please us. He is interested in and dominated by his own wants, his own pleasures. It is only later, and very gradually, that he becomes aware of other people's wants and needs, and still later that he becomes interested in contributing toward other people's satisfactions and happiness.

Becoming aware of other people in this sense is like learning to perceive depth and distance with our eyes. We have two eyes, and this gives us binocular vision, or vision in depth, but it takes some time for us to develop this as a mode of perception, and still longer to learn to judge distance accurately. To an infant everything he sees is within reach: he puts out his hand indiscriminately to touch his own foot or the toy at the end of the crib. Only by experience, by moving around and touching things, by having to go from touching this object that is near and that object that is farther away can he develop his perception of the third dimension.

In the same way the child normally learns that other people have feelings like his own, that a pinch hurts his playmate as it hurts him. At some point he learns that there is pleasure to be gained in giving another pleasure. And this of course is a great step into maturity, especially into maturity in love.

An individual who has not taken this step has been arrested at the childhood level of love, the narcissistic level of receiving love but not giving it.

The Superhighway of the Unconscious

The fourth in our list of neurotic signs is unconscious need or fixation. This, like immaturity, is a catchall phrase by which we mean the assorted baggage of childish or irrational needs which remain with us from earlier stages of development. We all have some of these, and they all deprive us of our freedom to some degree.

These inner forces restrict us in much the same way that we are restricted when we are driving along a superhighway, one of a steady stream of cars. We have to keep moving, have to keep going at the same speed. It may be a lovely day in spring, and a patch of flowers blooming beside the road catches our eye. We would like to stop and enjoy them, but we cannot stop. We must keep moving.

So it is with the lives of people who are driven by unconscious forces. They cannot stop. They cannot love except within the narrow confines of their most habitual mode of behavior.

Very commonly, for example, a person will grow up with a most impelling need to be right and yet remain innocently unaware of the existence, not to mention the imperativeness, of this need. Surely he owns up to the value of truth, justice, accuracy, but then what self-respecting person does not? He never sees that he *has* to be right; it is always the importance of some issue which he believes arouses him. What he fails to see is that *he* remains the central issue in every disagreement large or small.

As a result of repeated scrapes with guilt early in his life, threats of punishment, or the personal menace of some sense of inadequacy, a man may unwittingly *feel* that one wrong move is enough to decrease his status in the eyes of the world. Being wrong once is enough to betray him just as clearly as a single dollar bill might reveal the criminal of a million dollar burglary. Few own up to such distrust of the world and nobody owns up to such a fragile picture of himself—not out of dishonesty, but just plain unawareness.

The need to be right is mostly unconscious and, for this reason, our judgments about ourselves are frequently more partial than true. It is always the other person who failed to signal, made the wrong turn, or somehow involved us in the automobile accident—never, or rarely ever, are we primarily at fault. For many people, the same thing happens in their personal relationships. Every dent, every scratch is always the other person's fault. They simply cannot get off their superhighway of personal righteousness.

This lack of freedom is the most indelible mark of our neurotic tendencies. Whatever the specific symptoms may be, the limitation of our freedom to act in our best interests is always the general consequence. Anxiety, a poor self-image, immaturity, and unconscious fixations all conspire to limit the quality of our love no less than the quality of our life. A still closer look at the everyday expressions of this enslavement might help the cause of liberation.

CHAPTER TEN

Neurotic Love:
Its Everyday Expressions

NEUROTIC ELEMENTS IN our behavior no doubt spoil love for us, but do not eliminate it from our experience. It is important to recognize this because of our romantic tendency to call a relationship something less than love if it eventually fails to meet our expectations for it.

Being attracted, falling in love, and developing attachments are all inevitable, whether they are fulfilling or not. Some loves, and more especially some phases of love, are just like the story book descriptions. Others seem no better than life is itself from day to day. The reason, of course, is that *we* are the subject of our loves and, as such, we influence its character enormously.

We overlook this easily enough in a troubled relationship. People say, "But it is not *my* neurotic qualities, it is my loved one's which are making all the trouble. She (or he) is the one who—." And here follows a detailed list of complaints. This answer yields immediate comfort but it is not likely to lead to improvement in the love relationship. For if anyone can convince himself that he is not the spoiler, he does not need to change himself, and as for his beloved, he is not likely to succeed in changing her. Of course he can try. And so we often have two people, each expecting the other to become nicer, to become more loving in one way or another, and neither of them willing or able to do something about his own faulty contribution to the relationship. Many relationships endure despite this chronic dissatisfaction the participants have with each other.

This is not love as we dream of it or strive for it. But do we strive for it? More often than we recognize, our neurotic drives convert our love from an expression of desire to one

141
141

of need. We dream of one thing and act on another. Everyone wants beauty, tenderness, understanding, passion, but our neurotic needs easily usurp the attention and energy with which we approach life. Our fond desires soon seem to have little relevance to our everyday behavior. They are crowded out of the sphere of real influence back to our dream life, our last stronghold of freedom. Work, routine, and dissatisfaction quickly fill such a life and, more than ever, love seems utterly unattainable.

The first reason for this unhappy result is in the choice itself which people of marginal adjustment make. There is a somewhat cynical, but nonetheless frequently valid, saying that neurotic birds of a feather flock together. Under the romantic exterior, it may be neurosis calling to neurosis which brings two people together and even holds them together. They are not making a choice in their best interests, representative of their most stable values and tastes, but out of the strongest, least controllable forces within them. They seek each other out and cling to each other not out of the luxury of desire, but simply because they cannot help themselves.

A man plagued, for example, with the necessity of proving himself repeatedly in the eyes of all other men might easily be driven along two lines. He *must* make a million dollars and he *must* be seen with the most beautiful girls. I remember exactly such a young man who as a bachelor had always dated the most attractive and hence the most popular girls. The more popular a girl was, the more hotly pursued by other men, the more he pursued her. At any given moment, the girl of his choice was the one with whom it was most difficult to get a date because she was always dated up.

He finally married one of these desirable girls. He had to work hard at it for more than a year but at last he succeeded; he bested his rivals and captured the prize. And from the moment he had her, he lost interest. He no longer found her fascinating, charming, or even physically desirable.

What he failed to see was that he was never primarily interested in her. He was interested in the other men who pursued her; he was interested in the competition with them. He admitted, somewhat ruefully, that during the year he was fighting to win her he had had the best time of his life. If he could only keep getting married all the time he would be a happy man. Getting married was the fun; being married was a dismal mistake.

Obviously this young man's love had not been a free choice of a woman he desired. He had been driven by a neurotic need to compete with other men, regardless of what girl they were competing for. When he had won the race he was still not free to enjoy his victory. A neurotic need, not being in our best interests, fails to satisfy us even when we satisfy it. He could not be happy until he was in another such race.

The attractive young woman he won over was just as driven in her own way by needs she failed to control in herself. She did recognize, during her courtship, that her fiancé was happiest showing her off and that they were rarely alone together. It seemed odd that he was often gloomy and grumbling when finally circumstances did separate them from others. His gifts were always expensive, even to the point of irresponsibility, but never were they really understanding or sensitive. Still, having been lost in the shuffle as one of many children, she liked being shown off, fought for, treated as something special. Once she was his, her huge need for attention was neglected and rapidly became the source of painful disappointment.

Another example is the case of a young woman of modest background who fell in love with a charming man, good-looking, a scintillating conversationalist, with literally hundreds of friends. She was aware of his track record: he had been married three times, had been on the verge of marriage at least a half a dozen times besides; he owed everyone money including herself. Her friends warned her; the man himself kept postponing their marriage. Yet she would not be satisfied until she had married him even though everyone else felt the marriage was doomed from the start. This was a man who could support friendship, that is, friendship with a hundred or more people, but he could not maintain a few close and deep friendships and he surely could not maintain a love relationship with one individual.

He was attracted to this young woman in the same way that he was attracted to many others at the same time. Most people accepted him on the pleasant but superficial terms he offered them. But a young woman appeared who, driven by her own neurotic need, wanted more. She saw in him popularity, acceptance, charm, wit, all the glamorous qualities of which in her plain background she had felt deprived. For her, the man represented escape into a glorious new world, a dream world of sophistication, status, satisfaction. Being driven by these needs, she allowed her attention to wander from the desires she would inevitably have as a woman married to such a man. His very popularity later became a source for jealousy, his gregariousness a feeling of personal rejection, and his wit altogether too caustic for her comfort.

If you listen carefully to a man or woman about to marry, you can often hear not love but a neurotic need revealed in the description of the prospective mate. "Wait until you meet her," the lover says, "she is so sweet, so agreeable, she never says no, there isn't a more generous woman on earth." Now that may be so, and he may have found a jewel of a girl with a genuinely loving and giving nature.

Or he may be telling you that what he has found is not someone to love but someone to control. This agreeable girl may never say "no," not because she is so loving but because she is completely passive and in need of someone to do all her thinking for her. The lover, on the other hand, is unwittingly seeking not a partner, not a woman with whom to live a stimulating and gratifying life, but someone who will never disagree with him, someone who will never challenge him. He is a man so insecure that he feels threatened by the most trivial opposition. He may have found someone genuinely loving and lovable, or he may have found merely someone whose need to be dominated dovetails with his need to dominate, to have his own way.

It may work out, of course. When neurotic needs dovetail, the marriage may not be happy but it may last. Two such people may cling to each other throughout life. It is not that they do not love each other. It is just that their love for each other is dominated by and expresses their neurotic needs. And so, the love is not very rewarding. Instead of making them happy, it keeps alive what is wrong in them. Their relationship gives them the opportunity par excellence of continually cultivating, rather than curing, their neurotic needs and shortcomings.

Many a man unawares goes looking for a wife who will be his mother, a woman who will run a well-organized household that ministers to his comfort. There will never be a dent in a sofa pillow, the ash trays will be immaculate, the check-book will always be balanced, his shirts will be properly laundered and his suits will go out for pressing and come back to his closet without his lifting a finger. His marriage will have everything except humor, spontaneity, joy, surprise, and the kind of give and take that makes for a deeply satisfy-ing human relationship.

Such a man and woman may remain permanently married but their relationship is not with each other. It is a relation-ship each has with the mechanics of living, she to run the machinery and he to consume the conveniences it manu-factures. The arrangement satisfies each one's neurotic needs but it fails to fulfill their dreams of love.

And so it goes. What we think is our choice is really made for us. The more strongly neurotic an individual is, the more strongly do these inscrutable forces drive him. Not only are they unrelenting. These needs operate below the level of con-sciousness and, as a result, they fail to benefit from our own intelligent examination. More often than not, these needs are residues of a much earlier stage of our existence. Weaning ourselves away from them would be better for us than satisfy-ing them. Anything short of this amounts to marrying not for love, but to reduce anxiety.

The indulgence of our neurotic needs allows our own past to blackmail us. Not only is the choice for love and marriage corrupted, our conduct in marriage is similarly affected.

Neurotic Need Mars the Marriage

We need not be neurotics to have neurotic shadings to our personalities. We do not have to be dominated by neurosis to be nonetheless driven into modes of behavior which put a blight on our love.

We fall into patterns, habits of behavior, and the remark-able point about these habits is that they are so ordinary, so familiar that we do not even notice them. A true neurotic is likely to be original in his way of expressing his neurosis; the compulsive handwasher we discussed earlier is an example. But the rest of us tend to fall into unoriginal patterns of compulsive, neurotic, and consequently unloving behavior.

The common or garden variety of this is nagging. Let us consider a man who is discontented with the quality of his love, with the climate of his marriage, but he does not know why. He is not able or perhaps he has not tried to see the defect in his own contribution to this love. But he can see what is wrong with his partner. Why can't she be more thoughtful of my needs? Why can't she be a little less impulsive about our social life? He feels he works hard, comes home tired, and likes his comfort. If he catches her up on every small fault, he sees this as a justifiable judgment of her wrongdoings and not at all as nagging. He even admits that one of the things he hates in anybody is nagging.

His wife may fit the pattern and nag back with an equal lack of awareness. She innocently feels that all she wants is for him to love her but she wants love on her terms. She wants all sorts of little attentions. She wants constant evidence of his approval. She wants constant buttressing, constant reassurance.

These two people are obviously on a collision course. They may truly love each other, may truly be capable of a strong and rewarding companionship on many levels. But they have fallen into a self-feeding pattern of discontent with each other, and they are hardly aware of it. Each of them has allowed an unrecognized neurotic need to dominate a relationship that perhaps does not have to be so dominated and so contaminated.

Granted, the husband needs a little of the kind of thoughtful consideration for his comfort that he used to see his mother give his father. His father, too, needed this kind of attention, and his mother catered to it. She catered to her son, in the same way. His need for it is built into his personality. But it is not his whole personality.

Similarly, the wife has a trace of immaturity. She often does not stop to consider another's wishes before gratifying her own. If friends call and suggest going out to dinner together tonight, she does not think of consulting her husband first, because she wants to accept, and he may say no and then she will be deprived of her wish. This is childish and self-centered behavior. And it is combined, as it often is, with another childish characteristic, a need to be loved and approved no matter what she does.

Nagging is, of course, unloving. In this familiar pattern, both partners are essentially complaining about their unfulfilled needs in their attachment to each other. Neither is willing to meet the other halfway, so that they can express their love without the constant intrusion of their own unsatisfied needs. A husband loves his wife by recognizing her feelings of insecurity and satisfying her needs for reassurance. The wife loves her husband by accepting his wanting to be cared for and made comfortable, and does in fact give more thought to his comfort.

These are not such extreme needs that to satisfy them the partners must exploit each other. Each one unwittingly wants to be accepted by the other as he is, as she is, with the slight neurotic defect that each one has. We all have such defects. But we also have other strengths and out of them we can afford to coddle each other's neuroticism a little.

Many of us shirk the use of our own emotional resources. We fall in love, we marry, and then we forget that a human relationship is a living process requiring care. We slip back into the familiar pattern of thinking the way we did before marriage, about ourselves, about our own wants. Unconsciously, in the relaxation of marriage we give free rein to our own neurotic drives and at the same time turn a deaf ear to the needs of our partner.

Some Unloving Patterns

Some people make this very evident in their behavior while at the same time concealing it from themselves. They find admirable substitutes for their real role as lovers. They fall in love and marry but strong inner forces press their primary attachment not to each other but to goals which represent some relief from their own anxiety. They are simply not free enough emotionally to relax and enjoy love; they must reduce the pressure of their own vague fears. So, the woman, familiar to all of us, runs a beautiful house, devotes herself to her children, to the PTA, to good works in the community, to so many admirable activities that she wins plaudits from everyone who knows her and superficially this reduces her anxiety. Even her husband is proud to find her such a first-rate citizen, and he cannot understand his failure to enjoy his marriage as much as he thinks he should.

The masculine version of this is also familiar: the man who has gone all out to win his wife, and then goes all out to win something else. He courts his wife magnificently: he focuses all his attention on winning her, but when she is won she becomes merely money in the bank and he goes on to further conquests, not necessarily of other women. He expands his business, buys a more expensive house, takes more luxurious vacations, increases his status and his importance in every possible way.

His wife may be unaware of all this as competition, because she enjoys the benefits of his success. She gets a mink coat, later on a diamond bracelet, and this has the appearance of love. Meanwhile, she loyally carries out her end of the partnership. She runs his increasingly large establishment, bears and rears his children, joins the women's auxiliaries of his clubs, wears his mink and diamonds with good grace. She may feel something is missing; she may look back on his courtship with some nostalgia, but she keeps herself worthily occupied and it must be confessed that she enjoys her share of all this status and all this material comfort.

Then suddenly the children are grown up and out of the house. One of the strong cohesive forces in their life together has virtually disappeared. Their house seems enormous and their relationship distant. At about this point, the husband begins to look somewhat critically at his wife. She is older, heavier, more worn than he remembers, for he has not really looked at her for quite a while. In the same vein, she begins to ponder the fact that he is not very good company. He too has put on weight, he is getting bald, takes little interest in theater or the arts, and worst of all takes her utterly for granted.

These people had love to begin with, and both contributed to its loss. Both allowed their anxiety, the same trace of neuroticism, to press them relentlessly to make good from the social point of view. It became more important than their relationship to each other and finally destroyed the potential they initially saw in it.

The course of such events easily lends itself to blame and judgment, neither of which catches the essence of what actually happened. Although the pattern is familiar enough, the most moving parts of it lie buried in our unwillingness and inability to recognize either the anxiety we suffer or the inadequate goals we set to dispel our anxiety. The complex machinery of such behavior easily usurps enough of our thought and time and energy to chase our more purely romantic interests back to our dreams and our everyday expression of love virtually out of our life.

Lingering Immaturities

Just as traces of anxiety can contaminate our conduct in a way which despoils our love, so too can lingering immaturity breed a host of inappropriate reactions. There are men who bring into their marriage a reserve and reticence toward woman, still remaining from boyhood efforts to extricate themselves from a hovering, over-solicitous, over-inquisitive mother. It may be hard for a loving wife to break through this mistrust, but if she recognizes it and takes it into account as part of the husband she loves, she may help him to overcome it. There are girls who have grown up with a mother who dominated the household and a father who permitted her to do so. To such a girl, the image of a wife is a dominating woman like her mother, and that is the kind of wife she may begin to be. Her husband may find it hard to overcome this image, but if he recognizes the danger and accepts his wife as a wife and not a boss, she may gratefully come to lean on his love and his strength.

There is of course no guarantee that the mistrustful husband or the wife who tends to dominate can be won over to a less neurotic, more loving partnership. But we assume that these are not powerful neurotic drives, only tendencies, and tendencies can be encouraged or discouraged. We can let the weeds overgrow the garden, or we can discourage the weeds and cultivate the flowers.

This is not nearly so easy as it sounds. Our bad habits have a powerful grip on us. One of the most common of these is the habitual tyranny we allow immediate desire to exercise over us. Consider, for example, the importance and the use of timing in our behavior.

When we have had even a little experience of life, we know that one can say practically anything to practically anybody if one only chooses the right moment and the right manner. Yet many of us, who are most sensitive of this truth in our public relationships, are willing to ignore it fatally in our private relationships, our most significant relationship of love. Why is that?

It is, again, a neurotic pattern, a holdover into adulthood

of immature behavior. A child acts first and thinks later, if at all; he is governed by his feelings, his immediate desires and impulses. He cannot put anything off until a better moment, or frame his words or deeds in a better form. He cannot stop to think how his behavior will affect another person. He has not learned to empathize with another's feelings or think from another's point of view. He knows only his own.

In a child this is normal. It may cause us inconvenience, irritation, or embarrassment. It may get the child into difficulties. But we recognize it as childish behavior, even though we may feel we must rebuke or punish the child if only to teach him what he is obliged to learn.

In an adult it is no longer excusable as childish. It is an immaturity and therefore out of place. It is part of a neurotic pattern. It displays one's inability to accept adult responsibility. As a way of getting what one wants it is unrealistic, and often it is self-defeating and destructive. At the least, it is the unattractive behavior of a spoiled child.

The alcoholic, the gambler, or any person who is absorbed in an intense pursuit of some satisfaction of special importance to him tends to behave much the same way. Such a person is concerned primarily with himself, and self-concern dulls sensitivity to others. He cannot pursue his own all-absorbing desires and at the same time have very much thought to give to others.

Even the occasional compliance, the promises to do better, the extravagant gifts and gestures of affection are only placation. They are an appeasement of the loved one, a way to stall off disapproval and perhaps disaster. But at any moment, particularly if his desires are blocked or denied, he is either catapulted into a crashing rage or crushed into a whimpering state of self-pity. There are men who display this immaturity of reaction when a tired wife discourages their sexual advances at bedtime. Many a woman responds with similar immaturity to a husband's reluctance to commit himself to some additional financial burden in her behalf. In both cases, the reaction of the adult is no better than that of a child. Their own desires are almost too much for them to handle. Denial, postponement, compromise are too alien to their habits of response to have any appeal.

Popularly we label such immaturity childish or self-centered. It is true that one has to be free of oneself in order to give one's attention to another. A comfortable relationship requires a degree of freedom, something of oneself to spare, beyond what is required for one's own interests. We cannot be in love and in tune with the highly sensitive needs and desires of the loved one, if there is a constant clatter of static issuing from ourselves that we cannot turn off or turn down.

Tripping Ourselves Emotionally

Another major obstacle to the freedom we need for love is a poor picture of oneself. As a result of a host of damaging experiences, described earlier, people commonly enough approach adulthood feeling unworthy, diffident of their abilities, and trapped by a constant consciousness of self. The wounds of growth are of two general types: either they cripple us, limiting our ability to function, or they leave us still smarting from the pain of early threatening or damaging experience.

In either case, we are left emotionally in the condition of constantly tripping over our own feet. We get in our own way. We cannot keep ourselves sufficiently out of our own consciousness to focus on and attach ourselves to someone else. If faint heart ever did win fair lady, he could hold her only as a nurse or mother. Love is fed by what we give the object of our love. People who think poorly of themselves are all too willing to become charity cases and, more than they realize, develop a one-way relationship of dependency.

The subtle neurotic tendencies that creep into our love and infect it are difficult to eliminate not only because they are longstanding, but because they grow in response to unconscious needs. By definition, we cannot recognize them in ourselves. A woman does not see herself as emasculating or, to put it more popularly, as wearing the pants; all she is trying to do is to be helpful. She does not believe she has taken over, usurped many of her husband's functions in the family, driven him to a point where only inadequacy can show. She regards her requests of him with the same innocence an aggressor nation asks merely for two things: sea coast and interior.

Love, long before it eventuates in marriage, is frequently visibly discolored by the recurrence of certain harmful patterns of conduct by one or both of the lovers. Up to a point, they try to overlook such incidents, and absorb them by the healthier elements in their relationship. Before long, their rational behavior begins to yield to the persistent yet puzzling pull of unconscious traces of neuroticism. "What's happening to us?" the troubled lovers ask of each other. "Why do we hurt each other so often nowadays? There is no doubt about our love and yet we don't seem to have any fun any more." Translation: we have needs of which we are unaware which are damaging and incompatible with love, and they often slip through our good intentions and drive us to do things we later regret.

More than we readily recognize in ourselves, we grow up with an unsatisfied yet unconscious need to test the acceptance and love we enjoy from others. It is as though we were six years old, unsure of which we wanted more: love or self-assertiveness. The six-year-old still sees these desires as irreconcilable and his conflict over them gets him into trouble. One moment he asks for love and in the next he tests his assertiveness by some act of disobedience. Following a reprimand or punishment, he learns to doubt the love he receives at other times. Some of us never get over this and continue to question the genuineness of the love we receive. If our need to establish this is strong enough, we do not look for it in a way we are apt to find it. We unwittingly tax our lover by an act of marginal acceptance and then give her the third degree as though she were a criminal, to uncover the facts of her feelings.

Sometimes a person's predominant unconscious need has nothing directly to do with love as we ordinarily know it and yet it may have a continuing and deleterious effect upon love. As a result of a poignant sense of early deprivation, a man unwittingly may come to live his life exclusively under one banner: ownership is more secure than love. He may leave himself not enough time for the complex cultivation of those things which make for a worthwhile relationship with some member of the opposite sex. The fortress of material wealth with which he guards himself from the world protects him also from women. What he fails to see is that love at best needs no defences. The result is that his love remains, like everything else in his make-up, guarded and therefore partial and often strained.

All these crippled loves have the same tragic quality. Glowing expectations give way to strife, disappointment, a lack of fulfillment. The people involved are not villainous; they are largely the innocent victims of forces in themselves that they cannot easily see or control. They may be first-rate citizens of considerable accomplishment. People love to be with them. And this makes it all the more puzzling. How can one's private life and deepest attachments be so troubled by discord in the face of social success?

The answer, of course, is easy. We learn the rules and live by them. Society rarely demands as much of us as we do of ourselves. More important, social demands are clear-cut, whereas we are not nearly so sure of what we want in our closest relationships. No sooner do we conjure up a desire than we begin to feel the discomfort and restraint of guilt, not to mention other demands we feel we ought to meet. Our more purely social relationships generally do not involve these personal inner complexities. Society beats out its rhythm simply and clearly; it is much more difficult to keep in step with the more impelling but less easily understood tempo of our own inner needs.

Buttressing the Structure

What can be done about all this? How can we deal with our anxiety, our poor self-image, our immaturities, our unconscious needs—the traces of neuroticisms we all bring with us into adult life and adult love?

There are many professionals in the field who take the bleak view that there is very little we can do. Since anxiety, for example, begins so early in life, since it seems to be an inevitable component of our human experience—and the theories we have discussed seem to confirm our observations that this is so—then do we have much chance to overcome it?

The same is true of our other common neurotic tendencies. Few of us manage to survive a normal childhood without some trace of the sense of unworthiness, some immaturities, some unconscious fixations at an earlier stage of development. Perhaps ideally they could be avoided, but neither we nor our human societies are ideal. Every society that has been studied seems to leave something to be desired as far as individual development is concerned.

The pessimists point out that since these defects are imprinted so early in life, they become part of the very foundation of the personality. And just as the foundations of a building are covered over, so the foundations of personality are covered over. A multitude of experiences are piled on top. In a building, as stresses and pressures attack the superstructure, it begins to crack and show the distressing signs of faulty construction. Something must be done with the basic structure of the building to prevent its total disintegration and collapse.

So it is with our personality, the superstructure which must encounter the stresses of living. But how can we get to the foundation, to the basic structure of our emotional life by the time we are fully grown?

Freud devised a method, the method of psychoanalysis, but it is a long, painstaking process and not everyone can afford years of therapy. Nor is it an infallible method; no therapy, medical or psychological, is perfectly successful. Yet the prospect is not so gloomy. There are many supports that can be added to the superstructure, and these additions can be highly decorative, highly enhancing.

The architects of the great Gothic cathedrals found ways to support and simultaneously adorn their structures. The idea of the flying buttress was born when medieval architects raised the vaulted roofs of their cathedrals ever higher and higher, and the walls began to totter under the weight. They had no steel girders in those days, and so they invented the buttress, and designed it so that it not only supported the walls but seemed to fly and soar along with the building. The flying buttresses of the Notre Dame in Paris, which one admires from the Left Bank, were so much a part of the beauty of the cathedral that when it was refurbished and strengthened seven hundred years later in the 19th century, additions were made to these buttresses and not to the foundations or the walls themselves.

When a great artist achieves a work of art and, incidentally finds in it a release for his anxiety, he does much the same thing. He builds a flying buttress that not only supports but also enhances him. We need not be great artists to adorn and buttress our lives successfully. We may need some help at times, but there is also a great deal we can learn to do for ourselves.

Breaking the Neurotic Chain

The first thing is to use our free time in a more calculated effort to enjoy ourselves. We have mentioned this elsewhere in this book, but it merits repetition. We have a tendency to fall in a vegetative heap at the end of the day and an even bigger one at the end of the week. We allow our leisure to remain undirected and consequently unfulfilled. We become irritable, annoyed and soon use the people around us as targets for the expression of our vague dissatisfaction. As they begin to respond in kind to us the dormant neurotic elements in our personality flare up and the result is as familiar as it is unhappy.

Planning one's pleasures more carefully can help a person enjoy himself more thoroughly. Feeling better, he feels more worthwhile, more grown up, more giving. Parents recognize that when their children are healthy and happy and enjoying themselves, they also tend to be good, to be cooperative and willing to continue the pursuit of happiness.

Other cultures have done more and talked less than ours about pursuing happiness. We have been brought up in a social tradition that tends to frown on enjoyment; enjoyment for its own sake was sinful or at least dangerous. Pleasure opened the door to Satan.

But social attitudes change, although slowly. For generations, when the modern western world was being built, people had to work hard merely to survive, and even harder to achieve a minimum of security. Any time they took to enjoy themselves might cost them dearly; it might even bring disaster. Most people lived on the edge of destitution and starvation, as many millions still do in many parts of the world. But we today have a surplus of time and resources that we can afford to spend on enjoyment. And our attitude toward enjoying ourselves is changing in consequence.

Enjoyment can serve our purpose in many ways. Any form of enjoyment can take us out of ourselves, free us from our nagging anxiety and insecurity, give us a vacation from our neurotic burden. We rarely laugh alone, but we laugh with others. Laughter is more infectious than a cold. The most uproarious comedy can fall flat in a half-empty theater but when the house is full everybody laughs.

Happy children are nice, and so are happy people. People

are nicer to each other when they are having a good time. The more people enjoy themselves together, the fonder they become of each other. And so one of the best ways of dealing with neurotic stresses in love is to do enjoyable things together. So long as we enjoy ourselves, we remain within reach of happiness and, feeling this way, we crowd out the neurotic tendencies which otherwise damage our personal relationships.

The difficulty in all this is that neurotic means sick, sad, unhappy. The stronger the neurotic elements, the more difficult does it become to plan and calculate one's pleasures. There are people who habitually find what is wrong anywhere. "How can I enjoy anything," asks a college girl, "when my teachers are all dull, they give us far too much work, and there are no boys around?" Obviously not everyone feels this way. Other girls at the same place are enjoying themselves. *Their* attitudes and activities are worth studying if happiness means anything to the sad young woman. Better yet, their activities are worth imitating merely to start the process of feeling differently.

Our neurotic tendencies injure us, but they do not destroy us. Assuming we are average, there is much we can do for ourselves without treatment. We are not disabled. We function well and have good times. It is precisely this which helps us more than anything else.

There is a current emphasis on understanding what is wrong with us as though this guarantees freedom. Of course it frequently helps to become aware of drives which have been pressing us unconsciously. But awareness is not always enough for their dismissal. Redirection of these needs is a lot easier. Although unconscious fixations or drives do not lend themselves to deliberate conscious redirection, the process is enormously enhanced by the general richness of our lives. Simply, this means that the more interests a man has, the more channels of expression he has available for any and all of his needs. If he has a stronger need to be with men than women, for example, his love life need not be ruined. He may through his political or athletic interests come to spend enough time with men not to be vaguely restless and unhappy about the time he spends with his wife.

The picture is of course even more complex than this. Many

needs, many interests, many facets of our personality and many people and situations are all thrown together into the hodge-podge of our lives. This is why thinking about ourselves is so hard. We can and do a certain amount of evaluating and planning, but generally the decisions we make reflect our *mood* even more than our rational thought. This is why it is so important to protect our mood. Any small bit of pleasure we give ourselves and others does exactly that—it protects our mood and puts us in better position to limit the damaging effects our own neurotic tendencies might otherwise have on us.

CHAPTER ELEVEN

Love and Loneliness

LONELINESS IS LIKE the common cold—scarcely anyone is immune to it. Most people have experienced the infection at some time and some people seem to be suffering from it almost all the time. Some people are more susceptible, others less so, and we seem to fluctuate, too, in our susceptibility to loneliness as to the common cold. We are more likely to be lonely at certain ages, certain seasons of the year, even certain days of the week. For young people who are lonely, weekends and holidays can be the loneliest times, while for elderly retired people the weekdays when everyone else is at work may be the times when they feel their loneliness most acutely.

To push the analogy a little farther, loneliness is easy to catch, hard to cure, rarely fatal but always unpleasant and sometimes wretched almost beyond bearing.

There is an impression among observers of the social scene that loneliness is increasing. It is talked of as a social illness like unemployment or juvenile delinquency, not so dramatic in its effects as either of these but desolating for those who suffer from it and painful even for the more fortunate to think about.

Our cities with their swollen populations and cliff-dweller high-rise buildings are breeding places of loneliness. Neighborhoods crumble under the housing development bulldozers and families scatter in the pursuit of jobs and professions everywhere. In a world on wheels, old and comfortable groupings of people have disappeared. In the factories, computer-run machines replace the companionable work crews, and some unions are asking "loneliness pay" for the solitary machine-watcher to compensate him for the loss of human give and take on the job. Increased longevity adds a new kind of lone-liness among men and women who outlive their work, their friends, and their marriages.

These divisive forces exist along with others which sociolo-gists have described in great detail. Here we are interested in loneliness not as a social phenomenon but as a personal and individual experience. We would like to see how it comes about, why it strikes some people and not others, some ages more intensely than others, and how we can ameliorate and perhaps prevent it.

Alone Is Not Lonely

For all its obvious manifestations, loneliness is not a simple phenomenon. Being lonely is not the same as being alone. We may be alone by choice, or even if not by choice our aloneness can be productive, but loneliness is by definition involuntary and most often it is unproductive of anything but restlessness and discontent. For many kinds of work, some recreational pursuits, and indeed merely to think and dream, a certain amount of solitude is essential for many of us. Whether or not we like it, there can be great value in being alone. But there is only sadness in being lonely.

We may actually feel loneliest in a crowd, jammed physi-cally together in a bus or a subway train, side by side at a lunch counter or in a motion picture theater. The physical closeness of other human beings can intensify loneliness. There they are, all going about their business, going home to families or out with friends. To the lonely soul, everyone he sees seems preoccupied with living and involved with people; no one is lonely except himself. And yet many of those who seem so much more fortunate are actually going home to marriages or families in which they are as lonely as though they lived alone.

The lonely person may also be alone, and when he says that no one ever rings his doorbell or calls him on the telephone, the objective facts may bear him out. Yet he might have the same feelings if he were surrounded by a family, only he would clothe them in different words. He would say that in a house full of people there is no one he can talk to, no one who understands him, no one who really cares about him.

In another connection we talked about the mechanism of projection, that unconscious device by which we project onto others the failings that we find it unpleasant to face in ourselves. There is much projection in loneliness. The lonely individual who complains that no one cares about him may actually be complaining that he does not care about anyone. That his loneliness is self-created is very hard to admit.

And yet what difference does it make whether his loneliness is his own doing, or the result of others' coldness, or perhaps of impersonal circumstances? It is no less painful whatever its cause. Furthermore, whatever its cause, no one can do anything to remedy it except the sufferer himself.

Objective circumstances may contribute to loneliness; anyone can feel lonely in a strange place, away from familiar scenes and people, but that is a transient, situational kind of loneliness. If an individual remains for any length of time in the new place and continues to feel deeply and pervasively lonely, rather than temporarily homesick, it is then the unfortunate interior loneliness that one may suffer anywhere. This is the kind of loneliness one takes along wherever one may go with whomever one may be. This kind of loneliness or detachment may sometimes suggest deeper emotional disturbance. The anxiety associated with it may be masked from others just as successfully as the fantasy frequently connected with it. All we generally see in such people is their polite reserve.

True loneliness is a basic sense of unconnectedness with people. It is in essence the denial of satisfaction of a deep need that we all share, the need to form relationships, to become attached, to love and be loved in some way.

The Absence of Love

To say that loneliness is the absence of love may seem merely to state the obvious. But when we remember our definition of love as an attachment, some of the implications are not so obvious. A husband and wife may fight all the time; theirs is a negative attachment, but it is an attachment, and whatever else they may be they are not lonely. On the other hand, a husband and wife may never say a word to each other that is not courteous, and yet they go their own ways, indifferent and detached. Either or both of them may be bitterly lonely within the superficially unmarred, formal relationship of marriage.

Still another individual, without marriage or family, living entirely alone and perhaps in deprived circumstances, may form so many and such satisfying attachments on the level of friendship and companionship that he is never aware of living a lonely life. He is not, in fact, lonely.

The need to become attached in some way to other people is deep within us, part of our nature as human beings. The human species has a long childhood of comparative helplessness which enforces dependent relationships. The human individual also has a capacity for awareness of himself as an identity, and in our Western culture this awareness of the self, this individuality, takes on a special importance not at all found in primitive or Oriental cultures.

In the West we see ourselves less as members of a group, more as individuals. Yet our individuality is uncertain until it is recognized and acknowledged by others. The young child at the age of two or three years begins to demand this recognition of himself as an individual when he breaks out of bounds, refuses to come when called, refuses to obey his mother; his use of the word "no" is an assertion of his individuality. Much of the adolescent's rebellion is similarly a demand for recognition of his separate identity, his individuality.

Individuality is not easy to be sure of in a vacuum. Other people must signify their awareness of us, their response to us, in order to assure us of our identity. And beyond this, we would prefer them to respond to us positively, with liking or at least with interest, to reassure us that we are likable or interesting or worthy of favorable attention.

Most of the attention that we give and receive during our waking hours is formalized, institutional. We greet others with, "Good morning, how are you?" and we are not usually much interested in the answer; what is more, we are reasonably sure that the others are not much interested, either. Most of us have little opportunity in our daily relationships for the expression of important feelings. We need intense relationships for the expression of intense feelings, the kind of feelings that makes us truly aware of ourselves as individuals, as identities. We seek such relationships. And when we fail to form them, we are lonely.

The Individual's Progress

Despite our emphasis on individuality, our way of growing up actually gives us little preparation for it. From the beginning we are nurtured in groups—the family group, the neighborhood group, the church or Sunday school or perhaps country club group or summer camp group, the grade and high school peer group and, if we go away to college, the college groups of many kinds. At college all one has to do is raise one's voice, to have company. People live in groups—dormitory, fraternity, sorority groups, class groups, team groups, club and extra-curricular activity groups. Everywhere on campus there is a group of some sort and everybody belongs to at least one of them. Even the fiercest nonconformist nonjoiners have a group, the group of nonconformist non-joiners. The problem at college is how to get away from people long enough to get some studying done.

Then suddenly at commencement all these groups shatter, all the pieces fly off in every direction to home town or city, to jobs, to marriage, to separate and individual lives. It is the first year back from college that teaches young men and young women, at long last, what it is to be an individual, alone and without the automatic innerspring cushioning of membership in a group of some sort.

For the young people who live in small towns, the old group may or may not reconstitute itself after college. Many come home only to take off for a big city where job and perhaps marriage opportunities are more promising. For most of those who return to a home in the city, as well as those who leave home to make life in a city, there is literally no group, no neighborhood, no community of human scale into which they can fit themselves. The city is too large to be a community in itself, and city dwellers are too mobile, or too jealous of their privacy in crowded quarters, to make a friendly community of their apartment house or block or neighborhood.

There are exceptions. In our major cities there is a social elite, the equivalent of what used to be called the Four Hundred in New York, the Main Line in Philadelphia, Beacon Hill in Boston. For these families there are specific events at which young women ready for marriage make their debuts and young men attend, if only out of social obligation. At these events and at subsequent entertainments, at summer resorts where these families have their homes, and at various suitable and ritual occasions, the young people are expected to enjoy themselves at the same time as they look each other over with marriage in view. These young people, in other words, can return to the same group whenever they choose. If they like, they need never strike out for themselves as individuals; they need never pay the price of possible loneliness for freedom from the social forms of their group.

Young people who are not members of that statistically small and exclusive group have no choice. They must make their own social way. They take jobs, but the people they meet on the job are not homogeneous as all the other groups have been until now. They vary enormously in age, background, education, interests. And they all have their own orbits. After five o'clock they all vanish to their own homes, their own families and social groups, if they have them, or to lonely lives which they generally keep concealed from their office colleagues.

Lonely people are generally secretive about their loneliness, as though it were something to be ashamed of, a symptom of failure. And in a very real sense it is a failure not winning friends and love and marriage. It is a failure in not getting love and in not giving love, in forming attachments.

The brand-new Bachelor of Arts on his first job will not know at sight which are the lonely ones among his office mates. Indeed he may never know. All of them will manage to look very busy, very much occupied socially after hours. The only ones who will admit to knowing nobody and wanting to meet people are those few like himself who are also newly arrived in the city and on a job.

If he wants to avoid a similar secret loneliness behind a false façade of social success, the newcomer must work hard at forming attachments in order to fall in love and get married.

The Importance of Getting Married

Getting married may seem an illusory solution for loneliness, since some marriages do not banish loneliness for their partners. It may even seem a drastic solution, since marriage is after all a commitment to another human being, made in good

faith and presumably for life. Surely it is better to make many
friends and become involved in many relationships of lesser
importance until one is ready to make a mature choice of
a life-long partner. Shouldn't one be reasonably selective
about whom one chooses to marry?

Obviously one should. But it is also obvious that many
young people who pride themselves on their selectivity are actually demonstrating that they would rather be alone. For people who are wary of forming attachments, it is very easy to
find something wrong with all available candidates. If a person does not like the kind of people he is meeting, and yet
makes no discernible effort to meet other kinds of people
whom he might like, then clearly he prefers to remain un-
attached, no matter what he may say to the contrary.

Indeed it is better to get married. Even if the marriage turns
out to be a mistake, it is more of a mistake not to make this
mistake. People who marry are, at least, keeping alive the
ability to commit themselves to another human being, to form
an attachment and invest certain hopes and efforts in that
attachment. The longer an individual remains unmarried, the
longer he is avoiding a commitment, detaching himself, un-
relating himself to other people. And the more he is courting
that permanent detachment that we call loneliness.

Suppose the marriage turns out to be a mistake, let us dis-
passionately consider its cost. Ours is a mobile society, in
which divorce may be painful and is likely to be expensive
but it is no longer a permanent wound. There are many who
benefit from a first marriage which does not last very long.
From time to time we have referred to the beneficent traumas
of life, and this can be one of them. More and more we are
finding that a good and lasting marriage is the second marriage
for one if not both the partners.

For a man or woman who is widowed the same advice
holds; it is better to risk a less than idyllic second marriage
than to remain alone. A woman who has been exceptionally
happy in her first marriage may well grieve for what she has
lost, but she will do well to marry again even though she has
only a small chance of matching it with her second marriage.
In actual fact, if her first marriage was really a good one and
not romanticized in retrospect, then she has a better than
average chance of a good second marriage as well, for she
has already shown herself capable of being a good wife.

It is always better to have someone to think about, to be considerate of, even to be angry with, than to have no one at all. It is better to have a scapegoat for our discontents, and many a marriage is held together because it serves this purpose.

Building Bridges to People

It is all very well, no doubt, to advise young people, and widows and widowers, to go right out and get married. What if they can find no one to marry? Is there no such thing as poor luck?

Luck is unquestionably a factor. Even more serious a factor is the difficulty of meeting people, of making friends, of finding and fitting oneself into groups of likeminded, companionable people. We have already mentioned the divisive forces that keep people apart in the modern urban-suburban way of life.

Granted that it is difficult. But simply to agree that it is difficult is scarcely an answer. If the river rises and washes away the bridge it is obviously necessary to build another bridge, or at least to get a boat. If social forces divide people from each other, then they must find some way to circumvent the forces and come together in spite of them.

When we cannot form a group of our own, then we must join a group already formed. Americans have been so cruelly derided by their own social critics—Sinclair Lewis, for example—for being "joiners" that many of us cringe at the thought of joining anything, even the Democratic or Republican Party. We may vote the straight ticket year after year but we decline to write ourselves down as party members and still call ourselves independent voters.

For anyone who is alone, it is essential to join something. He does not have to join any group he does not like. There is bound to be one that is interested in something that interests him. If he likes sports cars he can join a sports car club; if he likes to watch birds there are bird watchers' societies. There are boating clubs, skiing clubs, clubs for miniature railroad fans and model airplane fans, for parachute jumpers and skindivers and kite fliers. There are amateur orchid growers' clubs and gloxinia societies and dahlia societies and societies for Japanese dwarf tree fanciers.

Whatever people are interested in, there is a group somewhere of those who share that interest. Very often there is a publication, and there may be an international society whose members write letters to each other about their interest. There is no reasonably healthy human being alive who has no interest or cannot develop one; most of us have secretly cherished half a dozen interests upon which we have never acted.

Building a bridge to people may mean taking inventory of oneself and one's life, and perhaps making substantial changes —a new job, a new neighborhood, another city. A young woman decides to look for a job in an engineering firm because engineers are mostly men and she wants to meet men. Another goes to Alaska for the same reason; it is one of the few states in whose population the men outnumber the women. In our highly mobile society the traditional groups of family and community may founder, but mobility also opens the way to new groups and new communities. In more rigid societies of the past, many men and most women lived out their lives in the place of their birth, whether or not they were happy there.

Taking inventory of oneself may reveal that some psychological barriers have been building up against people. Many a woman, young or older, dutifully accepts her friends' invitations and meets many men, but she comes away from each dinner party feeling that somehow all the attractive men are married, and the unmarried ones do not pursue the acquaintance. The chances are she is not interested in them. Whether or not she is aware of it, she is doing something to discourage them from becoming interested in her.

It is painful to face our defects. It is painful to do something about them, because doing something means changing habits of feeling and of behavior, and that is very hard. And so we explain away our inability to become interested in people by saying that people do not seem to become interested in us. We accept our solitude, and begin declining social opportunities— we feel tired, we have a hard day tomorrow, it looks like rain, the date is not really that interesting. Soon we are left with our solitude whether or not we choose it. A top whirling around on its own axis digs itself a deeper and deeper hole. The only way out is to accept someone's hand and let oneself be pulled out into an orbit that revolves around people, not around oneself.

For and Against Solitude

Being alone has its advantages. There are many occupations that cannot be shared with other people; we read, study, practice a musical instrument in solitude. There are many worthwhile tasks that demand long hours of lonely persistent effort. For thinking, contemplating, working out problems, making decisions—and paying bills or writing letters—it is necessary to be alone.

There are unique pleasures, too, in being alone, making no effort to accommodate oneself to another's needs or wishes, having no thoughts or feelings except for oneself.

These are dangerous pleasures. People too easily become addicted to solitude, to the relief of not having to bother about other people, and the solitary world becomes ever narrower and more inward. It tends to become distorted, in the same curious way that a word too often repeated becomes distorted. It sometimes happens while you are writing a letter, perhaps, that one word suddenly sounds strange—let us say, the word "and." You repeat the word to yourself—*and, and, and*. Try it now. Repeat *and;* keep it up for thirty seconds. This simple word, one that you use hundreds of times a day, soon begins to sound bizarre. You are not even sure of its spelling.

If that can happen in thirty seconds with such an ordinary, emotionally neutral word, imagine what happens if we spend not a mere half minute but hour after hour with highly charged thoughts and feelings about ourselves, going over them again and again without interruption, without distraction. Like the word repeated too often, our thoughts and feelings become bizarre. We lose perspective, proportion, balance.

When people are part of our world, they will not let us do this. They will not leave us alone to spin around on our own axis. They distract us, bother us, annoy us—and this is all to the good. They talk about themselves, and whether or not we are interested, even if they bore us to distraction, it is good for us. It shakes us off that continuous inward-turning axis, nudges us out into a wider orbit. People force us to objectify our perceptions, even of ourselves. Out of sheer politeness we are obliged to respond, to say something, answer a question, express an opinion.

It is better to spend more time with people rather than less. Even if they are people who annoy us, who bore us, who seem to be wasting our time, they do something for us; the time we spend with them is not wholly wasted. Best of all, of course, is to spend time with people whose companionship is stimulating or at least enjoyable, but if we cannot have cake every day we take bread or even dry crackers.

Anxiety grows on solitude, as we mentioned in another connection. Aloneness is the greatest breeding ground for the diffuse, unfocused, pervading uneasiness that makes us vulnerable to chronic worry. Almost anything can become a cause for concern to the solitary person; almost anything can make him fearful. People who spend too much time alone tend to jump when a telephone or doorbell rings. They become tense; their nerves become uninsulated and exposed. If they are not consciously fearful, they are likely to suffer anxiety in some part of the body. They overeat or have indigestion or are unable to sleep. They take less good care of themselves. Lonely people admit there is no point in fussing over their clothes, a meal, their dwelling place. We catch such glimpses in ourselves on an occasional night alone. The lonely person acts this way habitually, that is, he treats himself poorly more of the time. In clinical practice we see emotionally disturbed people, some who are gregarious and some who are not, but the ones who suffer most are those who are most alone.

Dead-End Individualism

We tend to equate a love of solitude with a strong individuality. Young people especially like to think of themselves as strong and independent in proportion as they can get along without the company of others. The cultivation of solitude can be a phase of emotional and intellectual growth, a last whirl around the egocentricity of childhood, before they step out toward the larger adult horizon. But it can also become an unhealthy habit of withdrawal, or rejection of others out of fear of being rejected oneself.

Questions of "What am I? Who am I? Where am I going? What is the meaning of life?" have always occupied philosophers in some form. The basic postulates of existentialism are of course great favorites with young people—in dormitory bull sessions they are almost as popular as discussions of the opposite sex. Questions like these are a stimulating spur to the exchange of ideas when they arise in a group of people, but when they float up out of solitude they have a pale shadowy quality, the very opposite of robust thought and feeling. They have the anxious sound of an individualism not strengthened but rather shaken by its aloneness. Such questions would probably not arise at all if the questioner were involved in relationships with others, if he felt bound to others. A young man or a young woman in love is not likely to ask, "Who am I? What is the meaning of my life?"

We see many examples of the mistaken exaggeration of individualism as a strong, solitary, go-it-alone way of life. It is a kind of dead-end individualism, not an expression of individualism so much as of emotional alienation.

The sense of oneself as an individual thrives best not on solitude but on interaction with other individuals. We might say that no one is a whole individual until he is part of another person, or of many people. This runs counter to mathematical law but it is good psychological law. When we are too much alone our identity tends to lose its dimensions, to become vague in its boundaries. We feel ourselves most clearly defined in our impact on others and theirs on us.

The Fully Developed Individual

Undoubtedly the individual realizes himself most fully in a single profound relationship with another human being, one with whom he is very much in harmony. This is the ideal, but not all of us can achieve such an ideal.

Those who succeed in building a good marriage probably come closest to the ideal, but even a very good marriage does not flow smoothly along in perfect harmony all the time. Nor does it necessarily meet all the needs of its partners. A marriage that left no gaps and offered no conflicts is unrealistic. We cannot expect such perfection, not even in our closest relationships. The more facets we have to our individuality, the more we extend our relationships to include other people and other interests, even though the principal activities of our lives may cluster around a single central relationship.

There are also people who do not achieve one single great

relationship in their lives, who yet live a very full life of relationships. They build up around themselves a whole constellation of attachments that meet many of their needs. Granted, they suffer loneliness at times, but everyone suffers loneliness at times.

Romantically we may dream of the single, all-absorbing, all-satisfying relationship, the one person with whom we could reclaim the lost paradise and live like Adam and Eve as though there were no other human beings in the world. But in reality the bride and groom quickly beckon from their Eden and invite in all their friends and relatives to share their happiness. Even a paradise *à deux* is the better for a few other people around, if only to take the blame for whatever troubles may arise.

To make the investment of one's whole self in a single relationship is hazardous. The relationship may not endure, or life may take one of its members away and leave the other totally bereft. A good, long-enduring marriage can exact this price of one partner who survives the other.

The fully developed individual is very likely to have such a central relationship in his life, but he also has many tentacles tying him to many aspects of other lives. Nor does he limit himself to relationships only with his peers. His friends are varied—younger, older, richer, poorer, all contribute something to his life and he to theirs. One kind of loneliness such a variegated web of relationships can protect him from is the loneliness of the long-lived, who find themselves in their late years with no friends at all.

The Inward Loneliness

A corollary of this sketch of the well-developed individual is that one who has not made many friends has not developed many facets of himself. The fact that he has not formed attachments to many people may well mean that he has failed to explore many potential attachments to activities and ideas as well, since such attachments form the very bonds of common interest by which we relate ourselves to people. And if we ask why this person has not developed his potentialities more fully, we may find ourselves coming back to a defect in the primary attachment of his life, his attachment to himself. A poor development of our basic love, self-love, is usually the first cause of a poverty of other loves, and its consequent loneliness.

The lonely person is not necessarily without loves. He may have very strong loves of ideas, of objects, of occupations that can be pursued in solitude. He may develop attachments to a few people, perhaps an attachment to one person of the opposite sex that is strong enough to lead to marriage.

From all outward appearances this marriage may seem to be a very good one, and yet this man may remain lonely within it. He makes no demands on his loved ones, and does not encourage them to make demands on him. He believes that he shows his love best by letting people go their own way. He unselfishly asks nothing, and the consequence is that he may be spared the need to give anything.

There is little exchange in such a life. Such a man's attachments to people, even to his wife and children, never become primary in his life. He is unable to relate himself to any human beings, even those closest to him, on the deep, empathetic level on which we experience our greatest attachments. He may be so diffident, so unsure of the acceptability of his love to these others that he does not permit himself to feel strongly about them, but takes refuge in a cold, detached formality. Or he may have strong feelings but be unable or afraid to express them, afraid that they will be rejected, or laughed at, or in some way turned into a source of embarrassment or pain to himself. The sum of all these uncertainties is of course the uncertainty of his primary attachment, his attachment to himself.

This is a deep-seated inward loneliness, and hard to resolve. Loneliness is more painful in the midst of a crowd than alone on the desert or the top of a mountain, and it is most painful at home with one's wife and children. This is the truly difficult loneliness, because eventually it is an expression of inadequacy, of inability to reach out toward other people on some level of feeling and understanding, and to draw their feeling and understanding comfortingly toward oneself.

The Habit of People

People who are lonely within marriage generally have a significant personality problem. People who are lonely because they are not married have another sort of problem. Are they lonely because they are alone? Or are they alone because they have the habit of loneliness? One way to answer this question is to go into therapy. A shorter, less expensive way, if possible, is to make a habit of people.

This is such a simple, obvious approach that we may wonder why lonely people do not seize upon it. We have no need to wonder—they tell us why. They give us a great number of reasons. They are much too busy with their work; they simply have no time for people. Or they find most people too uninteresting, most relationships too superficial and banal; they demand more depth and intensity in their relationships than most people are able or willing to give. Or—they tell us —they have been disappointed in people too many times; people are insincere, hypocritical, not really interested in anyone but themselves.

These are all very good and convincing reasons, except that we can recognize them now not as reasons but as rationalizations. The real reasons lie deeper and are not nearly so flattering to the self.

Another reason, one that we hear often, is that one does not have enough money to entertain his friends as he would like to. This may have some validity in a level of society in which one's style of entertaining is closely linked to status. But if we really want to see our friends, we are not deterred by lack of money. We make do. The most important single item in our entertainment of people is ourselves. We do not need the grand ballroom of the Waldorf Astoria to give a cocktail party. We usually have our best times in small places where we are all crowded cheerfully together so tightly that formality is difficult to maintain.

The best parties are the informal ones where everybody has something to do. The cookout is one of America's great contributions to entertaining, a perfect social device. It is no great art to give a dinner party with a catered meal and impeccable service. It is a less perfect but much merrier party when the guests serve themselves and each other and everybody talks to everybody else.

Young people at school, camp, or college sometimes make a discovery that is invaluable to them for the rest of their lives. They discover that they get to know and like other people best when they are working together in some common cause. Great friendships develop in times of war or disaster, not only because people feel more intensely in the face of danger but also because they are thrown together, crammed together in a common effort.

If we were to write an anti-loneliness manual for the unmarried, these would be some of the rules:

1. Keep moving. Let no week go by without giving or accepting an invitation. If no one calls you, call someone. No excuse will do. No occasion for meeting people is a waste of a single person's time.

2. Practice speaking to new people. If necessary, learn lines in advance: what to say at cocktail parties, buffet suppers, weddings, funerals. Some hostesses are skillful at introducing people so that they can talk to each other, but you cannot count on it. Learn how to introduce yourself and begin talking. Better yet, learn how to get the other person talking. The easiest social skill, and the most endearing, is to know how to listen.

3. Do not give up a steady date without a replacement. The desire to go out with people is mere wishfulness without the habit of going out. Keep the date, and keep going out. It is no triumph to have a good time with the man or woman of one's dreams; the real test is to enjoy a date with someone who falls far short of the ideal. Leave perfection to the perfectionists; keep alive the habit of responding to people.

4. Women may object to the foregoing rule on practical grounds. If one goes out with the man more than once, he soon begins to make sexual advances. The question of how to handle this arises.

What is the answer? The answer can only be that learning how to deal with this situation is part of learning how to be a woman. It is like learning how to wear clothes becomingly, how to make the most of one's hair, one's eyes, how to put on lipstick and how to get in and out of a car gracefully. This situation may take a little more skill and tact than some others, but women have been dealing tactfully with delicate social situations for many centuries. A rule that many knowledgeable women have adapted from a favorite perfume advertisement is to promise him anything but give only what and when it pleases her to give.

Loneliness Is Worse

The foregoing rules may seem to treat the problem of loneliness lightheartedly, but in fact they are offered in perfect seriousness. Making a habit of people means finding every possible way to be with people, to do things with people, to become involved with people. This is a habit most easily developed in youth, but it can be developed at any age and in any circumstances.

For those who are trying it for the first time it will surely seem artificial. It will feel awkward, uncomfortable, even a little ridiculous, the way we feel the first time we try to dance or swim or get on skis or ice skates. The older we are, the harder it is to develop a new skill or a new habit, not because we have lost the ability to learn but because we have developed so many other habits of inhibition and timidity and self-consciousness.

No matter how awkward it is at first to make connections with people, there is one thing to remember: it is never so painful as loneliness. And the longer we live with loneliness, the harder it is to change. The habit of people gets easier, once it is begun. Love remains remote without people in our lives. And the more people there are, the more likely it is that we will find those we can love. The more likely, too, is that we will be able to recognize the people we love and adapt ourselves to them.

CHAPTER TWELVE

Love and Friendship

CERTAINLY IT IS no mystery that the great loves recorded by history were always between members of the opposite sex. It is curious to note that the great friendships were always between members of the same sex. The presence or absence of sex in a relationship is of course no small matter and the result has been to think of friendship as very different from love. Yet if love is an attachment and friendship is an attachment, although this does not make them one and the same, it does mean they have a great deal in common.

The very word friendship originated in a verb of the ancient Teutonic tribal languages, meaning *to love*. In the subtle way that language has of linking related human experience, "friend" and "love" seem to have a common origin. As the dictionary defines it, a friend is "one who entertains for another such sentiments of esteem, respect and affection that he seeks his society and welfare."

Like love, friendship also has a grand tradition. David and Jonathan, Damon and Pythias are immortal by virtue of their friendship. Each was prepared to sacrifice life itself for his friend. Jonathan braved the murderous wrath of his father King Saul by refusing to betray David. Damon stood ready to suffer execution in his friend's place, and was within a breath of doing so when Pythias, who might have fled to save himself, returned to die. The tyrant of Syracuse was so moved by the love of these two friends that he revoked Pythias' sentence of death and asked to become a third in their friendship.

Platonic Love

In other societies than our own, friendship actually rivaled the value even of the love of man and woman. This was true in the age of chivalry in Europe, in the golden days of the Arabian culture, in the great years of ancient Greece. It was about friendship that Plato wrote when he described love in its ideal form. Platonic love came to mean something else, as we shall see, but not until many centuries later.

Plato examined friendship the same way he explored the manner in which we come to know things. Like all the major philosophers of his time and many others since then, he wondered about the ways in which we acquire our knowledge of the world around us.

How do we know, for example, that a tree is a tree, an automobile is an automobile? As we live our busy lives, we habitually recognize these objects and let it go at that. But if we stop to think about it, it can be puzzling. How *do* we recognize them? Or any of the thousand objects that we encounter in our daily rounds? They come in many shapes and sizes and colors; the variety in which objects present themselves to us is enormous. Yet we never mistake an automobile for a railroad locomotive, a dog for a horse or even for a cat. Ideas offer a still more striking puzzle. How do we recognize love, or beauty?

Plato set about solving this puzzle by developing the notion of the pure or ideal type, which exists in all things despite the variety of their external forms. He defined this as the essence of the thing. Platonic essences of ideas consisted of those characteristics absolutely essential to the idea of a thing. They made up, for example, the horse-ness of a horse, the tree-ness of a tree, the love-ness of love. This principle concentrates all the characteristics representing the essence of a particular object or concept, and pares away all the merely incidental, superficial, and frequently transitory traits of anything we attempt to identify. Thus, whether we are looking at a Rolls-Royce limousine or a teenager's jalopy, we do not have a moment's doubt that they are both automobiles.

This essence of the thing that we recognize is generally the sum of what our senses tell us the thing has in common with all other things of its kind. Sometimes this method of identification can get us into difficulties. When black swans were first discovered in Australia, the naturalists and the philosophers were thrown into confusion, for swans had been known for centuries and part of their swan-ness was that they were white. There was some question whether these Australian birds should be called swans at all. Finally the savants settled on calling them black swans, but to do this they had to eliminate from the ideal or essence of swan-ness the quality of whiteness, since whiteness was no longer part of this essence.

A Platonic ideal or essence was originally a purely intellectual or cognitive device designed to help us identify or classify things in the world around us. "Ideal" was not used in the ethical or aesthetic sense to mean "best." History, however, played a trick on us and what Plato deliberately left out of the essence of love, as he defined it, was subsequently misinterpreted as a more desirable or higher form of love. His exclusion of sex from the essence of love—from those characteristics essential to the recognition of love—prompted people centuries later to call sexless love Platonic.

Plato could not help but recognize two thousand years ago what we see just as clearly today, that sex often has little if anything to do with love. Personal pleasure is frequently the major motivation in a sexual encounter. A sexually aroused man might even feel hostile towards the woman from whom he seeks physical satisfaction. Other people, of course, feel differently and sex for them may be one of their deepest expressions of love. Yet these same people may also express their love in non-sexual terms. In other words, sex and love are often related and many times sex and love are not related. Plato could not include in the essence of love anything which was less than an *invariable* part of it. He saw sex as a powerful force but he did not believe that the attachments human beings developed to each other were exclusively or necessarily sexual.

History picked this up during medieval times when feudalism flowered into the age of chivalry. A concept of love developed which was called chivalric love. It was romantic love in its most extravagant form. Women were placed on a pedestal, and a knight undertook to serve his lady, write poetry to her, love her and perhaps die for her, with no more reward than a glance of approval and her scarf to wear in his helmet. The greatest love was for the most unattainable woman and physical separation or sexlessness was part of a medieval knight's love.

This aspect of love persisted into the next historical period, the Renaissance, where it was given still another boost. The growth of religion as represented in Christianity encouraged the acceptance of anything spiritual over the physical or

fleshly. The greatest woman who ever lived—and the holiest—
was the Virgin Mary and one of the greatest acts of all time
was the immaculate conception. This was emphasized repeatedly in the works of the best Renaissance painters. The Virgin
Mother was represented on canvas not as some ordinary
woman but rather as an idealized version of one. Serenity, fulfillment, and love were painted again and again into her face.
Many a church—Notre Dame—was named for her. Women
in general were encouraged to live by the lofty standards at-
tributed to her.

All this took place during a time coincident with a change
of attitude towards the human body. Although the unashamed
nudes of Greece and Rome continued to appear in Renaissance
sculpture and some painting, the prevailing tendency was to
glorify not the body but man's devotion to religious ideas.
Even the fig leaf, after awhile, left too much exposed. Not just
Adam and Eve, but the whole human race had been banished
from the Garden of Eden. Self-consciousness and modesty
created an imperative need for bodily concealment. Even bath-
ing went out of style. And sex degenerated in the minds of
people to lust and sinfulness.

Consistent with this change of attitude was an emphasis on
the more purely devotional aspects of love. Its natural origins
and expression gave way to more noble sentiments. The Platonic notion that sex was not an intrinsic part of love was
seized upon, but radically altered. Whereas Plato left sex out
of his definition of love, sexlessness was not installed as a major part of the definition. Platonic love redefined in this fashion
was not accepted merely as an essence or ideal. It was now
accepted as a reality and a better or more desirable kind of
reality at that. It became love in its purest and most noble
form, undefiled by base, animal desire.

Sexless Love

Platonic love, in the sense of sexless love, is no longer considered the ideal relationship between a man and a woman.
Freudian psychology even questions the possibility of its existence. Yet there are many excellent relationships today between
men and women which do not actively involve sex. This is not
because they aspire to a sexless love. Usually sex is excluded

because their relationship is built on other facets and either or both are sexually committed elsewhere—that is, they are married or in love—or because they have no sexual interest in each other. There is a constant, undying awareness that one of them is a man and the other a woman. As a result they behave differently and treat each other differently than if they were both of the same sex. No matter how markedly this sexual awareness affects their behavior, it remains very different indeed from sexual attraction. Certainly not every man and woman who develop a relationship become sexually attracted to each other even though their sexual awareness may remain undimmed. This can promote friendship between them despite history's neglect of such a possibility. As the social roles and functions of women become less strikingly different from men, friendship as we shall see becomes all the more feasible.

The sexlessness of Platonic love has still another kind of appeal among young people who are not yet ready to commit themselves to sex and marriage. Frequently a boy-girl relationship is easier to cultivate precisely because it is only partially cultivated. By calling their relationship Platonic, a girl and a boy can avoid the difficulty they initially face in overtly affirming their sexual interest in each other. It becomes a way of saying that their relationship is more one of friendship than love. Marriage too can then remain sufficiently distant to be unthreatening.

Teenagers today still engage in the game of Platonic love. In their first heterosexual encounters, both are likely to be shy of physical contact. They have only just emerged from a long period of sexual segregation in which boys played with boys, and girls with girls—what we call the latency period. In adolescence, when society and their own drives permit them to entertain their sexual aims for the first time, many girls and some boys approach the new relationship with great diffidence. Both are more comfortable if they can place their interest in each other on another level. They may do their homework together, dance together, listen to hi-fi together—any excuse to be together will serve as a safe substitute for another of their major interests in each other, which is sexual. By this avoidance of their own sexual desires and the anxiety created by these desires, young people easily see themselves as reaching up into the more distinctly spiritual quality of a relationship. If their attachment to each other lacks fulfillment, they enjoy compensatory feelings, in what they call greater sensitivity and mutual understanding.

This diffidence can persist. A young man may continue to be uneasy about revealing his sexual feelings to a girl he thinks highly of. He still has a lingering feeling that sex is wrong and that a nice girl will reject any sexual approach. The girl, hedged about with her own conflicting feelings, is grateful that he does not put her to the test of either accepting his sexual advances or rejecting him altogether.

Not that the young woman does not feel her own sexual desires. Still she may prefer that her boyfriend avoid rather than ignite them. Frequently she will more easily than not accept this as a sign of his love. It is as though he were making a sacrifice. His postponement of any sexual harassment of her is taken as a sign that he is a gentleman and that she is respected. And often he is just as relieved to a be a "gentleman" as she is that he is willing to assume this role.

And so both take refuge in an unspoken conspiracy to conceal the real nature of their attraction for each other. Instead of telling her how beautiful she is, he tells her about a beautiful theory he has on how to solve the problems of unemployment. The girl "knows" that his enthusiasm for such big issues is really his timid detached way of telling her how strongly he feels about her. She need only half-listen to enjoy his good looks and of course she must mean a great deal to him if he spends hours with her on matters of such great moment. The subject is by no means always impersonal. Family life, friendship, even sex may be discussed. But the pattern initially is generally the same: intellectual discussion precedes and is a substitute for actual involvement.

Sometimes the beginnings of love are not only overtly sexless, they are also verbally "loveless." A young man, for example, who has had a very close relationship with his mother might be strongly hesitant for a long while about using the word love at all. Deep down inside, he feels as though he were betraying his mother by saying, "I love you" to anyone else. It is very much like the difficulty many young married people have in addressing their parents-in-law as "mother" or "father." These words, like "love," are often so richly embroidered with highly special feelings that their easy usage is blocked by our own earlier experiences with them.

Still, love has its beginnings and before too long it is more courageously recognized for what it is. Calling it Platonic may delay its recognition, but not its emergence. It never was an attachment or love without sex. It is love with sex suppressed, for the present. For young people, Platonic love is less threatening than the real thing. They can move in and out of it almost as easily as though it were a wading pool. And this is basically what Platonic love is for them: a wading pool before they take the plunge into deeper waters. Sooner or later their love must develop its sexual side, or else it withers. Love without sex between a man and a woman in our time is not even a romantic ideal. At best, it can only be part of the preparation for the complete relationship.

This does not keep young people, during the sexually suppressed or Platonic phase of their relationship, from calling themselves friends. For all the glamour and romance associated with the word love, there is also a gravity about it which may postpone its use. Teenagers speak of "being pinned" or "going steady" rather than being in love. This helps them keep the marital consequences of their relationship at greater distance.

But "friendship" remains a misnomer. It is used here to suggest a relationship less than love. On the other hand, some people are extremely facile with the word "love" but, of course, its use does not always guarantee the sentiments we like to associate with it. A purely sexual relationship is rarely recognized and accepted as such. Instead people will often thinly disguise and justify their biological appetites by saying they love each other. Love, after all, is ennobling and can elevate promiscuous pleasure to the level of spiritual fulfillment. One of Hoffenstein's couplets muses over this obvious deception.

"If you love me as I love you
We'll both be friendly and untrue."

Friendship is dealt with unkindly in both these cases. Certainly it does not benefit from deception. Secondly, although it is less of a relationship than heterosexual love in being more circumscribed, friendship can enjoy extraordinary quality. Yet to some degree, it has gone out of style. We rarely see it in the movies. Literature too seems to neglect it. Generally there is only one protagonist and the rule is every man for himself. Friendship seems to command less of our attention and interest than other human relationships. Man and nature, man and money, man and morality, and most of all man and woman— these are the relationships most commonly found at the heart of our films and novels. Friendship exists but it is taken for granted as an ordinary part of daily life, never as a monument to our human experience.

It is true that if the relationship is between a man and a woman, friendship is more difficult to develop than between members of the same sex. Additionally, the friendship they do achieve never matches the quality of what men and women can and do achieve in a relationship of love. In this sense, friendship is less than love. Its consequences are far less elaborate. There is nothing in our experience which rivals the many-facetted totality of the involvement of family life for those of us who accept it. Friendship, on the other hand, is more finite so that no matter how great the dedication two friends may enjoy, they inevitably recognize its limitations and frequently feel the dead spaces even between the liveliest areas of contact.

Yet among members of the same sex, the friendship which can develop should not be underestimated. Sex, of course, is absent but even without this binding force and without this great potential source of mutual pleasure, an attachment of great depth and breadth can emerge. Many men are simply not candidates for love in the usual sense. Not that they are homosexual or otherwise sick. They may in fact be so strongly in love in our sense of the term, i.e., attached to some goal, that they have little or no room for a woman in their lives. A man devoted, for example, to the exploration of the Antarctic is a case in point. Another man and he might share a great deal in their adventures together but a woman might be a burden, someone who could not be included in this central area of his life.

In a less noticeable way, there are many men who find friendship more compatible than love with their way of life. The area of their choice, whether it be politics, business, or scientific research, does not matter nearly so much as the amount of devotion the man feels towards his choice. He may fall in love and marry only to find that these conventional attachments are minimally satisfying and frequently burden him with demands which keep him from what he really wants to do. He prefers being with his political friends or his business friends, whichever the case may be, because they are part of the world to which he is primarily and most strongly attached.

This does not mean that love and friendship are necessarily mutually exclusive. Most of the time, just the opposite is the case. Friendship is a type of love and as such most of our friendships keep alive and strengthen our ability to love. Love between a man and a woman does not feed on itself. It needs the constant nourishment of other human relationships. We enrich any one area of contact by what we bring from the others.

No matter how deep a love may be between a man and a woman, their different roles in life invariably separate them at least for their occupational and domestic duties. Ideally, these periods of separation are also fulfilling. But they cannot be without other people about whom we care, friends who share the interests and problems we face in these roles. Too much time spent without people quickly corrupts our ability to accommodate ourselves to them when they do appear. We become set in our ways rather than flexible so that even the person we love the most will easily rub us the wrong way. On the other hand, the satisfaction we derive from friends preserves our pleasant receptive mood. Additionally, worthwhile friendships spread other lives before us with which we, in turn, enhance the life of our loved one.

Although as we shall see, there are many devisive forces in society which separate us from each other, for many of us friendship is a natural product of growth. Our elaborate division of labor makes human contact unavoidable and, out of this contact, attachments of real value frequently develop. We often think of friends as people whom we choose, in contrast with members of our family who are just there—the "givens" of our life. Yet it is not altogether true, as in many other cases, that we have literally chosen our friends.

George Santayana, in his *Reason in Society*, offers us a most perceptive analysis of friendship. Using the word "society" in its sense of people associating with one another, he speaks of three different kinds of society: the natural, the free, and the ideal.

Natural society consists of those friendships which grow out of the forces in nature which bring people together. Suppose we lived in a small village, a hamlet in Switzerland nestled in a valley between the ponderous peaks of the Alps, and we spent most of our lives there because physical conditions made it difficult to go very far from home. Geography would account for the attachments we would make. We would share our joys and our troubles with our fellow villagers and we would make our friends among these same people. We would have little choice of friends from elsewhere. In any case these people with whom we grew up and lived so closely would become the most comfortable friends for us.

All of us have such friendships. People who go to the same college, live in the same dormitory very often become friends as a result of these natural forces that bring them physically together. They may or may not be good friends, but they often remain friends of a sort throughout life, simply because of this natural association during an exciting period of their lives. And they may derive much pleasure and comfort from this friendship. Yet clearly they have not made friends by a pure act of choice.

Santayana's free society is closer to what we think of as the untrammeled act of selecting our friends. People who choose each other because they have common interests or espouse common causes are members of this free society. People meet and pleasantly discover coincidences in their lives. They both like tennis, Mozart, modern poetry, and ancient history. They discover they have been to the same places and independently sparkled with enthusiasm over the same tiny details. They know people in common whom they enjoy, their work is related, or even more simply they laugh together easily and so they like being with each other.

Finally there is ideal society, a relationship based not merely on common interests which may be temporal, transitory, even trivial but on the ideal values for which people have come to stand. They may have been dead for centuries and still figure prominently among our ideal friendships. Santayana himself is a treasured friend to those of us who have read him with pleasure and profit, and address ourselves to the same philosophical ideals. Ideal society pulls people together because, as the name implies, they share common ideals. They have come to stand for the same thing in the philosophical sense of the term. Beauty and truth, to mention merely two such ideals, have drawn people into a friendship of ideas and goals even if they never actually physically met.

All of us can and do have all three of these kinds of friendships simultaneously. All of us are members of natural, free, and ideal societies. Unfortunately too many of us spend too much of our lives in a natural society which arises from minimal choice and offers at best less fulfillment than the other two types. We do not spend enough time deliberately cultivating friendship. We spend our time with people who live on the same street, work in the same office, belong to the same Parent Teachers Association. We talk to these people; we may like their company and even share many interests with them. But we have not selected them, nor they us. And we do not ordinarily develop with them the form of ideal love, the profound psychological and emotional relationship that constitutes friendship at best.

Our social lives are often just as barren of deeper friendships. A familiar complaint of husband to wife, or vice versa, is that they are forever having dinner with the same set of people, not necessarily the people they would ideally like to see. Socially we also fall prey to natural forces, and spend our leisure with people with whom we become associated more or less by accident and geography, not by conscious choice. We like them, we discover some interests in common with them, we enjoy their company and they enjoy ours, but we do not draw from the relationship the deep satisfaction of love which friendship can offer. We elevate our society from natural to free, but not to free enough or ideal.

The Uses of Friendship

The art of friendship is worth cultivating because friendship has many uses. The French cynic, La Rochefoucauld, wrote that people maliciously took some private pleasure in their friends' troubles. The chances are that more of us would be distressed and deeply believe that "a friend in need is a friend indeed." One of the great values of friendship is the company it gives us if and when we need it. The fact that friendship is not so all engrossing and demanding as heterosexual love is one of its virtues. It is a limited partnership at best and this very finite character gives us the freedom to enjoy our friends when we need them or want them and not hurt them when we choose to be by ourselves.

This does not mean that friendship is without frictions. Friends disagree and friends quarrel. Friends make a great variety of demands on each other, and sometimes the demands put a strain on the friendship. But friendship is flexible. Friends can pull apart and draw together. They can see each other or not see each other for a while. They can turn to each other for companionship, or out of need, or they can go their separate ways for a period.

Friendship not only ideally begins as a free choice of two people for each other, it continues by choice. The friends set the tone of their friendship at will. Its depth, its intensity changes according to their desire or their need for each other, their willingness or ability to respond to each other.

There are intense and demanding friendships, and there are friendships so easy, so relaxed that such friends turn to each other as a relief from other relationships. Men friends often seek each other out regularly, for a respite from their more intense and demanding relationships within marriage. This does not mean that they do not love their wives and children. It only means that it is good, now and then, to put your feet up on the desk, or lean on a bar, and talk shop or politics or anything whatever with a trusted friend with whom one does not have to be on guard for business, or status, or emotional reasons, and with whom nothing more is involved than the personal expression of opinions or a free-wheeling exchange of funny stories.

Women friends seek each other out with the same relaxation in view. They let their hair down and enjoy women's shop talk. Friendship is thus a form of love with little or no tension. It is a relaxed kind of love, a release from the intense relationships that we need and want but cannot sustain every moment of every hour.

Friends also fill out our lives with the kinds of companionship that even the most satisfactory marriage cannot always provide. The interests of a well-married pair dovetail at many points, but they can scarcely meet at every point.

For one thing, in our society our interests do divide to some extent on sexual lines. This may not be true in all human societies. Perhaps in some Orwellian culture of the future, women will do all the things that men do, the biological roles of the sexes will be taken care of by test-tube automation, and the agreeable differences that add so much variety to our lives will disappear.

For the present we can continue to enjoy the differences between the sexes when we are together, and we can also seek our separate interests with members of our own sex, with our friends. Men continue to play poker or golf together, women continue to meet for lunch and a matinee or an afternoon of shopping, and both are refreshed by their separate activities when they come home to each other again.

As individuals, too, they are surely entitled to their individual interests. A husband who is an amateur musician can play string quartets with his musician friends, a wife who is an amateur artist can go to her painting or pottery class where she meets friends with similar art interests. One may have more intense community interests than the other, or different recreational hobbies. Some excellent wives really do not care for fishing, football, politics, and some devoted husbands remain indifferent to Mah Jong, high fashion, flower arranging.

The richer we are as personalities, the more facets there are to our interests and the more we need friends to share them. No one needs to be all things to any one friend. Each friend brings something of his or her own into a friend's life.

Some Deeper Uses of Friendship

Friendship has some values that go still deeper than the pleasures of relaxed companionship and shared interests. There are profound psychological uses for friendship in our lives.

Friends help us to deal with our anxiety. Anxiety is present in all of us to some degree. Love and marriage are our most sought-after solutions, but we also bring our anxiety into those relationships, and those relationships generate anxieties of their own. Friends, especially groups and circles of friends, are an excellent antidote to anxiety. In a group one's individual ego expands; in a group one feels the support of allies. When we meet for an evening with friends, we may laugh, argue, dance, play games, enlist in causes, engage in whatever activity that particular circle of friends likes to share. Whatever it is, we become part of a group and our anxiety is allayed, put aside for the evening.

Friends help us to maintain an objectivity about ourselves. A person in trouble, in pain, worried about something, angry about something, or simply depressed, is discontented with the world or his lot, and tends to turn inward upon himself. The same highly charged thoughts begin to go around and around, an endless long-playing record, until everything he thinks or does is colored by that emotion. Being with friends takes one out of this repetitive concentration on oneself. It takes the needle off the record.

It may even put on another record. A friend talks about *himself,* and one begins to think about him instead of *oneself.* When he finishes telling his troubles, one's own troubles may seem less important. Often one comes away from a session with a troubled friend so deeply concerned for him that one's own concerns, so burdensome an hour ago, have become lighter than air. They have simply floated away.

We have found in group therapy that people experience enormous relief simply from the discovery that they are not unique, that other people are struggling with the same problems, making the same mistakes, suffering from the same wounds and bruises. Friendship can serve much the same purpose.

There is a possibility that we can benefit from our friends' mistakes. There is no guarantee, but it can happen. We might even benefit from our friends' wisdom. At the very least, a friend can act as a sounding board. Talking out a problem with a trusted friend is sometimes enough to let in the daylight so that we ourselves see the solution. A friend who will simply listen is sometimes the perfect answer to our need.

All these values exist in friendship becaus at its best it is a free association between equals, a free choice. Friends help each other, but they do this because they want to, not because they have to. Of course, there are corruptions of this. Some people seek others out for help in one's profession or business or job, or because they know the "right" people and can advance one socially, or because they know a lot of girls and can get one dates. This is not friendship; this is opportunism. There is nothing especially wrong with asking and returning favors. We do it in our business and social lives every day. We all perform various services for each other. But that is not what we mean by friendship.

Friendship exists for its own sake. Friends are loyal and helpful to each other, not for what they can get in return, but out of love.

The Nurturing of Friendship

So friendship is, indeed, valuable. People testify to this in the friendships they have. They may complain but they also enjoy them. Some have a great many friends. Some enjoy only a few friendships but they are deep and enduring. How can we go about developing this asset?

Developing friendships means overcoming many of the divisive forces in both society and ourselves which keep us from each other. This is not easy. It basically involves a change of attitude towards ourselves and the world. Certainly it is easy enough to memorize techniques of behavior which have helped people win friends but if we remain diffident and fearful, how can we bring ourselves to do those things? The first step toward friendship is to expose oneself to it. But this is also the most terrifying and difficult step for someone who is shy.

The trouble, too, is that shyness all too often is mistaken by others for snobbishness. One socially apprehensive person looks at another equally defensively and they each impute to the other a superciliousness which neither feels. If only one had plastered a smile on his face, the ice might have been broken. But it is hard to act friendly if one does not feel friendly. A person may want friends and, yet instead of feeling friendly, he mostly feels anxious about possibly being neglected and even harbors some small anger in advance. Unfortunately their silence preserves these feelings as well as their social distance. The recitation even of nonsense syllables would call forth a response from the other. Once there is interaction, however small, exposure is less painful.

The more widely we reach out from ourselves, the more people we encounter on some level of mutual interest. The easiest way to develop friendships is on the basis of a shared pleasure or a shared cause. People who are interested in the same thing are likely to be interested in each other.

We do have to be willing to take a first step toward each other. A shared interest or activity does not automatically grow into a friendship. Two people may work together for months on a community project or a political campaign. They may like each other and work well together. But like railroad tracks they may simply run along side by side and never actually meet, never draw close enough to each other to build a friendship. They remain "contacts," in the cool but accurate Madison Avenue phrase. They do not become friends.

Some of us who are football fans have sat side by side, season after season, watching the same games, rooting for the same team, yet never talking to each other. We may nod in greeting after the third or fourth encounter, but we never explore each other further to see whether there may be more points of meeting than the physical contiguity of occupying two adjoining seats.

To make friends, we have to be friendly. Unless we develop an attitude of acceptance toward ourselves and others, the mechanics of social intercourse will not reward us with worthwhile relationships. We have to begin by expecting to find something we like in people, in strangers. When I was a little boy my mother taught me that "even a clock that does not run is right twice a day." If we have patience, if we are alert for it, we can catch the moment in each twelve hours when the stopped clock tells the right time.

I was somewhat older when the meaning of this bit of homely wisdom dawned on me. People, too, can be right some of the time, even people who seem always to be wrong. It takes patience, it takes alertness to catch the moment when they show some appealing aspect of themselves. *We have to be willing to discover the worthwhileness of a stranger.* It is up to him to put himself in evidence as a person, but it is up to us to invite him to do so. The same musical score can be played very differently by the same orchestra, depending on the inspiration and leadership of the conductor. There is something more to be found in everyone if we take the trouble to bring it out.

Even the most unlikely encounters may produce a moment of rewarding communication between human beings. Two people may seem to have nothing whatever in common, but there is one thing that they have: their common humanity. To come upon a momentary revelation of this is enriching, and may even be memorable. Extraordinary times, such as war times, can yield such extraordinary moments.

Men have built long-lasting friendships out of shared experience in wartime. They may have nothing in common after they return to private life, and they may not remain friends on a day-to-day basis, but having known each other through hardship and danger they have won each other's respect and affection. A man will put himself out to help his old buddy who needs help. This is not mere sentimentality. They did not choose each other as friends, but a bond of friendship was forged out of their common human need in extraordinary circumstances.

Surely we should not have to wait for disaster to bring out our common humanity and link us together as friends. We should be able to look for possible links without any greater pressure than our own readiness to make friends.

Protecting Friendship

Friendship can be durable or not depending on how we treat it. The same neurotic tendencies that can contaminate love, as we shall see in a later chapter, can spoil the love of friends. Good friends use each other in a variety of ways. They can call upon each other in time of need, for actual services. They can use each other as conveniences on occasion. They need each other for confidences, for pouring out troubles, and at times we may use a friend mercilessly for this. This is itself a good test of friendship. We may turn a friend into a dumping ground for our miseries in a period when we feel overwhelmed. But the score evens itself, for when his turn comes to need a dumping ground we are ready to serve.

This does not strain friendship. Friendship becomes strained when it is no longer between equals, when one friend uses the other but is not available to be used in turn. Friendship is harmed when one friend dominates the other, or exploits the other for some neurotic need. We no longer feel the same toward a friend who uses us only to pour out his troubles but forgets to share his good news with us as well.

Friendship is damaged when we become blind and insensitive to the feelings of our friends. In their enjoyment of each other, people sometimes take the affection they receive for granted. They overlook the amount of feeling many people invest in their friendships and thoughtlessly they are sometimes hurtful. In still other cases, these strong feelings are simply not shared. We have heartbreaking experiences not only in love, but in friendship too. The arrogant little princess in Oscar Wilde's *Birthday of the Infanta* disavows any interest in the feelings of others and proclaims, "For the future let all those who come to play with me have no hearts."

We begin to learn the art of friendship from an early age. If our parents have friends, if as children we are exposed to their friends and are encouraged to fill the house with our own friends, we are well on the way to a life of good friendships. Some of us, who have not had this early experience, must work harder at nurturing friendship. Like our loves, our friendships reflect ourselves; they take their place among our loves as part of our autobiography. Whether we have many friends or few, we all know what a source of pleasure they can be. A world without friends is a bleak world indeed.

CHAPTER THIRTEEN

Romantic Love

TWO OF THE characteristics that distinguish human beings from lower animal forms are, first, that we drink when we are not thirsty, and second, that we have no mating season. We make love and we mate throughout the year.

And yet, although it is true that for us love has no season, one season does claim a peculiar compatibility with it. In the spring, we are told, a young man's fancy lightly turns to thoughts of love. It is, of course, a rather special kind of love for which the spring provides so apt a setting. We call it romantic love.

Romantic love often arouses the disapproval of sensible people. It is impulsive, excessive, irrational and frequently unwise. It even scorns reality and feeds on illusion. It is impermanent, usually short-lived, and frequently it ends in heartbreak. It is almost a kind of temporary insanity. Yet for even the most sensible among us it has enormous appeal. If we never experienced it we wish we had, and if we ever did we remember the experience with fond nostalgia. If all the world loves a lover, it is a romantic lover that the world loves.

Any aspect of human behavior that is so downright contradictory merits special attention, and since it is an aspect of love, both the behavior and our irrational response to it are clearly part of our present investigation.

Why is romantic love, with all its evident folly, so appealing? Or perhaps we should first ask: What is romantic love?

Although its origins are most prominently associated with the period when knighthood was in flower, it was not until many centuries later that romantic love was given its most robust expression. At the close of the 18th century, on the heels of the Age of Reason, the term "romantic" emerged as an important concept concerning a whole way of life and love. The Romantic Era bloomed with wild extravagance for the first few decades of the 19th century. Then almost overnight it gave way to the materialism of the scientific and industrial revolution, and never again regained the philosophical respectability it briefly enjoyed. Yet it bore splendid fruits, which we still enjoy, in all the arts and especially in music and poetry. Schubert, Beethoven and Brahms, Shelley, Keats and Byron are part of our romantic heritage.

The Rebellious Romantics

In their own time the romanticists were in rebellion against classicism. Classicism was the mood of the 18th century, the century that worshipped reason, order, restraint, the discipline of form.

We use the word "classic" today to mean a model, a perfect representation of a type. A physician speaks of a classic case of some disease; he may even in his enthusiasm call it beautiful, to the patient's distress if he should happen to overhear. What the doctor means is that it is a model of the disease, one that shows all its known symptoms and follows perfectly its characteristic course. More often than not, when we are sick we present a few symptoms of a condition but not all of them, and we may even suffer a few symptoms of something else. Our individualism prevails even in illness, and we do not make diagnosis easy for our doctor. Only rarely do we oblige him with a classic case of what ails us.

Classicism expressed itself repeatedly in the effort to achieve stability, order, predictability. Time tested formulas, conventions, and classifications were accepted as the basis for the most desirable harmonies in life. The romantics extolled the opposite of this orderliness. They broke out against the restraints of form, of classification, and sought not the typical but the individual, not the conforming but the unusual, the picturesque. They turned from the discipline of reason and intelligence to the expression of feeling and passion. Finally, the romantic spirit spurned the hard world of reality and took flight with the imagination into an extravagant and unreal world of fantasy. The romantics not only mounted the winged horse—they threw the reins on his neck and let him go. They soared to heights of ecstasy, plunged to depths of despair. No exaggeration of feeling was too wild. Experience became the romantic reality of life; reason merely a pale reminder of it.

Enter Mephistopheles

Goethe was the giant of the romantic era, and in his own person he embodied its contradictions. Like a colossus he bestrode both worlds, the world of reason that would give birth to the scientific age, and the world of passion and poetry. He contributed to science a brilliant classification of botanical forms and some respectable discoveries in the field of optics. At the same time he wrote a wildly passionate romance, *The Sorrows of Young Werther,* which allegedly set off a wave of suicides of despairing young lovers across the continent of Europe.

His immortal creation, *Faust,* was the perfect summation of romanticism. Faust as we first meet him is an old man. He has devoted his life to study. He has given all his years to classic order, and form, to restraint, control, predictability, to the use of intelligence and understanding. He knows all there is to know. And yet, he feels, he has not gained mastery over the universe or himself. He has missed the essence; the heart and core have eluded him. He writes:

> "And here, poor fool! with all my lore
> I stand, no wiser than before:
>
> ———
>
> And see, that nothing can be known!
> *That* knowledge cuts me to the bone."

Doubt and a sense of unfulfillment so deeply felt are the Devil's home grounds and surely enough Mephistopheles appears. He tempts Faust to abandon reason so that life will be at last revealed to him. While Faust retires to another room to weigh the bargain he is about to make, Mephistopheles borrows his cloak and "advises" a new student on the proper course of life.

> "See that you most profoundly gain
> What does not suit the human brain."

and then he adds that couplet which is probably the most succinct and yet fullest statement of Romanticism in all literature:

> "My worthy friend, gray are all theories,
> And green alone Life's golden tree."

Faust, as we know, at the sacrifice of his immortal soul, seizes the opportunity to return to the world of the senses and passions, the world of which his intellect cheated him.

Romanticism Equals Love

Everything we have said to define the term *romantic* seems to apply equally to the common definition of love.

People think of love as a free choice, an expression of their own individuality. Others do not choose our love for us. We may let a friend arrange a date for us, but when it comes to falling in love, our own desires and feelings assume the dominant role. We even have to struggle with our intelligence, our own judgment. Who falls rationally in love? The mind has nothing to do with love. The heart, we say, has its reasons. Love for us means extraordinary feelings, emotions too big for us to manage. In love we forget to eat, forget to sleep, cross the street against the light unmindful of screaming brakes and imminent destruction, walk into a subway station with an umbrella open.

Love is something we cannot control, cannot contain. It is the highest of our desires, the grandest of our experiences. And when it happens to us, it is unique. Lovers at the height of their love are certain that theirs is like no other love anyone else has ever experienced.

Who Can Describe It?

All these characteristics that we associate with love are typical actually of only one kind of love: romantic love. We do not find it discussed in psychology books nor in the literature of the social sciences. The reason is obvious. Anything romantic defies investigation by its very nature. The most that is said, therefore, is that romantic love is poor preparation for marriage, a statement with which we may or may not agree when we come to the end of this chapter.

Yet our interest in romance is certainly great enough to

justify an effort to understand it more thoroughly. If scientists back away from it, let us turn to the artists. And here we find all we want about romantic love, and more. The most articulate of all have been the poets. They have analyzed it to its final sighing dithyramb.

The first thing the poets tell us is that it is no use to try to understand, no use to bring intelligence to bear on life and love. We cannot know, we cannot understand; life and love simply happen. Thus Omar the tentmaker, in the *Rubáiyát of Omar Khayyám*, tells us:

> "Into this Universe, and *Why* not knowing
>   Nor Whence, like Water willy-nilly flowing;
> And out of it as Wind along the Waste,
>   I know not *Whither*, willy-nilly blowing."

He does not know why he is here, who put him here, where he will go from here or when. He knows nothing. Events simply take place.

The romantic lover, then, is not only ignorant, he is incurious. He does not know and does not seek to know. He accepts his ignorance not in despair or resignation but with a kind of delight. Since he does not and cannot know, he is free of his thinking mind, free to let his emotions whirl him where they may.

He is free to follow his desire. In romantic love we experience the sharpest awareness of our desires, and they acquire a value that in classic literature they do not enjoy at all. They are not material desires; the romantic lover wants nothing that the world considers worth wanting. Thus Omar, again, in his most quoted lines:

> "A Book of Verses underneath the Bough,
>   A Jug of Wine, a Loaf of Bread—and Thou
>   Beside me singing in the Wilderness—
>   Oh, wilderness were Paradise enow!"

The most meager fare, the barest comfort—if comfort it is at all—are Paradise if only the loved one shares them. Not a thought about the mosquitoes, the ants in the bread; not a thought about whether the wilderness is chilly or parched with burning sun. None of this matters. None of this even enters the lover's thoughts. His consciousness has room for only one thing, for his desire. Even if the most generous symbolic meanings are imputed to the famous quatrain, it remains a dream of romantic desire, and not a statement of reality.

Reality Is Oppressive

He is dreaming his vision of Paradise, the satisfaction of his desire. In romantic love we are allowed to dream. It has to do only with our dreams, our desires, our world of fantasy. In romantic love we shut out reality, because reality is oppressive, reality holds us down. Omar tells us so:

> "Ah Love! could thou and I with Fate conspire
> To grasp this sorry Scheme of Things entire,
>   Would we not shatter it to bits—and then
> Re-mold it nearer to the Heart's Desire?"

Reality is a sorry scheme of things, reality is hateful and he would smash it if he could. But since he cannot, he simply leaves it. He departs into the world of his own making, the world of his desire. Keats asks, at the end of his *Ode to a Nightingale*, "Was it a vision, or a waking dream?" He wonders, "Fled is that music: do I wake or sleep?"

This is an apt question for the romantic lover. Much of the time he cannot tell whether he is awake or asleep. Some of the romantics, as we know, even took opium. There is some evidence to suggest that it may have been socially and medically more acceptable then than now. For the romantics, all experience was equally part of their reality whether it was induced by drugs, alcohol, sleep, or plain everyday consciousness. An opium-eater found he could make his flight to *his* reality that much faster. Coleridge wrote *Kubla Khan*, we are told, on awakening from an opium dream, and it has the detached eeriness of such a state. He begins:

> "In Xanadu did Kubla Khan
>   A stately pleasure-dome decree:
> Where Alph, the sacred river, ran
> Through caverns measureless to man
> Down to a sunless sea."

And further,

> "It was a miracle of rare device,
> A sunny pleasure-dome with caves of ice!"

And finally,

> "For he on honey-dew hath fed,
> And drunk the milk of Paradise."

This is surely a striking departure from our reality. It is not the way in which we ordinarily express our desires, and our feelings do not ordinarily invite such fantasy. Of course, we are not Coleridge. Yet he has not left us far behind. It is the poet's task to interpret for us what we feel and cannot or dare not say. He clothes our desires in words; he takes us by the hand and shows us our dream of delight, lets us live in it for the length of the poem—as Mephistopheles showed Faust the world of passion and love.

Suffer and Die for Love

The oppressiveness of reality is beyond the power of the romantic to change or escape from, except in dreaming, and so he suffers. Suffering is an essential ingredient of romantic love—without this ingredient it would not be the authentic article and could not wear its brand label. To understand romantic love we must understand not only that the lover suffers but that he is willing to suffer. His suffering is sweet; he takes pleasure and pride in his suffering. He courts it. Says Keats:

> "My heart aches, and a drowsy numbness pains
> My sense, as though of hemlock I had drunk,
> Or emptied some dull opiate to the drains
> One minute past, and Lethe-wards had sunk . . ."

The somewhat earlier Cavalier poet Robert Herrick dwelt in a more macabre fashion not only on suffering but on death:

> "Love brought me to a silent Grove,
> And shew'd me there a Tree,
> Where some had hang'd themselves for love,
> And gave a Twist to me."

The "twist" or noose was no common rope but made of silk and gold, a dainty yet nonetheless lethal instrument. In what grander tradition can the final curtain of an opera fall? Dying is a perfect culmination for the romantic lover. He dreams of dying for love and many, at least in romantic literature, took the drastic step of making that particular dream a reality.

This is going far. In our most intense romantic moments we do not nowadays seriously consider dying for love. Anyone who did would strike us as not romantic but sick. The poets follow this path to the logical end, however, and they extract every ounce of heart-wringing emotion out of their final scenes.

Consider the love-death of Isolde, soaring in ecstatic soprano tones above a whispering orchestra. Consider Romeo, gazing on his dead love, as he believes, and lifting the vial of poison to his lips: "Here's to my love! (drinks) Thus with a kiss I die." And Juliet, waking from her drugged sleep to find him dead, chiding him for leaving her not a drop of the fatal potion, kissing him to suck the poison from his lips, rejoicing as she finds his dagger. In our books and on the stage we do not consider this sick. We glory in its excess, its unbridled exaggeration, its glorious freedom from intelligence or prosaic common sense.

Love's Philosophy

Still, attempts are made to glorify romantic love not only by singing its praises but by giving it philosophical justification. Shelley would have us believe it is an inexorable part of nature. In a poem entitled *Love's Philosophy,* he writes:

> "The fountains mingle with the river,
>   And the rivers with the ocean;
> The winds of heaven mix forever
>   With a sweet emotion;
> Nothing in the world is single;
>   All things, by a law divine,
> In one spirit meet and mingle.
>   Why not ī with thine?"

What better way to approach the business of making love than to assume we are acting "by a law divine"?

Love was also insatiable. It devoured the lover; he could not give enough to it. We scarcely think of the sober New England essayist Ralph Waldo Emerson as a romantic lover, and yet he wrote:

> "Give all to love;
> Obey thy heart;
> Friends, kindred, days,
> Estate, good fame,
> Plans, credit, and the Muse—
> Nothing refuse."

All these expressions of romantic love are excessive. They go to lengths of exaggeration that are not characteristic of our everyday discourse and our everyday feeling. Taken out of context, they even have a quasi-psychotic quality.

And yet we find them appealing. Would any wife object if her husband came home one evening and said to her,

> "Helen, thy beauty is to me
> Like those Nicean barks of yore,
> That gently, o'er a perfumed sea,
> The weary wayworn wanderer bore
> To his own native shore . . ."

Would she mind? Surely not. What if these exquisite lines of Edgar Allen Poe are an exaggeration? If a husband did this only once in all his life his wife might be a trifle suspicious. But if he approached her somewhat more often in this fashion, even though she recognized its excess, she could not help but enjoy it.

Hurry, Hurry

Finally, to all these characteristics of romantic love we must add one more: its urgency. It is fiercely imperative; its impatience stems from the youthful, impulsive awareness that time is running out. Young lovers often decide that the only way they can preserve their love is to get married. They may be utterly unready for marriage in most every respect, but they feel they must get married because they will never again find a love like this and if they do not seize it now they will lose it forever.

This sense of urgency is expressed in romantic literature more than almost any other quality. Andrew Marvell protested,

> "Had we but world enough, and time,
>   This coyness, Lady, were no crime . . ."

And he adds,

> "But at my back I always hear
>   Time's wingèd chariot hurrying near."

Furthermore, he warns,

> "The grave's a fine and private place,
>   But none, I think, do there embrace."

Herrick put it into a quatrain that we all know well:

> "Gather ye rosebuds while ye may,
>   Old Time is still a-flying:
>   And this same flower that smiles today
>   Tomorrow will be dying."

And to come back to the Rubáiyát for one more verse,

> "Oh threats of Hell and Hopes of Paradise!
>   One thing at least is certain—This Life flies;
>   One thing is certain and the rest is Lies;
>   The flower that once has bloomed forever dies."

Do not delay, snatch love now—life passes, love passes, all is fleeting, all must end. This desperate awareness of time, of the transience of all lovely things and of love itself, is still moving to us, even though we no longer feel the same urgency we knew during our adolescence. We realize that we have a good deal more time than we imagined in those impatient years.

The Do-It-Yourself Art Form

When we describe romantic love as having all these irrational characteristics—exaggeration, impatience, willful ignorance and defiance of reality, a yielding to desire, suffering, even death—we are describing a kind of folly if not actual insanity. Yet this is not to denigrate romantic love. Romantic love is the most widespread art form known to man.

Not everyone can paint, not everyone can do sculpture or write poetry, but everyone can love. Romantic love is an art form available to all of us; we are all capable of this creative expression. It is a do-it-yourself kit that we do not even have to go out and buy. We can create it without any materials other than our own dreams, and if we need directions, literature is full of them.

Romantic love meets virtually all the criteria for an art form. Like art, it supersedes the facts. It is not interested in the literal truth of science but rather in the symbolic truth of art.

Consider the very romantic novel, *Wuthering Heights*. If we were to look at it literally as a factual record, we would be obliged to say that what it most closely resembled is the clinical case history of an obsessional neurotic. And it is not even a good case history. There are far better ones in the psychological literature.

But if instead of reading it literally, we accept it as superseding factual reality we can then see in its exaggeration an even greater truth—a truth about all lovers. Heathcliff's wild, bitter, self-defeating love for the lost Cathy degenerates into a purely destructive force which many others have felt who are equally incapable of controlling the strong desires out of which love grows.

To express its symbolic truth, romantic love selects and exaggerates the significant characteristic and virtually ignores what is not directly to its purpose, This, too, is true of art in general. Michelangelo, for example, knew his anatomy at least as well as any physician of his time and probably much better than most. He may have done the drawings for some of the Renaissance anatomy texts, in the same way that Titian and his students did the plates for the great anatomy text by the physician and teacher Vesalius at Padua. Yet when Michelangelo did his statue of David for the city of Florence, he made his David fifteen feet tall, which is biological nonsense. He modeled David's body tenderly and delicately to show that he was young and still uncalloused by time and the inequities of life. And then he seemingly contradicted this by making the youth's right hand disproportionately large.

He did this because somehow in this delicate figure Michelangelo had to indicate strength, the strength behind the sling that killed Goliath. Michelangelo took liberties with the facts in order to state symbolically the truth about David, his youth and tenderness and at the same time his strength, a strength of the spirit as well as of the hand. He did, after all, go courageously forth to do battle with a gigantic, well-armed, battle-scarred warrior, even though he was merely a boy. To model David simply and accurately as a boy might be good reporting but it would not be art.

For another example, Brancusi's *Bird in Flight* is a gleaming cylindrical object that does not even look like a bird. And yet it catches the essence of flight. It departs from the facts and selects only that which conveys motion—that of a bird in flight. It selects and exaggerates that single aspect, and builds the entire sculptured form out of it. And in the end we feel the flight of the bird even more knowingly than if we had examined a photograph of a real bird in real flight. We catch the essence of flight.

And this is precisely what we do in romantic love. We too select some part of our feelings and we exaggerate their expression. A man in love proclaims to his girl, "You're the only girl in the whole wide world for me." This is not literally true. He happens to be there and she happens to be there and perhaps the glands are working and it is spring and there may be all sorts of factors at work.

He may also be a very practical-minded man operating on the advice in a song from *Finian's Rainbow,* "If you can't be near the girl you love then you love the girl you're near." If he said that to a girl, it is doubtful that she would become predisposed in his favor. When he says, on the other hand, "You are the only girl in the world for me," not only does he have a favorable response from her, he has a favorable response from himself as well. He is giving his feeling a grandeur of dimension, and he is enlarged by it. He too feels the character of love more fully.

Love Adorns, Love Enhances

The lover sees more in his loved one than anyone else sees in her. He adorns her image; he exaggerates her beauty of body or face or personality. He puts into it what may not even be there but no matter; he wishes it there, he sees it there, and he loves her for it. Quite often, as we know, the romantic lover creates a completely non-existent image of the loved one. He hardly knows the real girl. What he is in love with is his ideal image of her, or of someone he would like her to be. Conversely, the loved one does the same with the lover; she loves what she thinks he is, or wishes he is.

Now this is not rational. In terms of what comes after, when perhaps the lovers marry, it is most impractical. But in addition to the rational, practical, efficient aspects of life, there is also a decorative side, an artistic side.

This need to decorate, to make beautiful, is a powerful one in us all. We can trace it back to Stone Age man in his cave. He painted deer on his cave wall. He also adorned his weapons, and his tools. He made a knife blade out of reindeer antler and then he decorated it. He whittled and carved a design on it.

We might call his first knife an example of craft or applied art. But when he was well fed and safe in his cave, he had the leisure to express something else in his make-up. He adorned his tools, adding a purely decorative element to his life. We call this pure art.

If romantic love is an art, it too must have this decorative quality. And so it does. It adorns the lovers and every aspect of their love. The girl next door may be just good old Elaine. Fall in love with her and she becomes, "Elaine the fair, Elaine the beautiful, Elaine the Lily Maid of Astolat." One teardrop from the loved one's eyes has more power to move us than all the water in all the seven seas. Greeting the loved one is a moment of high drama, and parting is pure tragedy.

For the Emancipation of Feelings

Perhaps one reason for the appeal of the romantics to us is that they fought a battle for the sake of all of us in defense of feelings. Their rebellion against the restraints of reason is still poignantly felt among us. The fact is that we have little opportunity to express feelings. Many times we scarcely dare recognize that we have them. We live in a society that permits us to express emotion only under very special circumstances. In most situations, even highly emotional ones, it is a mark of good manners, of civilization, to keep a stiff upper lip in the face of trouble, grief, or pain and bravely express our ability not to express ourselves.

Such discipline may help us to manage our painful emotions. The display of grief permitted in other societies, such as the wild wailing grief of a Neapolitan mother over her dead son in an Italian film, is sometimes threatening to us. We deal with our emotions not necessarily better but differently.

When the feelings are less lacerating, or when they are actually happy feelings, we exercise the same restraint. We expect it of ourselves, as of others. Implied in this restraint is that there is something not quite nice about feelings. They are perhaps childish, or primitive, or subhuman, or in any case uncouth. When a man pounds the table in anger or protest or simply out of strong conviction, people jump; he is behaving like a bully. But the romantic lover has permission to express his feelings, and in terms as dramatic as he can muster. For this freedom alone we would have reason to wish we were romantically in love.

The freedom to express our feelings is now part of our political tradition. The American and French revolutions established the value of the individual, right down to his most irrational feeling. This was stated at least in principle, and the rights of the individual are most carefully protected by our Constitution, the first ten amendments, and the many interpretations of the courts since these were written.

Yet for generations there have been equally binding laws, though unwritten, against the expression of feelings. There are subtle social forces, standards of behavior, that keep the emotions hemmed in. Today, when we understand somewhat better what happens to repressed emotions, we try to permit our children the expression of their strong feelings.

Not too long ago a child who said something disrespectful to his mother or father was soundly spanked, or he had his mouth washed out with soap. Today we frown on these punishments. If a child never says anything which expresses strong feeling, it generally means that we are exercising a control that is too heavy, too authoritarian for his best development.

The child psychologists have had to fight for this freedom of emotional expression for children. They have had to teach parents how to manage this freedom wisely for the child, for of course they cannot permit physically harmful or dangerous behavior in the name of self-expression. As adults, however, we allow ourselves and each other very little leeway.

Feelings Become Respectable

To all this the romantic lover is a glorious exception. In love the feelings need not be denied. In love we let ourselves become intensely aware of our feelings. We dwell on them, enlarge on them, cultivate them, and of course express them —to the loved one, to our friends, or if no one else will listen, to ourselves. For lovers are also permitted to talk to themselves without any doubt being cast on their sanity.

When the lover expresses his feelings, feelings in themselves become more respectable. We are charmed by their expression, even in others. We look upon them with tender amusement and perhaps with nostalgia. Other feelings that people may express we find threatening, such as anger, hostility, even outspoken grief, as we have observed. But not love. When we see two young people, in a roomful of others, fixed hypnotically upon each other, unaware of anyone else's existence, we smile; we feel warm and kindly. We may think they will get over it, we may regard it as a temporary sickness, we may be utterly cynical about its outcome, but we do not recoil from it. On the contrary, we like it.

The Fool of Love

Romantic love gives us another freedom, the freedom to be awkward or inept. If we suffer from a feeling of inadequacy about some aspect of life—as who does not?—we frequently overshoot the mark and our behavior is likely to be awkward, excessive, overdone. In romantic love this at once becomes acceptable. The lover can rave, he can rant, he can stumble over his own feet, bump into things, forget to say hello or goodbye, forget appointments, make nonsensical conversation, play the fool in a thousand ways, and no one will rebuke him.

A famous fool of love is Rostand's hero in the play *Cyrano de Bergerac*. Cyrano's enormous nose made him overwhelmingly self-conscious. Did he go and hide? On the contrary, he made himself as conspicuous as possible. He wore a great white plume in his hat, his *panache*, which became his trademark. He made himself an excellent swordsman and went about provoking duels in which he could display his skill. He became a notorious braggart and swaggerer. When he fell in love with Roxanne he did not dare to court her for fear of rejection. Instead he poured out all his ardor in the name of his handsome but dullwitted friend Christian. This he did in highly literary fashion, and since Roxanne had a proper appreciation for romantic sentiment poetically expressed, Christian won the lady.

For all his folly we love Cyrano. Even Roxanne loved him, as she reveals in the last scene when he lies dying and she kisses him in farewell.

Flight from the Mind

A third freedom that romantic love brings us is the freedom from judgment. Romantic love is not critical and not judgmental. It is a perfect flight from intelligence and reason. The lover follows his feelings. He does as he feels like doing, and at the same time he has the perfect excuse. It is not his choice, not his will that he is following. He is a helpless victim of forces far greater than himself, the forces of love. With this splendid justification he can thoroughly enjoy himself.

The romantic lover indulges himself in love somewhat like a cat. A cat does not caress you; he caresses himself against you. So with the romantic lover. He thinks he is in love with his beloved, but more often he is in love with love; he is enjoying being in love, indulging himself in the joys of romantic love. The object of his love seems to be the beloved but in fact what he is in love with is often an image he himself has projected on the beloved, as on a screen. He is in love with his own creation, with a part of himself.

If he were to see his beloved for the person she is, he would have to use his mind and his judgment. He would be considering whether this beloved is going to wear well, whether she will satisfy his needs, provide the kinds of companionship he wants. He might even consider whether she will be a good mother to the children he hopes to have some day.

In romantic love he is free of all this good sense and good judgment. Santayana described the romantic lover as free as air to "love what he imagines and worship what he creates," his own individual work of art. He added, and with some truth, that romantic "love is nine-tenths the lover and only one-tenth the object loved."

Add to this the excitement, the drama—for romantic love is nothing if not dramatic. To be in love takes us out of the humdrum, the routine of every day and puts us on a roller-coaster. We swoop up and down, we soar and we plunge. In love we are part of the drama of life. We cannot plan, cannot think ahead. We have no script; we play every scene *ad libitum*, for obviously feelings cannot be planned, emotions take their own unpredictable course. A silence, a pause, the very emphasis on a word or a syllable changes the course of an evening from joy to gloom or vice versa. Whether the loved one says "yes" or "YES!" makes all the difference.

The drama is still better in retrospect; impassioned recollections of the loved one are even more enjoyable than the presence of the loved one herself. Many lovers actually prefer to spend less time with the loved one and more time musing over her, recollecting the last meeting and anticipating the next. When lovers are together they spend much of their time just looking at each other without a word. If they talk, the probabilities are that one of them will say something sensible, something that recalls reality, and the dream is shattered, feelings are hurt, the meeting ends in a quarrel.

The literature of romantic love gives this secret away. Most of it involves dreaming about the loved one; very little is concerned with being with the loved one. How much time did Romeo and Juliet actually spend together? Dante's great love for Beatrice grew on a mere thirty seconds of actually seeing her, yet he dreamed of her in poetry for the rest of his life. Dorothy Parker, in a romantic short story, describes a young woman suffering from unrequited love, who takes a taxi and rides downtown, not to see the man she loves but merely to keep driving around the block on which he lives and think about him. It is a painful, agonizing time that she spends, and yet, although she suffers, the reader understands her and sympathizes thoroughly with her.

The Mechanism

In all this there is a particular psychological mechanism at work, something analysts call the process of idealization.

Translated bluntly, it is a form of sexual overestimation. The lover overestimates the beauty, the virtue, the qualities of the beloved. He does not make an accurate, rational, or mature assessment of the love object; rather his evaluation is hasty, exaggerated, and likely to be full of error.

And the analysts suggest to us that when we fall in love romantically—that is, without thought or judgment, without trying to discover what the love object is really like—what we are doing is developing a hiding place for our sexual aims which are still basically narcissistic. We choose a love object as that hiding place.

In childhood, as we have noted, we first fall in love with ourselves as our primary source of pleasure, and then we love the food, the hand that feeds us, the parent to whom that hand belongs. The child comes to love his parents and others, but basically his love is still infantile, still narcissistic; he loves his parents and others mainly for what they can do for him by caring for him, giving him pleasure and comfort. He is not yet interested in their happiness or well-being, only in his own. Essentially his love is for himself.

During his early loves he feels the need to turn to a member of the opposite sex, and yet his capacity for love is still not very mature. In these early relationships, he is still mainly in love with himself. He loves being in love. The young lover is still indulging his self-love; he is still interested in his own emotions, his own joys and sufferings in love. He is not really interested in the loved one's feelings, except as they affect his own. He is not really interested enough to know what she is really like; he likes his own image of her better than the real girl she is.

This is idealization, and it is the psychoanalytic interpretation of the process we know as falling romantically in love.

Meanwhile, of course, the world is fooled and the lovers themselves are fooled, because here are two people of opposite sexes and they are putting on a dramatically convincing performance of being in love with each other.

An altogether different process easily confused with this is sublimation. Here the infantile or narcissistic aims are replaced or redirected along other channels. In sublimation the individual's sexual aims are not necessarily expressed sexually. They may be partly blocked, but in a pleasurable way, and then tenderness, understanding, care for the loved one grow out of what began as purely a narcissistic and pleasure-seeking impulse. When love is sublimated in this fashion, the psychoanalysts point out, only then does the relationship develop toward stability.

Without this step, we have two people who are using each other for the purpose of satisfying their own needs and desires, their own pleasures. Not until they substitute, for this narcissistic aim, the more mature aim of seeking to understand the loved one's needs and caring about the loved one's satisfactions, not until then are they on their way to a relationship they can maintain. We may say that this is the way that romantic love develops into mature love. By the process of sublimation, the self-love of childhood develops into the outgoing love of maturity

Love as a Guarantee

Romantic love may thus serve its purpose as a first step toward mature love, and serve it well. It bridges the wide and possibly frightening gap from loving oneself to loving another. The emphasis that romantic love places on the strength of one's feelings is highly appealing. It suggests a guarantee of love; it overcomes fear with a promise, however illusory, that this is a love that one can trust.

Through the childhood years, we remember, the child received a kind of conditional love from his parents. They loved him provided he accepted their way of doing things. He takes this conditional love, since it was all he could get in the world of harsh reality. But he still longs for unconditional love. He would like to be loved no matter what he is, no matter what he does.

Romantic love gives him that guarantee. It is not a thirty-day guarantee; it is not even a guarantee for life. It is nothing less than a guarantee forever. He is totally loved, totally accepted. No matter what he may do, no matter how badly he may behave, he will be forgiven, he will be loved. This is the premise, we noted, of romantic love.

With such an exaggeration of love and with all the promises that accompany it, both the lovers feel that they will never be hurt again. This is the love they have longed for, the love with no strings attached, the unconditional love.

When they contemplate marriage, they begin to ask themselves questions. They ask, "How do I know I'm in love?" The answer to that is simple. If they raise the question at all, then they are in love. But that is not the question they really want to ask. What they want to know is, Is this the real thing? Is this love great enough to survive all the difficulties of marriage, to solve all the problems of marriage?

The answer to that is, No, it is not. It takes only two people to fall in love, but marriage involves much more. It involves relationships with many people besides the two at its center, for they bring other relationships with them and they must be dealt with—parents, brothers and sisters, cousins, friends, and eventually children. Marriage involves many intangibles, such as values and principles and ways of living and backgrounds that may be similar but are not likely to be identical. It involves money and management. It involves the passage of years and the changes that time brings. Marriage is not a part-time amorous liaison but an arrangement for living a life together.

Loving and Marrying

How then does romantic love relate to marriage?

We must first acknowledge that for all its delights, romantic love is pre-marital love. In all the romantic literature it would be hard to find a story of romantic love in marriage. It happens occasionally in real life. But it is rare indeed in literature. In literature, the great romantic lovers never find happiness; they are doomed from the start. The fairy tale lovers of course marry and "live happily ever after." The rest of their life is summed up in a single phrase. Obviously there is no more to tell, for romance ends with marriage.

The writers and the poets are right. Romantic love in its pure form is utterly inconsistent with marriage. It begins with the choice of a love object, not for any realistic reasons but despite reason, despite reality. It implies a love so strong that it will overcome all, but the love is built on dream and fantasy and the obstacles it is prepared to overcome resemble fairy tale dragons more closely than the prosaic matters of paying the rent and taking out life insurance. Romantic love is ardent and intense, but that is no indication of its permanence. It is experienced on a level of ecstasy, and ecstasy is hard to maintain for any length of time. It has the quality of stolen kisses

—or stolen week-ends, in our more forthright times—while marriage is a public arrangement in the eyes of the world as well as the law.

Finally, romantic love teaches the lovers nothing about how to preserve their love. It tells them nothing about what to do in time of trouble. It gives them no guidance on how to make up when they have had a difference of opinion, or hurt each other's feelings, or misunderstood one another. There was nothing about understanding each other in the original guarantee, only the promise of loving each other. Understanding was the last thing they thought of, when they fell in love.

Romantic love is thus a delicious art form but not a durable one. In the end, its most persistent practitioners confess that they would like to escape from its patterned illusion into the next, more realistically satisfying stage of an enduring relationship. For romantic love can become stale with endless repetition. And despite the cynics it is married love that can keep green and fresh the best romantic elements. Like all art, no form ever totally monopolized all available beauty. Every period of art offered something of value, yet no period ever fulfilled the needs of everyone. The romantic period gave us a great deal. With selection and tempering, we can add much of its richness and adornment to the substance of married life.

CHAPTER FOURTEEN

Love and Marriage:
Its Conflicts

IN THIS ROMANTIC world of the West, no expression of love has the validity of getting married. Yet it is curious how little has been written about love within the framework of marriage. The great writers and poets lavished their finest talents on romantic love, and sometimes on adulterous love, as in *Anna Karenina* and *Madame Bovary*. But they have not been inspired to write about the love of two people married to each other.

Married love seems not to attract film makers, either. When people are portrayed making love on the motion picture screen they are almost never married, or at least not married to each other. One would think we were embarrassed by the sight of a husband and wife behaving lovingly toward each other, as though we were still children locked out of our parents' room.

There is, of course, a great deal of clinical material on the subject. But this kind of literature has little to tell us about the joys of married love. It deals rather with the problems, the disappointments, the failures of love within marriage. Now and then we come upon a literary effort such as the prize-winning play of Edward Albee, *Who's Afraid of Virginia Woolf?*, but once again the theme is non-love in marriage, not love.

Is married love too dull to warrant our attention? We make a hasty disclaimer—"Oh, no, not at all!"—and yet many people feel that it is. What has married love, fulfilled love, that can compare with the sweet anguish of romantic lovers? When married lovers suffer we do not find their anguish attractive. It is more likely to be threatening, since it signifies disappointment and defeat. It strikes us as not literary or poetic but clinical, even sick. We would prefer not to look at it. And when married lovers are happy lovers, what is there to say? Only what the fairy tales say: "and they lived happily ever after."

It is also true that when we think of married love we are no longer thinking of love so much as of an elaborate institution of which love may or may not be a part. Marriage is so many other things besides love, as we commonly use the term, that love becomes almost incidental.

Marriage, when we examine it seriously, is a whole pattern of attachments, only one of them being the attachment we call love. When people speak of the problems they have in marriage they generally mean problems having to do with money, with children, with in-laws. When they talk of the comforts of marriage they mean the satisfactions of a well-run home or what a good cook one's wife is—more recently, one's husband. We almost never hear married lovers speak of loving each other or being loved.

Perhaps the reason is that love within marriage is too intimate to discuss, except with marriage counsellors and lawyers when it goes wrong. Those who are discontented with their love either acknowledge defeat and seek divorce, or find other compensations for a relationship which keeps them unfulfilled and forever restless. And those who rate themselves happy in their married love have no need to talk about it; their happiness finds expression in the many satisfactions that life has when a secure love is its core.

What Does Happen to Love?

Marriage soon reveals the kind of lovers we are. Human nature is the same in marriage as it is in other areas of life. Marriage does not create difficulties. We bring our difficulties with us into marriage.

If the partners bring into marriage neurotic patterns too rigid and unyielding, too inimical to love, then the feelings of love simply cannot grow. Consider for example the man who is so secretive, so suspicious of everyone, that he does not give his confidence even to his wife; she never knows who his business associates are, how much money he makes, or even precisely what he does for a living. In a word, he never lets her know *him*, the man, the human being in all his dimensions; how then can she love him? And how can she respond with warmth to the limited, even miserly part of himself that he offers her, the attachment weakened by the lack of confidence, in which so much is withheld?

Or consider the kind of wife who does everything perfectly; she is a perfect housekeeper, a perfect hostess, a perfect citizen in the community—a spark plug in the PTA, a leader in local good works. She never reveals human weakness or fallibility. When an individual seems that perfect, when she never lets down, she seems unreal. We have the feeling that this may not be the real person that we see, but a cover for her.

The real person, for all we know, may be harboring all kinds of hidden feelings, perhaps hostile and even destructive. She will not allow us to see them; she will not allow herself to see them. She is unable to tolerate feelings that may conflict with her standard of perfection. Her husband and children will feel unloved, and at the same time they will feel deeply guilty because all the external signs of love are constantly displayed before them.

These are two extreme examples, and it is a question whether love can flower in a marriage handicapped at the start by such profound personality disturbances in one or the other partner. Yet we all bring some neuroticisms into marriage, and marriage is an unflattering mirror that mercilessly magnifies them. We see our immaturities and our inadequacies thrown right back at us, in the reactions of our marriage partner.

The reaction may be outright angry criticism, an open rejection of this aspect of me that my loved one never suspected or never took seriously until now. Or perhaps she conceals her dismay to avoid a quarrel. Perhaps she buries it under a show of acceptance, telling herself that that is the man she married and she will have to make the best of it.

If she really is able to make the best of it, to accept this unfortunate trait in her husband and love him anyway, defects and all, then she is truly pulling her weight in this partnership. And if the man can do the same for her, if he can accept her weaknesses with her strengths and love her altogether, then they have the beginnings of the kind of love they both long for, the dependable love that marriage promises.

Unfortunately, it does not always work that way, at least

not in the beginning. More often, both partners feel let down; they lose confidence in each other and begin to blame each other for not fulfilling the promises of their courtship. During courtship they exaggerated each other's charms and virtues; now they begin to go to the other extreme, and exaggerate each other's shortcomings. They criticize each other, in their minds and sometimes openly. One may blurt out angrily after a party, "That was a terrible thing to do, in front of all those people." During courtship, if one of the lovers wanted to correct the other, it would be done gently, lovingly; now the correction comes out barbed with blame and disappointment. Very likely it calls forth an angry defense in the form of a counterattack—and the lovers find themselves on opposite sides of a widening chasm of non-love.

The Abuse of Love

Even when love becomes contaminated in this way and perhaps irreversibly corroded, the partners do not necessarily separate. They go on together, carrying out their marital obligations although grudgingly. Men take to poking fun at the married state; they remember the good old days of bachelorhood and make sour jokes about not having known when they were well off. Women tend not to make fun of marriage —with all its faults, it is still better than the spinsterhood from which it rescued them—but they remember with nostalgia their dream of what it might have been. A wife complains about her husband to a confidante, who very often responds with similar complaints of her own, thus deepening the pervasive atmosphere of discontent for them both.

And more and more the partners seek their satisfactions apart from each other. They may go out together and enjoy themselves, but they enjoy themselves separately rather than together. Their enjoyments do not depend upon each other. They are like railroad tracks, running parallel side by side but never meeting.

They do bring their disappointments to each other but not like lovers seeking comfort, seeking understanding and drawing strength from each other. Their marriage becomes the dumping ground for all the griefs that assail them in the outside world. From their initial disappointment in each other, they go on to blame each other for everything that goes wrong, both within and outside of their marriage.

If a husband runs into heavy traffic on the way home, and perhaps suffers a scratched fender, it is because his wife does not have enough consideration for him to serve dinner half an hour later; the rush hour scramble is her fault. If his boss has given him a rough time, again it is her fault, for if he did not have her to support he could quit this job which is giving him ulcers. She is no longer his beloved companion but a millstone around his neck; a vaudeville comic's synonym for "wife" used to be "ball-and-chain."

Naturally she repays him in kind. She saves up all her griefs with the children, the neighbors, the house, the household help if she has any, and she lays them all before him with his dinner. If she does not blame him directly for everything disagreeable that has happened during the day, she at least implies that it is all a consequence of being married to him.

Obviously these partners are using each other in a most unpleasant way. Yet this abuse of their love as a dumping ground for all their discontents is what holds many marriages together. The attachment such people have to each other can actually grow even though the pleasure they give each other decreases. Love, in the romantic sense, disappears but love as an attachment of two individuals frequently thrives on the unhappy, unwitting needs marriage gives them the opportunity to express. If they did not have each other to blame, they would be left with no one to blame but themselves, and that would hurt even more.

The fact is that either we have scapegoats or we have symptoms. Marriage spares us our symptoms by giving us a ready-made scapegoat in the form of a marriage partner.

But we pay a heavy price. Love so abused loses its luster. After an enraged attack and counterattack, it is very difficult to make affectionate advances, either because one does not feel affectionate or because one is far from sure that a show of affection would be accepted. Making up after a quarrel becomes progressively harder; in such a climate of discontent with each other, the more pleasant side of love can no longer be expressed freely, spontaneously. Love gets to be expressed almost solely within the narrow confines of its habitual expression, as a dull attachment of mutual grievances. This is very far from what marriage promised.

The Prison of the Self

The heaviest price, however, is the effect upon the personality of the partners. The failure of their attachment of love forces each of them back into his or her own limitations. This makes for the flowering of whatever neurotic tendencies they have brought with them into marriage.

The failure to find reliable love with another person drives us back into the first love we ever knew, the primitive, infantile self-love which we long ago found so dependable. And this kind of love, or narcissism, can take many forms. Usually the form it takes for the partners in a disappointing marriage is the form it took with each of them before marriage.

A man who was ambitious before marriage now becomes even more ambitious. Such a man is after all blameless and beyond criticism. Society applauds him, and no one stops to ask how much of this drive for success is due to his failure in developing love for his wife, his children. In the old days a man might also react to his failure in love with a drive for power in the home—he would become a domineering husband and father. The authoritarian head of the household used to be more acceptable than he is today; nowadays we would find such a man old-fashioned, almost grotesque.

A woman may also develop a drive to achieve outside the home, and increasingly she can find opportunities to do so. More often, she is driven to express this form of self-love in some aspect of her role in the family. She may come to dominate her husband and children, making all the decisions, ruling the home with an iron hand with or without a velvet glove. She may take an apparently soft line, and dominate her children by overmothering and overprotecting them, keeping them passively dependent upon her long past the age when they should be striking out for themselves. We have learned to look askance at too obvious a display of this kind of mothering, but the devoted mother still has a respected place in society, and this retreat into self-love may never be questioned by herself or those around her, despite its destructiveness to her husband and children.

The disappointment in love can take the opposite form: instead of dominating, it becomes dependent. If one cannot win love as an equal, by giving love, then love can be exacted by helplessness. Women did well in the past with the role of helpless femininity. Although elements of this role remain part of a woman's attractiveness to men, manifest ability is rapidly becoming far more desirable than helplessness. Sickness is another matter, and it is a game that both sexes can play. A man can drag himself bravely to his work each day despite ulcers, chronic headache, fatigue; a woman can perform her duties in the home stoically regardless of migraine and lower back pain, and all must sympathize and applaud or be judged heartless. Psychosomatic medicine has given us considerable insight into many ills that have no apparent organic cause. The sufferer is both his own enemy and his own victim; the somatic expression of emotional difficulties is a trap that is most difficult to escape if one is caught, for the pattern frequently draws upon some of the very earliest childhood difficulties.

Whatever our pattern before, that is likely to be the pattern into which we are more deeply driven by a failure to enhance our love in marriage. A withdrawn man, whose shyness was one of his charms to the girl who fell in love with him, retreats into still deeper withdrawal; his one heroic effort to emerge into love of another person has failed, and so he gives up and goes back into his shell. He reads the newspaper at breakfast, sits silent at dinner, spends the evening watching television; he rarely suggests an evening out with his wife and discourages her from inviting friends or accepting their invitations. There are married couples who almost never really speak to each other.

Other individuals find anodynes in excesses of drinking or gambling, short of addiction. Since their love fails to absorb them, any excess is like a splash of color in an otherwise drab existence. It seems to them: What difference does it make? Nothing really matters. They feel that whether through their own or another's failure, love has failed them, and without love nothing has much value.

Failure is hard to live with. These are examples of extreme responses, but we all flee from our failure in love to some degree, and we flee along the road that we have already explored.

To put it another way, either we grow and expand into a positive attachment to another person, or we retreat into the narrower world of ourselves and become increasingly the slaves of our own neurotic needs and drives. It may be that we fall prey to a need to dominate somebody, to feel superior to somebody, to abuse somebody, to complain to somebody or about somebody, to become passively dependent upon somebody. All these needs are potentially inimical to love. If love is strong enough, it can afford to live with them without becoming damaged. But if love is weak, then these needs become strong, even overpowering, and they come to dominate us and shape the relationship into something other than a satisfying attachment.

Our love is often weaker than we realize because many of us enter marriage with attitudes toward it which we have never clearly defined and of which we may not even be aware. Many of these attitudes are inimical to the flowering of love in marriage.

What Many Men Marry for

Many a man enters marriage with genuinely strong feelings of love which unfortunately he fails to adapt to the new needs of his new life situation. During his courtship, he shares his good times with his fiancée, and their mutual enjoyment of these pleasures confirmed the value of their attachment to each other. Now that he has to share everything from his closet space to his pocket book, sharing becomes, more properly, caring. He cares for his pet dog because he knows the animal is helpless. When he married his wife, it did not occur to him that he was undertaking to give her all this loving care. Quite the contrary—he assumed not only that she would take care of herself but even more, that she would take care of him. She would cook and clean and see that he had freshly laundered shirts in his dresser drawer. Nor did he dream this up all by himself. This is what she said she would do.

For her part, the girl had every indication from him that he was going to care for her in suitable husbandly ways. Now both may be fulfiiling their promises to the letter. She does indeed keep house and cook and see to his laundry, and he dutifully brings home his salary and pays for the rent and the groceries. But the spirit falls sadly short of the expectations with which each entered the marriage. Each of them would be more patient, more tolerant, more giving—indeed each would take much better care of some dumb animal they had taken into the house than they do of each other.

Another man marries in the blithe expectation of continuing the part-time love that he has been enjoying. To him the bond of holy matrimony is merely a social and legal confirmation of the agreeable companionship that has been brightening his leisure, a perpetuation of Saturday night love. He expected that he would continue to live pretty much as he had been living, and have a wife besides; marriage was simply a way to confirm the arrangement. After a few months he is shocked to realize that marriage is something very different, that it is taking up too much of his time, his energy, altogether too much of his life. His wife is no longer there to give him pleasant companionship only when he wants it; she is there all the time. This is more than he bargained for, and it may be more than he is willing to accept.

What Many Women Marry for

These attitudes inimical to married love are not exclusive to men; they exist among women, too. A girl may unwittingly look forward to marriage as a solution for her feelings of social and economic insecurity. She is not alone in this; her mother and very likely her father as well have impressed on her from childhood that in this world a girl's only hope for security and status lies in marriage. She marries to escape the hazards of spinsterhood and gain the security she seeks and, interestingly enough, her marriage does exactly what she asked of it. It gives her social and economic safety.

But now, it appears, safety is not enough. She wants romance. She thought she had it during courtship; someone cared enough about her to take her out of her singlehood, her state of limbo, and this she interpreted as an act of love. Now she expects all the other acts of love to follow, acts of attention and cherishing all directed toward her. She is to be the recipient of all this, as she has been the recipient of the social and economic advantages she sought. There is nothing in her concept of marriage that stipulates what she is supposed to contribute to it. She wanted marriage; she was ready for it in practical terms. But now she finds herself unhappy because these practical satisfactions are not enough; a practical attachment is not enough.

Another woman marries expecting that the utter devotion she has enjoyed from her swain during courtship will continue to be the pattern of her marriage. Now obviously if a man falls in love with a girl who wants him to show devotion, he is willing and able to devote himself to her for as long as it takes to get her to the marriage ceremony and a little longer, say, for the honeymoon. But devotion is not a serviceable pattern over the months and years of marriage, and a woman who looks for this in marriage is bound to be disappointed. It is doubtful whether she would get the devotion she dreams of, even if she were able to give it in the same exacting measure. But we note that the dream of having someone bound hand and foot in devotion to oneself does not usually call for a return in kind. The woman who expects the tribute of slavish love is rarely prepared to give it.

People Are Different

Besides these individual attitudes which may interfere with married love, we also have troubles with each other simply as human beings. One of the prime sources of trouble people have with each other stems from the obvious fact that they are different from one another. They have differences of opinion, differences of taste; they do not necessarily want the same thing at the same time. Suppose your host at a dinner party greets you enthusiastically with a pitcher of exotic Daiquiris he has just made—and all you want is an ordinary Scotch and soda. He is bound to be disappointed. He may even feel that he never liked you very much altogether. If you like a play someone else dislikes, or dislike a book he praises, he may behave as though you have attacked him personally.

We all give lip service to the glory of our individuality and all our separate and individual differences, but we do not find it easy to accept these differences. We feel threatened by them, because anyone who is different from ourselves is likely to be unpredictable. Unpredictability is in some measure still alarming to us as adults, just at it was in childhood. A young child hides behind his mother when a stranger approaches; the child is uneasy, if not actually afraid, because this unfamiliar person is an unknown quantity and no one knows what he is likely to do.

A man and woman in love are of course aware of one basic difference between them. That is the one, as the humorous story has it, that the French Chamber of Deputies unanimously saluted "Vive la différence!" when they were debating giving the vote to women. The lovers are even willing to accept in a general way the likelihood that there are other differences between them. Yet courtship is a continuous and delightful discovery, not of their differences, but of how much they have in common.

The man will say, "And you know, this girl actually prefers the even-numbered symphonies of Beethoven!" Everybody chooses the odd-numbered symphonies, but she shares his unique appreciation of the even ones! Or she likes, not merely Rembrandts, but early Rembrandts, as he does. And at that moment he feels he has found the only girl in the world for him.

No matter how many of these similarities the lovers discover—or unwittingly manufacture—during their courtship, the differences remain. And these differences, which they feel obliged to ignore or minimize before marriage, become potential sources of conflict afterward.

One difference that people seem rarely to resolve is the one about money. Men and women have many individual attitudes toward money, but one clear distinction between the sexes is their traditional difference of orientation. Undoubtedly this is changing, now that more and more women work not solely in careers but in jobs for needed family income, but historically the husband earned most of the money, and the wife spent most of it.

Thus a man ordinarily comes to measure money in terms of the time and effort he has expended in earning it, while a woman measures it in terms of the needs she does not have enough money to satisfy. Out of this apparently built-in difference can arise endless quarrels. No matter how little or how much money they may have to spend, the partners may fight forever about how to spend it, without ever getting to the root of this evil. The root is actually not money itself but their unresolved differences in evaluating it.

And People Are Alike

Inevitably—and irrationally—we also discover in marriage that people are not so very different, and we may not like that either. Samuel Hoffenstein put it this way:

> When I took you for my own
> You stood 'mongst women all alone,
> When I let the magic go
> You stood with women in a row.

While he had nothing else to do but gaze at her adoringly, the young man in love liked to think his beloved was the only girl of her kind in the world, a unique human being. It was a wonderful feeling, because if she was unique, then he was also unique in appreciating her, and their love was like no other love. Her uniqueness set him and his love apart from all other lovers and their loves.

But now they are married, and life settles down to a day-to-day level. Now this unique girl is washing dishes, putting her hair up in curlers, wondering how much she will be able to spend for a new winter coat. In a word, she is a woman much like other women. Even worse is the young husband's discovery that he, too, is like other men, wrestling with the same commonplace tasks, feeling the same ordinary discontents, behaving in the same familiar ways.

The wife, too, is disillusioned to discover that a greasy pot is still a greasy pot, no matter whether the dinner it held was eaten by the man she adores. The holiday feeling of being in love is gone; the leisure-time enjoyments that filled all their hours together are now only a small part of their life. They once believed that just to be together was enough to make every day seem like Christmas, but their romantic rocket has come back to earth, and they are suffering from much the same despondency that children feel on the first day back at school after vacation.

Old Clothes in New Closets

These are comparatively superficial obstacles to the flowering of love within marriage, and all but the most unrealistic lovers can come to accept them. What may more seriously stunt the growth of love is that we bring with us into marriage all our previous patterns of behavior, all our habits, fortunate and unfortunate, of dealing with life.

As Freud told us, the course of any love depends upon all the loves that have gone before. In the closets of the split-level house, hiding behind the bride's trousseau and the husband's spanking new suits, are all their previous loves, all their previous attachments, all the ways they have experienced of loving and non-loving up to now.

A man whose great love before marriage was his work—whether for the work's own sake or because he is driven by a need to succeed—may have given a fine performance of love for the woman he wanted to marry. Once married, he is very soon spending the same long hours at his office that he did before. Many a woman considering divorce has told me, years afterward, that on the first morning after the honeymoon her husband hurried out of the house without even a goodbye kiss; he could not be late to his desk even though he owned the company.

It may be not his work but his leisure patterns to which he returns, and these may not include his wife. If she protests at his spending all day Sunday at the golf club, he generously invites her to come, too. She can swim in the pool, play cards, even play golf if she likes—she will find plenty of women companions. It is very clear that he is not inviting her to join him, but only to fit her life to his in some way that will not interfere with his habitual pleasures.

Disagreeable surprises of this kind are not necessarily the result of a lover's deceitfulness before marriage. More often they are the consequences of self-deception. Lovers brush aside troubling traits in each other, or they see such traits in the most attractive light. A man may have made no secret of his antipathy, for example, to family relationships. His childhood experience of family life may have been unfortunate; he may have extricated himself from it at an early age and he may have every intention of remaining free of it. In his eyes, family attachments may seem to impose obligations without any return in satisfaction or pleasure.

During courtship the girl understood all this perfectly. Indeed, she overflowed with sympathy; how he must have suffered as a child! Now that they are married, she makes engagements for them to entertain her family in the new apartment, to visit back and forth with sisters and cousins and aunts, to go to dinner at her parents' house once a week.

He reminds her that she understood his feelings and was even sympathetic, and she answers yes, but that was different. The only difference is that now they are married. It was all right for him to reject his own family, but to reject her family is too much like rejecting her. In fact, for all her avowed sympathy, she never did accept as genuine his strong feelings against family involvement. If she had, she would have considered whether she was prepared to give up her own close family relationships, or at least to dilute their closeness by not involving her husband in them. But she entertained no such prospect then, nor does she now. She wants to keep her old, close family ties, and she wants him to fit himself into her pattern.

Many a young woman looks upon marriage as an escape from her family and especially from her mother's control. She may earnestly confide this to her young man. She may tell him how profoundly she disagrees with her mother's principles of child rearing, how different she herself will be as mother to their children. She can scarcely wait for their wedding day, when she will at last be free and independent. And the young husband discovers when they return from their honeymoon, that the first person she telephones is her mother, the first person she consults for advice on anything and everything is her mother, the first person she turns to when anything goes wrong with her marriage is her mother. She calls her mother every day; if not to consult her or confide in her, she calls to fight with her. This dominant figure in her life marches right with her into marriage.

Methinks the Lady

Like Shakespeare, we should be on guard when the lady doth protest too much. Illogically, irrationally, and almost inevitably, the very trait of behavior against which we most strongly rebel is the one we are most in danger of adopting as part of ourselves, part of our own personality.

In the dynamics of human development, this apparent paradox has its own logic. The girl in our story has spent eighteen, nineteen, twenty years of her life being guided by her mother, having all her decisions made by her mother, long past the time when she should have been deciding these matters for herself. For a time, with marriage in prospect, she has been making a stand for independence, spending intense emotional effort on the same relationship although apparently in an opposite direction. Whether she leans or whether she fights, this girl's attachment to her mother remains unresolved, and a husband will have to be very loving indeed, with all the patience and persistence that implies, to undertake the task of weaning her from it.

Another lady who may protest too much in our time is the so-called career girl. Many, perhaps most young women nowadays have some experience of holding a job between graduation and marriage; some have even launched on a profession. Many and perhaps most such girls truly believe that work is only an interim occupation, and for many it probably is.

But many girls who protest that what they really want is a husband and children are innocently deceived. They show this by their pervasive discontent with the narrow confines of married life, especially in the intensive early years of child rearing. Some of them indeed, can hardly wait to get out of the house and into the working world again. They are feeding the baby with one hand and planning their escape with the other.

The French have a saying: "Not everyone who dances is happy." Similarly, not everyone who marries really wants to be married. Being a woman in our society still means, for most girls, that by a certain age one must be married. At the same time our girls are impressed with the ideal of independence. We give them the same education as we give our boys, and if they do not marry in college or immediately after graduation we expect them to get jobs and be self-supporting and independent. We even encourage them to have ambitions in the working world; we are proud of a daughter who embarks on a profession or develops a career. And without a thought of the contradiction involved, we expect her to drop all this at the altar, and devote herself thereafter to housekeeping, cooking, and raising children without ever a glance backward at what she has given up.

Some young women accomplish this sleight-of-hand with apparent ease. Like well-schooled ballerinas or high-wire artists, they do not let the effort show; one would think they had been preparing all their lives for nothing but baby care, casserole cookery and the operation of home appliances.

But with some the opposite conditioning finds more fertile soil. They have breathed the ambitious, competitive air of the working world, have dreamed of personal achievement, and now they find this stimulating atmosphere hard to relinquish for the narrow world of husband and children and the other young wives with the same narrow concerns. They do not need the promised financial security of marriage, since they can support themselves and have proved that they can. They like the idea of having children but chafe at the limitations it places on them. What they really wanted of marriage was not less than they had, but something more—something more which came from love, not from sacrifice.

Everybody enters marriage full of the desire for and the promise of security in love. Under and over all their other needs, real and fancied, runs this theme that has haunted them since childhood. Whatever else they may want, they want the security of being loved unconditionally and with no strings attached.

The marriage license does not guarantee this. Love and marriage are attachments which, as we have seen, easily conflict. Yet many people fit these attachments together so harmoniously that each of the elements is mutually enhanced. Marriage is better because of their love and love is better because of their marriage.

It would be unrealistic to suppose that this is accomplished by some single special effort. Let us look instead at how love does fare favorably in marriage and ultimately grow towards the fulfillment of our hopes in marriage.

CHAPTER FIFTEEN

Love and Marriage:
Its Satisfactions

"LOVE IS BUT a prelude to life, an overture in which the theme of the impending work is exquisitely hinted at but which remains, nevertheless, a symbol and a promise."

Thus wrote Santayana of love and marriage. How many people entering marriage look at their love as an overture, as a symbol and a promise? Very few. Most lovers consider their love a guarantee. They have fallen in love and have so proclaimed themselves, and now that they are married they can fold their arms and wait for marriage to deliver the happiness that is theirs by contract. How surprised they are when they find that what they have entered is not a perpetual party but a working partnership.

There is work to follow, says Santayana, a creative effort whose theme has yet only been hinted at. Many people feel that the work is already completed. They have captured a mate; they have made it to the altar. But the marriage license is not automatically a passport to happiness. It is more like a driver's license, a permit to drive but not a guarantee of the safety and pleasure of the ride.

The Marriage Trauma

Marriage is only potentially one of society's masterpieces. What it produces depends upon what we bring to it. We bring into marriage our whole selves, strengths and weaknesses, maturities and immaturities. The mere fact that we have committed the adult act of getting married does not make us adult. The best that we can usually say for ourselves at the beginning of marriage is that we stand on the threshold of our most grown-up relationship.

We can remain infantile and narcissistic in marriage; there is no guarantee against it, and if we do, that will be the quality of our love and of our marriage if it survives. But marriage may also be traumatic—in the beneficent sense. It may make such immediate and urgent demands on us to behave in adult ways that it shakes us out of our infantile patterns and hastens us along into emotional maturity.

Just as life can be damaging, it can also be corrective, and marriage presents us with both kinds of episodes. Some of the most happily married couples have had to go through exceedingly difficult episodes in their marriage, and by dint of surviving and maintaining their marriage through these very episodes they reach a degree of maturity that might have taken them a dozen years on the analytic couch.

There are people who have been so infantilized by over-protection at home that marriage, instead of fulfilling the dream of greener pastures, is soon no easier to accept than the general difficulties encountered in the outside world. The difference, however, between the problems of marriage and those of life in general is that the troubled individual has someone with whom, at least occasionally, he can face these difficulties. His wife may upbraid him but she also frequently helps him. The jointness of effort can be of great therapeutic value for him.

The episodes of marriage need not be dramatic in order to have a maturing effect. The mere impact of daily living with another human being—with a college roommate for example, or any person other than parents and the siblings we grew up with—can inch us along toward adulthood. Parents and siblings, of course, help us to mature in many ways, but they also evoke our most infantile behavior, if only because our immaturities are part of the old, repetitive pattern of our family relationships. Furthermore, our loving families are likely to be more tolerant of our childishness than is a stranger—after all, they are used to our nonsense!

With a stranger, merely in order to get along peaceably, we have to learn to accommodate ourselves somewhat to his needs and wishes; we have to think of his comfort or pleasure occasionally, not only of our own. If we want to develop the casual relationship into a friendship we must yield still less to our self-centeredness, pay a little more attention to the other's welfare and well-being.

Now suppose this person is not merely a roommate, who only temporarily shares one's life, not even merely a friend who at best shares only a part of one's life. Suppose this person is your girl, the one whom you have been urging to share your whole life with you. Suppose this is the person you have chosen, the one with whom you expect to find happiness, and to whom you have promised happiness. Think what an investment you have already made in her, of hopes and dreams and expectations. And she has made the same investment in you.

Because we make such an investment in each other, most of us enter marriage with powerful motivations to make it work. At the same time we bring into marriage everything we are—and some of this baggage, as we have noted, is of the kind that will get in the way of love. We are bound to stumble not once but many times over this baggage, these impedimenta of the past.

In the everyday world of marriage we unthinkingly slip into our everyday behavior and our everyday emotions. Everything we were, before the exalting interlude of romantic love, we now become again. Everything we hid from the loved one, and from ourselves, during courtship is soon glaringly revealed.

Saturday Night and Monday Morning

A happy love within marriage is in fact not easy to come by. It is so different from the love which most people bring to their marriage that it may as well be two different emotions. We are speaking, of course, of romantic love, the falling in love and being in love that usually ushers in a marriage.

Love before marriage is romantic love, part-time love, for which the lovers put on their Saturday night clothes and their Saturday night manners and even their Saturday night feelings. No matter whether they are seeing each other on Wednesdays and Fridays and perhaps Sunday afternoons as well—their meetings are still planned. They not only arrange the date and what they will do together but they arrange their feelings and their behavior. They show each other only their nicest, most agreeable, most interesting selves. Sometimes they show not themselves at all but some other kind of person, someone they would like to be or think the loved one would like them to be.

Love before marriage is a time of great intensity of feelings, and of great awareness of one's own feelings. The lover hardly for a moment relinquishes his awareness of himself, of his joys and pains, his thoughts and feelings, his hopes and dreams. Love before marriage, despite all it claims to be, is largely narcissistic.

Romantic love, we remember, also exaggerates; it inflates not only the lover's feelings but the qualities he loves in his beloved. And these qualities, however delightful they are before marriage, are usually of the kind that will have least importance once the lovers are married. For their courting time is spent in leisure-time pleasures, pleasures which are much enhanced if one's sweetheart is pretty or witty or a good dancer or skier. Obviously these talents will never be so important in their lives again.

The lovers also exaggerate the qualities that first attracted them to each other. And if they discover other characteristics which perhaps they find not quite so attractive, the discovery gives them little pause—the intensity of their love will surely overcome their differences!

Married love is of course unlike all this. Marriage is not only a matter of Saturday night feelings but also of Monday morning feelings and all the rest of the week's feelings. Now the lovers must not only delight in each other but also work with each other. Nor are they any longer isolated from the world in their romantic chrysalis; each has family, friends, colleagues.

Now they are called upon to fulfill all their promises of undying love, at the same time that each is confronted by the everyday reality of the other as a human being. From intense and exclusive self-awareness, each now is forced into daily awareness of the other. From two separate first persons singular, two *I*'s they must somehow move together toward a new entity, a common entity of *We*.

The metamorphosis from pre-marital to marital love is thus to a large degree a conversion from self-love to love of another person. It is a conversion from the *idea* of love to the *reality* of love, from an attachment to the *idea* of marriage to marriage itself.

The Care and Feeding of Love

How do we foster this transition and develop a strong married love? The answer unavoidably involves the whole history of our love life, the most significant part of our autobiography before marriage. Rarely does any single amorous experience, any number of zealous intentions, any one piece of luck or the most pious hopes and deeply felt longings guarantee the success of love in marriage. All this is wonderful, but it is as irrelevant to the ultimate value of marriage as a frame, however decorative and even appropriate, is to the value of the painting.

Love is a complex attachment. Contrary to popular belief, we do not suddenly fall in love. All we do suddenly is to recognize and entertain urgent feelings and desires about it. But feelings are fickle. They arise quickly and change or disappear with equal speed. Our relationships or attachments or loves have a slower developmental rate and are much more resistant to change. They emerge out of what already exists among our attachments. The difficulty in understanding this stems from our romantic belief that the many relationships which absorb us daily were not deliberately chosen by us and are therefore not representative of how we would behave in one of our choice. Our romantic love, we believe, is the one of our choice. Of course we make more willing promises about our choice but our behavior is very much a product of previous behavior than promises for the future.

This does not mean that romantic beginnings necessarily doom a marriage to disappointment and failure. Most any man initially idolizes the woman to whom he is attracted and inescapably entertains any number of delicious notions about her virtues, which may be somewhat unrealistic and are decidedly exaggerated. If his significant attachments of the past have been mostly pleasant, satisfying, and lasting, the chances are that he can accommodate his ideals to reality. Such a man's love depends not on the *exaggeration* but on *what* he exaggerated. He has enough flexibility, emotional resources, and freedom from nagging inner demands to accept less and work for more simultaneously. The result is to nurture the ideals he initially saw in his wife not by romantic boasts of his good fortune but rather by creating such a rich, sunny climate that her virtues find easy and habitual expression. Reality is thus used to embody and enhance romance instead of destroying it.

This kind of achievement is not easy. Often what we call romantic is a misnomer for neurotic. Idealizing can easily be invalid wishful thinking. Neurotic love feeds on infantile needs which so strongly conflict with the real world around us that we simply cannot reconcile the two without friction, pain, and a sense of loss.

More often than not, people develop relationships somewhere between these extremes of best and worst. They recognize changes in each other as they move from courtship to marriage. But they are not sure. A man reflects: in reality his wife is probably not so generous as he thought her before they married, nor can she be so self-centered as he thinks she is now. Most of us cannot be described in such black and white terms. We are made up a little less of one quality, and a little more of another. Which quality will become uppermost in a relationship depends upon both partners. What does he ask of her that she seems too selfish to grant? Is he perhaps giving too little weight to her needs, and too much to his own? Does she seem selfish to him when in reality he is acting rather selfishly?

Such questions suggest that perhaps these two people are not reaching each other. What strength of attachment can they expect to develop when an impenetrable air space remains between them, a yawning abyss of misunderstanding, unexpressed or improperly expressed needs and desires—in short, a lack of communication?

We hear a great deal about communication these days. The focus of our major interests seems to have shifted from institutional forms to an intense preoccupation with the individual. It is as though Jeffersonian democratic principles had been translated from political life to personal life, and—following Freudian lines—not only the way a man votes but every nuance of his personality, conscious and unconscious, now commands attention. We are more than ever concerned with what he is, what he means, what he stands for from his most remote and primitive yearnings to his most noble aspirations.

The more our own individualism becomes important to us, the more difficult is it to understand another individual. Worse yet, we seem to become less interested in trying. Naïve self-assertion frequently replaces the more sophisticated effort to understand. People bluntly dismiss their difficulties with the announcement, "I just had a need to . . ." Why? What other needs might be served? Is this really the need involved? Do one's needs exist independent of the social situation in which they are expressed?

The love two people have for each other can certainly benefit from greater willingness to understand each other. Yet people are often torn by the conflict of how much of themselves to reveal—not only to others, but to themselves as well. Even in marriage people do not easily let their hair down. They may want to but habitually they do not know how.

Is Love Everything?

We may well ask ourselves, not only whether we are demanding too much of each other in marriage, but whether we are demanding too much of love, perhaps even of marriage. At the risk of apparently contradicting ourselves, we must face the fact that our ordinary feelings about love are not all that there is in marriage; they are not even the only sound basis for a marriage. Historically, marriages were arranged with no consideration for how the prospective bride and groom felt about each other—often they did not even know each other. A marriage would be made for economic or social reasons; on dynastic levels, for political reasons. It might bring prestige or land or business resources into the family; it might be made to protect or enhance property or simply to produce heirs. It might accomplish any number of ambitious or prudent purposes, but rarely was it designed to unite two people who were attracted to each other.

Frequently, marriages arranged for such extrinsic purposes worked well. The partners were of course conditioned to accept marriage in these terms, and were not inclined to rebel; the girls indeed had no alternative. And we are bound to note that, although affection did not exist at the beginning, a strong and rewarding sense of acceptance often developed out of the compelling need to function well together within the institution of marriage, or suffer dire misery and perhaps disgrace.

Today we do not accept arranged marriages; we assume that romantic choice is the only possible basis on which two people marry. But is it so in fact? Many people still marry for practical reasons, for common interests, companionship, home and children. To begin with, they nurture a strong resolve to get along with each other. And if they succeed in this, their common purpose binds them ever closer until what they feel is, in fact, a positive romantic acceptance of each other. If they now had to choose, they would choose each other.

No matter how intensely we feel about love, it is not so broad and general an attachment as marriage. Love is a private relationship; marriage is an institution, and a public institution at that. Marriage involves many other people besides the married partners; the act of getting married to one person does not automatically dissolve all ties with other persons, with family, friends, groups of various kinds. Each partner brings into the marriage all these other ties, and the love these two have for each other must in some way accommodate those other attachments as well, or their love is threatened by them. For the old relationships and the old interests are bound to reappear after marriage, just as the old habits and personality traits reappear no matter how thoroughly they have been suppressed or ignored during courtship.

The new phase of their love, the married phase, can be threatened by the invasion of these other interests and relationships. But it can also be enhanced by them. It can grow on the way in which each of the partners accepts the other's involvements with people on the periphery of their life—with family, friends, business and professional associates, hobby pals, all the varied cast of characters of their separate premarital lives. Each must be willing to sacrifice some relationships to the other's taste or preference. But each must also be willing to accept some that are important to the other.

When a man sees his wife taking the trouble to make friends with a friend of his, one with whom perhaps she has little in common, he is bound to be pleased, even grateful. He knows she dislikes the way his friend drops ashes on the new carpet, forgets to use the coaster and makes rings on the table; she may know little and care less about the subjects he discusses. But she sees that this man's friendship means something to her husband and she includes him in their circle. She does not martyr herself in doing this, and thus she also spares her husband the pangs of guilt. She has shown that she loves her husband as he is, together with his taste in friends. Her attachment or love for him does not create conflict with his other attachments or loves.

This may seem a trivial instance; probably her husband would give up his friend if she asked him to, and not suffer too much loss. But the kind of love which enhances the value of marriage is built upon just such trivial instances of accept-ance rather than rejection.

Love and marriage are only a part of life and not all of it. The success of marriage, and the flowering of love within it, depend upon how well we harmonize this relationship with the other aspects of our lives. The enduring love of marriage grows out of the ability of the partners to deal with everything else. It grows out of how they get along with in-laws, with friends, how they manage the children, how successfully they work out their differences about money, how they weather stormy times together and how they enjoy good times to-gether. These are the building blocks of love within marriage.

Romance in Marriage

Many people see all this as fine but still bewail the loss of something they desire. What happens to romance when lovers marry? Many believe it must die. The mystery is gone. When a man sees his wife with her hair in curlers, or waddling through her pregnancy, or wrestling with pots and pans, vac-uum cleaners, diapers, it is not easy for him to think of her as "Elaine the fair, Elaine the beautiful." Even a true lover's imagination cannot make her so, for the moment. The lover's blissful ignorance, his readiness to love his beloved without in the least understanding her—these quickly vanish in marriage. If marriage is anything, it is a coming to know each other, to understand each other.

Sooner or later, married lovers respond to the gravitational forces of reality. They see each other in terms of what each really is, not in the radiant colors of the imagination. In mar-riage it is no longer practical to exaggerate feelings and be irresponsible to real demands. And finally, when we reach positions of responsibility in business or professional life, we acquire the appurtenances of comfort, and it is pure nonsense to dream of the loaf of bread and the jug of wine in the wilderness. We no longer suffer the deprivation or the uncer-tainty of each other that seems to be a necessary setting for romantic love. We no longer want to suffer it.

All this is a roundabout way of saying that the cold, gray

light of reason can chill us into a shivering acceptance of reality. Yet is it really so regrettable? How many of us actually want to stumble around all our lives in the flattering but much too dim light of candles, to the repetitious strains of gypsy violins? We talk nostalgically of romance but we are not prepared to give up our comforts for it.

We do not even, really, want to be swept away by the grand passion. We want it in the way one says, "I wish I could play the piano," or "I would like to get on a plane tomorrow and go to Europe," or "Some day I'm going to walk out of this rat-race and be a beachcomber." We do not do anything to realize these fantasies—or very few of us do—because we do not really want to do them. They are idle wishes.

Most of us truly want our stable relationships and our orderly lives in marriage far more than we want the wild ride on the winged steed. This does not mean that we never want romantic love. Early in our lives we not only want it but we can scarcely keep from falling into the pattern.

For the rest of our lives, although other more practical goals possess us, we do long to have a touch of romance still. We do not want it to dominate our lives. We prefer to have some measure of control over our destiny. But we would like to preserve romance without paying the price of total disruption.

And this is not inconsistent with marriage. It is, indeed, entirely consistent with a secure and lifelong relationship. The two essentials for romance within marriage are for the partners to survive knowing each other and to maintain an element of novelty in their daily lives.

That is what so many of us fail to do: we are unable to survive the knowledge of each other that comes with making a life together. Romantic love, pre-marital love, is part-time love. A romantic image is created and the lovers have nothing to do but love each other.

They cannot maintain this illusion forever, even without marriage. Many a liaison becomes as routine and unromantic as an old shoe. Within marriage the illusion is usually more quickly penetrated, because marriage itself is a thoroughly real and practical institution and it makes immediate realistic demands on both partners.

The romantic lovers, unprepared for this cold reality, suffer shattering disillusionment with each other, perhaps even more with themselves. They are not the perfect lovers they thought themselves to be. Knee-deep in the shards of their dream, they need romantic love more than ever. They need the promise of unconditional love as they never needed it before. But each unmet demand that they make on each other, each failure to respond with the unconditional love they had promised each other, builds the wall between them higher and higher. The longing for romantic love bounces off the wall, and unfortunately it often bounces off at an angle and in an opposite direction, toward another love object with whom the illusion of unconditional love can once again be nurtured.

Married people can survive the experience of learning to know each other. They can even come to enjoy each other as real and living human beings instead of as creations of each other's romantic dreaming. It is possible. It has been done. If they like the game of love, they can continue to play it. They can continue to court each other as long as they live. In fact they get better at it all the time; they become old hands, experienced and skillful.

This is most obvious in the sexual aspects of love. It is a notorius fact that the sexual experience of honeymooners is often anything but a pleasure, and yet this is the time when the lovers are most intensely romantic about each other. What is true of the sexual relationship is equally true of the other facets of love. Once the need to maintain an illusion no longer exists, every aspect of companionship can be more skillfully, more enjoyably developed.

Purely romantic love can become boring. Many bachelors are ready to admit this. If they have fallen repeatedly in love and for various reasons they have not married, they begin to weary of the amatory red tape of romantic courtship. No matter how delightful, no matter how enticing the new girl may be, the experienced suitor shudders a little as he embarks on the repetitious performance of romantic pursuit. In all probability, the delightful and enticing girl has much the same feeling. If for some reason she has been living the free life of modern singleness for a few years, she is as fed up with the repetitious pattern as her gallant pursuer.

Repetition, in short, can be as boring in romance as it can be in the marriage. The reason people sometimes look beyond the framework of their marriage for romance does not always suggest marital failure. They have simply allowed their activities with each other to become repetitious and boring. They are people given to repetition and the same thing will happen, after awhile, in a romantic affair.

Happily married people work out the ratio of sameness and novelty to fit the needs of their life. They season their lives as we do our food. In the same way, their love remains constant because of its diversity. The comfort they enjoy in each other does not prevent them from remaining attracted to new ideas, people, places, and activities. They lend themselves gracefully to the different episodes and interests of their life together. They are like many, rather than merely, two people to each other. The element of sameness gives their life together continuity and the element of novelty or change gives it freshness and vigor.

The Uses of Love in Marriage

There is good reason to believe that a later, more mature form of anything is better than its early, immature form. Of course we can all think of exceptions. The older a lamb gets, the more sheepish it becomes. Many people like kittens better than people. But people who really know cats, dogs, and people tend to like the grown-up version at least as well as the immature one, and in many cases better. Ripe fruit is usually better than unripe.

Love within marriage enjoys this process of ripening, and it can come to a fine fruition. It comes to be the later, more mature, more dependable and sustaining version of love rather than its early, sometimes ecstatic but mostly rather bungling form. It becomes more understanding, and the understanding lover gives love in the form that meets the needs of the loved one. He does not come home with a pair of expensive earrings when what she needs is someone to mind the baby regularly so that she can take the advanced courses she longs for. Good lovers within marriage come to learn each other's real needs, and do their best to meet them for each other.

This kind of love within marriage gives each partner the feeling of being tended, of being cared for. It is love almost without strain. Suppose, as a man sat working on a lecture he had to give the next evening, he were suddenly transported back into his early twenties, and the girl he was in love with called him up and said she simply had to see him that night. He might say he was sorry, he was working on a lecture he

had to give the next evening. She might insist; she might behave as though the whole world were about to crash unless he
came right over. If he stood firm, clinging to his responsibility
to deliver that lecture—or pass an exam, or finish a paper on
time—she might say, "Then you don't love me." And she
would mean it. Furthermore, at twenty he might drop the lecture notes, the study outlines or the paper, and go running
right over to prove his love.

Immature love involves all kinds of demands, all kinds of
irresponsible behavior with its attendant strains. Love within
marriage is spared such strains. A wife knows that her husband has work to do one night and she expresses her love by
being willing to let him be loving tomorrow.

Those of us who have adolescent children know the kind of
tensions with which they live, and how tiring it would be to
live with such tensions through a lifetime. The excitements,
the self-generating crises of immature love are wonderful—in
the years of immaturity. But life is much easier, much more
productive, and indeed much more enjoyable, in the steadier
relationship of mature love, when crises do not spring up
every hour.

One of the deeply satisfying joys of mature married love, in
contrast with the love of unmarried people, is its freedom
from the urgency of "good times." Young lovers frequently
have the same compulsion "to live it up" whenever they see
each other that people have about New Year's Eve. Even if
they do not feel this strongly about their time together, they
do not easily reconcile themselves to pleasures which do not
involve constant interplay with each other. Married lovers do
not have to sit and look at each other all the time. They can
enjoy a warm sense of each other's presence even though their
activities demand little or no response from each other. They
can read, listen to music, pursue their own interests freely.

Even more gratifying is the fact that such lovers feel and
confirm their love not merely from the pursuit of pleasure but
also from the work they do together. They purchase an old
barn in the country and work hard and lovingly together
painting and fixing it up for delicious weekends out of the city.
Their child develops a problem, and, worried but patiently,
they think, analyze, experiment and work out a solution for
him.

Unlike young love or the part-time love of an enduring affair, each of which in its way can be deeply felt, married love is very much more an integral part of life. It is not a stolen, isolated part of life, but part and parcel of it and, because of this, married love brightens not merely a corner of life but life itself.

Durable Love

The love that we develop within marriage has another quality: it is durable. We have a certainty of feeling, our own and our partner's. Suppose a wife makes a mistake; suppose she gets up on the wrong side of the bed one day and makes a wounding remark. Her husband's entire world will not collapse at his feet, as it might in the early, the romantic phase of love.

Married lovers do not abandon each other over one quarrel, one crisis, one fierce and bruising battle. They have survived such encounters; they will continue to survive them. They have something that can withstand everyday frictions and even occasional tempests. They may be stunned, momentarily shaken, by an explosive outburst, but their moorings to each other remain intact.

Love within marriage meets the many needs of our lives; it is consistent with those needs. It allows for the rational, productive side of life; it provides the climate in which we can do our work. It provides also for the irrational, impulsive side of life, when husband and wife find in each other a ready partner for "playing hooky" from some social obligation or dashing off to a country inn one day to have lunch before breakfast just because they feel like it. Marriage just as easily allows us to relax and put our feet up and think, or not even think, just loaf. It leaves room for friends, hobbies, sports. It accommodates periods of hard work and periods of tension, periods of exuberance and periods of strain.

When something goes wrong, married lovers count on each other. They use their love to great advantage in dealing with life, solving problems together, facing grief and loss together, sharing bad as well as good times. They reassure each other that the pain of loneliness is gone. Married lovers are no longer alone. Each has the support of a trusted partner, and a partner's strength to draw on when his or her own fails.

Married lovers grow within love; they develop into better human beings. We have seen what happens to people who are disappointed and unable to fulfill their love within marriage: they are thrown back into the prison of themselves, chained by their old patterns of adjustment, limited by the neurotic tendencies which take control when love has failed.

When love does not fail, when it grows, the lovers also grow. They grow as a result of what they live through together. They grow on each other's strengths and the strengths they develop to meet each other's weaknesses.

That is why, all things considered, marriage is society's masterpiece, and those who nurture love within marriage are potentially the happiest lovers of all.

CHAPTER SIXTEEN

Parental Love

UNTIL A MERE generation ago, nobody considered it necessary to question parental love. It was a foregone conclusion that parents loved their children and knew what was good for them. When Moses descended from Mt. Sinai with the tablets of the law, they included a commandment for children to honor, if not to love, their parents, but nothing about parents honoring or loving their children.

Nowadays we are so accustomed to questioning the quality of our love for our children that we can scarcely realize how novel an attitude this is. In the whole of human history, such a notion probably never occurred to parents. This practice of self-doubt among parents became common when today's generation of young parents were children. Particularly since World War II, with the growth of psychiatry and clinical psychology, we have been examining the nature of parental love. We realize now that the kind of love a child receives in his early years is a powerful influence in shaping the kind of adult he is going to be. Out of his experience of parental love come his later feelings of optimism or pessimism, his reaction to the world as threatening or friendly, his notions about his own adequacy.

We have already reviewed in this book the effect of our parents' love on our own adult ways of loving. We already have some notion of parental love from the child's point of view, how he learns both love and non-love, how anxiety enters his life, how his future relationships can suffer distortion because of fixations at an early level of emotional development.

What about the parents' side of this love story? What kind of love do we experience in relation to our children?

Love Without Choice

The first thing to recognize is how we come to have them. Some people want children and want them dearly enough even to hasten their marriage. Most people have children because, after awhile, they are expected to have them. Such a mechanical reason has little appeal compared to the lofty goals we like to believe we sponsor. People flatter themselves with all sorts of reasons for having babies, right up to an interest in the preservation of the human race.

The fact is, it is customary to marry. We are repeatedly asked, "When are you going to settle down?" And so we marry. If children do not follow after several years, we are asked again, "When are you really going to settle down?" And so we have children. This is not inimical to the enjoyment of marriage and children. It is a romantic exaggeration to believe that we cannot enjoy anything we do not choose.

We live in a society where, right from the start, we are conditioned to accept family life whether we like it or not. When we grow up and fall in love, we dream of living together and raising a family as the most valid expression of that love. This is the pattern of behavior defined for us in virtually everything we see around us. And so we follow suit. Our conformity may include and express the desire to have children or it may merely establish the fact that we have been conditioned to act like others regardless of our desires.

In actual fact, a variety of things happens. Some people plan to have children and do not have them. Others have them and do not plan. Some plan not to have them and do. Many of us do not even ask ourselves whether we want them. Being married, we expect them, the world expects them and we have them.

The really significant limitation on our choice comes in the next stage: we do not choose the kind of child we are going to have. Whether it is a natural or an adopted baby, it is a baby or at most a young child, and it is an enigma.

We cannot predict what kind of human being it is going to be. There are few if any signs of how this small bundle of inherited traits is going to respond to the kind of people his parents are and the kind of life they will offer him. When we choose a friend or a lover or a marriage partner we are generally choosing a peer, someone whose personality is at least as far along in development as we are ourselves. If we make a mistake, we have only our own lack of experience or judgment to blame. But with a baby all is mystery. We know little about our child at birth except its sex.

We can make a few general predictions, say about complexion and hair and eye coloring. We can expect some family resemblances in the general cast of features. We can assume that when both parents are small and come of families whose stature is small, the child is likely to be of short or medium height—although nowadays American children, and especially California children, are tending to tower over their parents. None of these predictions is very dependable. The human species is so mixed, and the American heritage is so widely blended, that we cannot be sure which genes will emerge most prominently in our children's physical development.

The forecast we would most like to have, of course, is not physical but psychological. And here we have a crystal ball, of a sort. But it is one in which we can almost never read the message clearly.

The crystal ball is ourselves, the parents. What kind of parents we are goes far toward determining what kind of child we will have. The outcome is not so very predictable, even so, for the child's own inborn capabilities are the other half of the story, the half that remains shrouded. Furthermore, we can only guess at the kind of parents we ourselves will turn out to be.

Yet perhaps we can read something of our own image as parents in the crystal ball. As Freud suggested, our psychological biography can be told in the history of our loves. The quality of our parental love will be not too unlike the loves that we have already recorded in our lives.

The Romantic Beginning

Whether the baby is planned or not, the world is quick to congratulate us on the blessed event which awaits us. This unanimity of good wishes helps us to fall romantically in love with the idea of having a baby. We approach parenthood as we approach romantic love, in a state of blissful ignorance, full of hope, full of promises to ourselves and to the unborn love object, full of exaggerated notions of what the baby will be like and how we will feel toward it. At this point the pleasure of parenthood is enormous, for we are living in a romantic dream.

Exactly as in romantic love, reality comes as a jolting intrusion. Reality begins with the wife's pregnancy. During these months, as we have noted, the prospective father often finds that he is the forgotten man, and the prospective mother just as often suffers doubts about her adequacy. Once the baby arrives, the physical realities of its care are decidedly uncomfortable, disruptive, and very far from unalloyed pleasure.

But we are still bemused by our romantic vision. We endow the baby with all the charm and beauty, all the endearing ways and loving responses, with which we endow the beloved in a romantic love affair. This is, or soon will be, the cooing, prattling, adorable dream child, the handsome little boy or beautiful little girl, the artistically gifted or intellectually brilliant offspring that will do us honor, the well-mannered, obedient youngster that will win the admiration of all our friends and neighbors.

This is the early quality of our parental love. We love what we expect the child to be. We love, in short, our romantic image of the child.

For a beginning this is not bad. It is the way we, the child's parents, fell in love with each other. It is a promise of love, not love itself. But as a promise it gives us the courage to go through the early weeks and months of diapers, formulas, feedings, the loss of sleep, the loss of freedom, and all the hard labors of caring for this completely helpless and completely demanding little love object. Our romantic love serves its purpose as an introduction to parenthood, just as it served its purpose as an introduction to marriage.

First Steps in Parental Love

During our first months of parenthood we learn ways to express love that we never knew before. We cannot express love toward our baby as we express it toward a wife or husband, a relative or a friend. We cannot take the baby out to the ball game or to dinner and the theatre; the baby has no use for flowers, books, records, a fur coat, or a trip to Europe. We cannot regale a baby with the latest funny story, engage him in political discussion or share our artistic or intellectual pleasures with him. We can only take care of him.

To say that we never knew these ways of expressing love before is fairly accurate, but we have experienced them before, in our own infancy. Love first came to us in this form, the form of being cared for. But then we were the recipients of it, not the givers, and it came at a time that is buried far below our conscious memory. So when we in turn give this form of love to our brand new first baby we feel like rank amateurs. We feel we are groping our way in a new language. We do not even recognize what we do as an expression of love. Feeding the baby, keeping him clean and warm and dry, protecting him from harm and from discomfort—how can this be love? This is simply the obvious thing you do when you have a baby.

Yet the way in which we do these obvious things for our baby is the first and one of the most important expressions of our parental love. In all the baby's vegetative life—his eating, eliminating, sleeping, being active, being quiet—in all these basic physiological functions of simply being alive, the baby depends upon us. He can manage none of them without our help. As we have said earlier, in this first phase of his life he does not need love. He needs only care.

Naturally, we give him this care. Any parent who does not respond to this need of the helpless little creature seems an unnatural parent.

The question is not whether we care for our baby. The question is, how do we do it? Do we meet his needs? Or our own? In this primary expression of our love as parents, do we somehow convert the act of giving to one of taking? Do we unconsciously manipulate the situation into a source of gratification for ourselves, rather than for the child?

We have been told often enough that our management of the child in his early months and years goes far toward determining the kind of person he will be. As parents, our dearest wish is to have him turn out healthy, happy, capable, interesting, the kind of son or daughter in whom we can take pride and pleasure, who will—yes, most definitely this, too—reflect credit on us as parents. Yet so often, in this first expression of our love, we persist in taking a turning that must end by bringing us dissatisfaction with our child, if not actual pain and grief.

Let us see how this works. One of the first acts of love that we perform for our baby is to feed him. To the baby, food is the closest thing there is to love; it brings him relief from his hunger pains, the bliss of a full stomach. From our earliest hours of life, food and love are equated. And we go right on equating them.

Food Equals Love

We show this in our relationships with adults no less than with children. When we invite friends to dinner, we would not think of setting before them the same meal we would serve ourselves on any ordinary Monday or Thursday. We prepare something unusual; we go to some special shop for an exotic tidbit or something out of season. And we heap food on our guests. We not only take trouble with the quality of what we serve but we offer it in quantity.

If they are good guests, if they eat more than they want and complain that they can scarcely get up from the table, we are gratified. The more uncomfortable they are, the more successful we feel. But if they consider their own comfort first, and eat only as much as they want, then we are the ones who suffer. After all the trouble we took, see how we are rewarded! Our food, our care, everything we have put into this expression of our regard has gone for nothing. Our offer of love has been rejected.

Our friends can put up with this on the occasional evening when they come to dine. They can overeat to please us or they can make excuses and escape indigestion until the next time. They can subject us to the same excess of love when we go to their house to dine. But a child has to suffer this kind of love three times a day, and still oftener in infancy when he is eating every three or four hours.

Every mealtime, mothers and sometimes fathers go through an extraordinary performance. They. coax, wheedle, entertain, distract, deceive or bully the child into opening his mouth so that they can shovel in food. They display the talents of a television comic and the guile of a confidence man, just to get another and another spoonful into the child's mouth. They threaten him and sometimes they punish him for not eating the foods they think he should eat, or the quantity. If he tries to wriggle away they strap him into his high chair.

The child, of course, learns equally effective ways to defend himself. He spits up, he clenches his jaws tight, he chews the same mouthful endlessly or lets it dribble down his chin. He puddles the food in his plate, tips over his cup, spatters the walls, makes pools on the floor. When all else fails he learns the infallible device of throwing up the whole meal.

Turnabout Is Fair Play

Some experts are fond of saying that there are no problem children, only problem parents, and we may well quarrel with that generalization. But in the matter of eating we have good evidence that they are right. It is the parents who make food problems. This repetitive performance at mealtimes can transform a healthy child into a poor eater.

And the consequences can be far-reaching. The mouth, the feeding organ which has been so abused, can become abusive; at six, seven, and eight the child may no longer throw up his food but he may throw up abusive language at his mother. In adolescence he may do a complete turnabout and use his mouth for excessive eating. We have observed that the compulsive trips to the refrigerator usually follow an argument between the child, girl or boy, and the mother.

In earlier pages we followed a girl into adulthood and saw how such mismanagement of just one of her childhood physical needs, feeding, later made difficulties for her as an adolescent and then as a wife. What about us, the parents? Surely the mealtime tussle is far from a pleasure for us. Surely we would rather have our child eat cheerfully, with good appetite, and grow up with a healthy attitude toward food. Surely we would rather have a friendly, cooperative boy or girl than an abusive and even foul-mouthed one. And surely we suffer agonies trying to keep our overweight teenager on a diet, just as we suffered agonies trying to get the same child a few years earlier to put on a little weight. We suffer anxiety, and we suffer shame. Our too-thin or too-fat child does us no credit. We feel we have done a poor job as parents.

Love on Whose Terms?

How do parents, with the best intentions in the world, manage to go awry? They begin lovingly enough, trying to do everything correctly according to the baby books. Why do the results so often fall short of their hopes?

The reason can be stated simply enough, although the mechanisms involved are not simple. We offer our children love but it is love on our terms, not theirs. We express our love in caring for them, in meeting their physical needs, but we too often ignore their true physical needs in an unconscious drive to satisfy our own emotional needs.

When a mother persists in feeding a child even after his hunger is appeased, she is satisfying a hunger of her own. It may be a hunger for the satisfaction she will have in showing off a fat dimpled child, bigger and fatter than any other baby on the block. She may have a hunger to overwhelm her child with love because she is poor in other forms of love. She may overfeed her child out of anxiety about being a mother. Many mothers, as we have noted, approach motherhood with considerable anxiety, and some are driven by it into a succession of errors in the early years of child rearing.

Mothers today are likely to be preoccupied with their young children morning, noon, and night, with only occasional relief by a baby-sitter. The young child is demanding, but the mother's needs are also demanding, and for all her overt attentiveness to the child she is pressed by her own needs to be inattentive to his genuine physiological needs. She simply does not recognize the physiological limits of his ability to do as she wants him to do, to be as she wants him to be. She feeds him to satisfy her love, not his hunger. She says, in effect, "You let me love you, or else!"

They Become Harder to Love

Eating presents the clearest demonstration of how we can lay up trouble instead of gratifications for ourselves in our ways of expressing love as parents. Naturally we have concentrated on the mother, since she is usually the one who feeds the child. Child psychologists tend to regard feeding problems in children as an act of protest against the mother. Stool training is also generally her task, and the afternoon nap. As the child develops, other paths open up along which our parental love can take a wrong turning, and father as well as mother can be led astray. Bedtime becomes difficult—some parents never seem to get their children to bed at all. The child begins to walk. He climbs on things, pulls things down, breaks things. He is often in danger. His curiosity takes him into many kinds of mischief. The growing sense of his own identity makes him resist restraint and control. He bursts into sudden rages and sudden tears. He experiences his first fears. He becomes harder to love.

Our parental role is also changing. From merely vegetative care, we are now charged with the task of civilizing this little animal. We must teach him how to live in the world into which he was born. We must train him in safety and hygiene and, sooner or later, good manners. We must inculcate consideration for others as well as a reasonable attention to his own best interests. We are the channel through which the standards and values of our culture are brought to the child. We are the first and, for better or worse, the most powerful influence in his life.

This is very different from other kinds of love. In other loves we may do a little teaching, we may exert a little influence and change the loved one in some small ways. But only in parental love do we carry the whole responsibility for the loved one, at least for the first five or six years of the child's life. We feel this responsibility and often we unwittingly allow ourselves to accept it almost as though we had no others. After all, a conscientious parent is a fine human being. Little do we realize we are over-playing our role. The authority of our position as parents, the enormous age differences between us and our children, even our good intentions all seductively conspire to inflate the sense of our own importance and unknowingly we may put undue pressure on our child.

Some of our attitudes toward the child and ourselves do change as he enters each new stage. He may be increasingly interesting as his individuality begins to emerge; he surely becomes more companionable as he begins to talk. But we rarely stand back and merely observe this with pleasure. We carry our children's pictures around and we tell our colleagues at the office their latest tricks and remarks; some of us even hang their nursery school art work on our office walls. But the fact remains that with growth the child becomes less dependent and we inevitably reinterpret our parental role.

This change in attitude is neither rapid nor always for the

better. Within two or three months after our children take their first steps, they are transformed from the round rosy cherubs of the baby food advertisements to frightened little old men and women. They have good reason to be frightened. By the single act of walking, they have taken themselves out of the Garden of Eden and the gates have clanged shut behind them. Their parents stand between them and their desires with a lexicon of *do's* and *don't,* frowns, threats, and punishments. Although learning to walk helps children to be less dependent, the impact of this on their mothers is to make them more, rather than less, authoritative.

Does it have to be so hard, both for the child and for ourselves? When he begins to be curious and to go exploring, we could take the attitude of introducing him to his new and wider world instead of blocking his efforts. Instead of hurrying him in his stool training, we could stop and remember that sooner or later a normal healthy child does become stool-trained with very little help from us. If we were less impatient we might even achieve quicker results.

Usually it is under the pressure of our own emotional needs that we put undue pressure on the child. We do not always know the sources of the anxiety that makes us overprotective one moment and over-demanding the next. We cannot always cope with our feelings of inadequacy and guilt which make us now too permissive and now too severe.

It would be unrealistic to expect that our own difficulties will not interfere in this most intimate and demanding relationship. Our parental love, we remember, is like our other loves in that it, too, is the product of all the loves we have experienced before. We cannot demand perfection in this love any more than in any other. But perhaps we can establish a kind of policy of parental love that will keep it closer to our children's needs and more gratifying to ourselves.

Less Is More

One of our outstanding modern architects, Ludwig Mies van der Rohe, knowing how a plentiful technology could clutter construction, made a great plea for purity in the form of a principle: less is more. The same might easily become the first point in this new program of parental love despite the fact that it may sound surprising, even immoral. It is a policy of being less parental, less conscientious, of doing less rather than more.

Let us see how this would work in the matter of vegetative care. If a mother could be a bit lazy, a bit absentminded about what the baby eats and how much—if, after preparing the right food and presenting it to him at the right time, she could look the other way—she would actually do a better job of feeding him. She would come closer to meeting his physiological need; by not attending so closely, she would be less likely to force him beyond the limits of his natural appetite.

If she were less conscientious about his stool training, she could let him set his own natural pace and thus avoid many a painful tussle, to say nothing of possible effects upon the child's later personality. If she were less concerned about his afternoon nap, she could accept the possibility that he may simply not be tired or sleepy today; tomorrow he may nap again. Or he may be outgrowing his need for a nap, and a short period of quiet play after lunch may be enough. Children's sleep needs, like their food needs, can be very different, and they change almost overnight. The baby books give us average behavior but every baby is an individual.

Nowadays we are very knowledgeable about sibling rivalry. We know that the stories of Cain and Abel, of Jacob and Esau, are duplicated in our own families. The behavior may be modified but the emotions are scarcely less violent. The battle begins with the birth of the second child, and it goes on with varying intensity as long as the children share the parental home. As each new one becomes big enough to realize he has interests to defend or advantages to gain, he declares war on the others.

Parents complain more bitterly about their children's bickering and fighting than they do about almost any other aspect of parenthood. To keep peace, they get into the fray themselves and deal out punishments right and left.

The results are far from satisfactory. Apart from the fact that this is not a very loving way to behave, and that it raises our own blood pressure, to say nothing of our voices and tempers, it actually eggs the children on. The moment we enter the scene, each combatant strives to win us to his side and put his adversary in the wrong. For our own part, we often have a sneaking feeling we have punished the wrong one. Sometimes the child who looks most like the victim is actually the *provocateur*. Trying to do justice in these situations is extremely wearing on a parent's nerves.

How much better to look the other way, keeping only one eye or one ear open to see that nobody gets really hurt. Children settle their differences remarkably well when parents are not around.

Hard Times

Along with being willing to do less, we can also be willing to let time take care of some difficulties for us. Although we cannot expect all problems to solve themselves, some do. The child, like the weather, is constantly changing. If we are not happy about the way he is behaving this week, we may only need to wait until next week, or next month.

In the most normal child's development there are times that put parents' patience and understanding to the test, to say nothing of parents' love. The toddler years are not always the hardest. The school years may begin with the child's painful display of separation anxiety, when he cannot let his mother leave him in the kindergarten class, or perhaps he develops a headache or stomachache just when it is time to catch the school bus. Later come the friendships we may not like, the battles over homework and music lessons, the rebellions against control, the impudent and sometimes offensive language. When adolescence looms, we all face it with trepidation; it is notorious for stress and conflict.

These are hard times for parents, but they are also hard times for the child, and it is salutary for us to realize just how hard they are. It is also salutary to realize that these hard times do pass. Even the most painful stages in the normal growth of a child inevitably come to an end. The child does not know this, but we do. Inexperienced as he is, he cannot look ahead to better times, but we can. Instead of adding to his troubles and ours with a miasma of anxiety, tension, disapproval, we can achieve a measure of calm with the confidence that the weather is bound to change. In such a climate the child can actually do better with his troubles. Our willingness to be patient while he works out his difficulties is a much more productive expression of our love than nagging and punishment, and it is surely more agreeable for ourselves.

Great Expectations

A singular error we make in our parental love is to fall into the trap of our own expectations. We neglect to revise them in the light of reality.

Many men and even a number of women are accustomed to revising their expectations of the stock market almost daily as they read their morning newspapers. People in business have to revise their expectations of sales and profits regularly, or they will soon find themselves in trouble. In marriage we survive by revising our romantic expectations of our loved one and accepting the reality of what he or she is in fact rather than in fancy.

When it comes to our children we are strikingly poor at this. The image of what our child will be is built in long before the child is born, and the unfolding of this new individual is very gradual. The fully formed product may not appear until our boy or girl is twenty, twenty-five, even thirty years old. During all those years we may continue to nurse our expectations of a child who will match our dream. With a child we do not have the ultimate test of reality to bring our dream down to earth. While he remains a child he is still developing, still unfinished.

Or so it seems. If we allow ourselves to know the child, his potentialities may be shrouded in the future but his inborn gifts become apparent very early. To take an extreme case, if he were going to be a prodigy we would discover the fact soon enough. And if we had any notion of what it is like to raise an exceptional child, we would be grateful that our child is normal, not to say average.

If we expect our child to do us credit according to our preconceived image, we are probably doomed to disappointment. He may one day surprise us by making us proud of him but usually not in the way we planned. In the meantime we torture him and ourselves by trying to make him into something he is not, and we miss the unfolding of what he is. Along the way we deprive ourselves of the genuine satisfactions of parental love and we may mark our child forever with a poor image of himself.

The harm of unrealistic expectations begins with the vegetative care of the child's first months. Because we expect an outstanding performance, we put pressure on the child to eat better, become stool-trained sooner, sleep through the night at an earlier age than the children of relatives and neighbors. When he goes to school, we increase the pressure on him to do well because now his performance is public and openly competitive.

There are fathers who buy their boy a baseball glove before he is out of diapers, and if by the age of ten or twelve the boy is still not playing baseball, such a father is genuinely disappointed in his son. It may be difficult for a boy to grow up in America not playing baseball but there are many fine healthy boys who never learn to care for the game. They may enjoy tennis or track or swimming. Or they may have only a small interest in competitive sports or athletics and stronger interests in electronics, history, or mechanics. The important thing is for the child to be interested in something, and for us as parents to be interested in the child, whatever his tastes may turn out to be. If we can share his interests or he enjoys some of ours, we can count ourselves lucky.

While in other ways we ought to pay less attention, in one way we do well to pay more—and that is, to the child himself. We do enough molding and influencing in the ordinary course of child rearing; we cannot avoid it. What we can avoid is overdoing it. Just as we need to recognize the validity of the child's desires, his individual capacity for food, for sleep, so we need to recognize his individuality in other ways. We relieve much of the tension of parental love if we can let the real child unfold, and make the most of him as he is, not as we wish he could be.

The Light Touch

Elsewhere we have observed how much better we like people, how much nicer they are, when we are having a good time together. How often, when we are with our children, are we having a good time together? If we were to make a day by day survey, the results might be deplorable.

Out of guilt, insecurity, all sorts of real or fancied shortcomings that we feel in ourselves as parents, many of us devote ourselves inordinately to our children. If we do not spend the time with them we spend it thinking about them, talking with our friends and each other about them, worrying about them.

In the good old days before modern child psychology, parents had the escape clause of heredity. A child was "born that way." In every family there was some unfortunate or disagreeable relative whom the child "took after." Since the Freudian revolution, parents feel as though every word they speak, every move they make has magic power for good or evil in the children's development. They are afraid to turn their backs for a moment lest something should go wrong.

Obviously as adults we cannot spend all our time with a child without becoming bored. Merely because of the difference in age, if nothing else, the child is unable to respond on our level and we become wearied with scaling our responses down to his. And if we spend so much time thinking and worrying about him when we are not with him, we obviously can bring little joy to the time we spend with him.

If we took parenthood less solemnly, we could have a good time with our children. We would not feel it necessary to rebuke every lapse from good behavior. We would not confuse the child by slipping, in a moment, from kindness and affection to anger and scolding. We could afford to smooth the relationship with courtesy—we could actually be polite to our children! If we treated the adults in our lives the way we treat our children, we would not have a friend in the world.

Politeness has its uses even in a relationship with a child. We find it hard to behave courteously to a small creature we always look down on; in our culture we are respectful of sheer size. We have to remind ourselves to say "please" and "thank you" to a little tot. We do it, very self-consciously, when we are trying to teach these forms to the child. But how polite do we really feel toward him? We like to say that good manners come from within, from feelings of respect and considerations toward others. If we are constantly driving ourselves to manage and mold our children, to stand guard over them and wet-nurse them to adulthood, we can hardly maintain feelings of respect toward them.

As soon as we stop playing the heavy parent, the pressure lets up, the atmosphere lightens. True, we are not the sole determinants of that atmosphere. Sometimes our children are sullen for reasons of their own. Other times they make issues important and request things we have to deny them.

Still, we can try to be tactful and pleasant even when we disagree and feel obliged to say "no". More often, we can afford to laugh and play. We can afford to have a good time with our children.

In the art of having a good time, children actually merit our respect. They can laugh more easily than we can. They can enjoy leisure and irresponsibility as we too often forget how to do. Children can bring a freshness and gaiety into our lives, if we will only put aside our heavy parental role and enjoy them.

Putting Love in Evidence

We have talked about expressing our love by managing the child's vegetative life with care, and this is all very rational. But there is an irrational side of love, too, an extravagant and impulsive side, and we need to put that in evidence.

We need not wait for the moment when a child performs well, in order to love him. We can pick him up and love him any time, just because we feel like it. When we make love a reward, when we equate it with approval, it often gets a very poor showing in our treatment of our children. We rarely remember to approve good behavior—we rarely even notice it. The good child is often the forgotten child. He usually wins our attention when he misbehaves, and then what he sees is nonapproval and non-love.

It would be a wonderful thing for babies if parents would simply put them down in the middle of the living room floor and let everyone who comes into the room pick them up, fondle them, talk to them. For a time parents were so frightened of germs that they hardly dared to let anyone touch the baby. One Hollywood couple built a glass nursery for their child and kept him literally under glass; people could see him but not touch him. We discovered long ago in hospitals and foundling homes that a baby who is not handled becomes a vegetable; he stops growing and developing, he withers away and he can even die. One New York hospital made a rule that anyone walking through the children's ward had to pick up a baby long enough to sing him a nursery rhyme before going on about his business. They found that the children got well in half the time.

Children thrive on being physically handled, physically

loved. They grow faster, develop better physically and mentally; they stay healthier. The more they are loved, the more lovable they are. Obviously a bright, alert, healthy and happy child is easier to love than a pale, dull, unresponsive one.

Showing love—direct, irrational, no-strings-attached love—is one of the surest ways of making our children lovable and loving, and hence making parenthood enjoyable. Children need the show of love, toward themselves and toward others. Children learn best by imitation; when a child sees his parents showing simple physical love, for him and for each other, he learns to love. We said in another connection that we teach our children to receive love but not to give it. The uninhibited demonstration of love is one of the simplest ways of teaching them to give as well as to receive.

As they grow older, especially in the latency period, as we call it—the middle years between kindergarten and adolescence—the physical show of love becomes less welcome, and in adolescence it is not welcome at all. These are also busy years, when we have to make appointments with our children in order to see them. We do make appointments—to take them to the doctor, the dentist, the music or dancing lesson, and most often to deliver a lecture to them on their poor grades or late hours or extravagance with their allowances. We hardly ever make appointments to show our love in the ways that are still acceptable to them, such as having a good time together.

We allow ourselves all too easily to fall into the routine of doing the same unplanned things repeatedly. Week-nights and weekends dribble away in a monotony which dulls our awareness and enjoyment of each other. Any small imaginative effort to break this pattern is generally rewarding. It is not hard to interest our growing children in many areas of our own world. Almost any teenager, even if he is still too young to drive, would welcome the chance to help select the new family automobile. And, having selected it, he could enjoy with equal enthusiasm the planning and making of many trips, large or small, with the family.

Inviting our children, as they get older, to share in our decisions and actively participate in our lives has many advantages for our relationship with them. It helps them open their own lives to us more fully. It subtly transforms our role from the authoritarian to the more acceptable one of friend, co-worker, and welcome leader. It makes our memory and experience more available to our children at the same time that we enjoy the benefits of their greater daring, vigor, and novelty. Most important of all, the mutual respect developed between parents and children clears away the last vestiges of dependency and allows children the maturity of expression ideally present in parents.

Of course, we cannot be more mature with our children than we are with ourselves. Our knowledge of what is best for them can be just as frustrating as our knowledge of what is best for ourselves—if we do not have the emotional freedom to act on our good intentions. The techniques of our daily behavior deserve more frequent examination than our goals. Relevant to this, the mere frequency of our laughter together is one of the best signs of the kind of rapport we enjoy. Although planning things together is important, so is spontaneous laughter. To do this with our children, we must first of all maintain a generous ability to laugh with or without them.

Perhaps the best expression of humor is the ability to laugh at oneself. This takes humility and, mostly, perspective. Another expression of this perspective is self-restraint in our relationship with our adult children. They want to try, they want to decide, sometimes they even want to fail just to see what happens as a result. One of our more mature expressions of love is to let them. If our relationship is a good one, our children give us a front row seat in their lives. We do best by staying there and enjoying the performance. We can cheer, applaud, even weep. But ideally we keep off the stage unless they specifically—and we should make sure of this—invite us to take part.

The Self-Liquidating Love

Parental love is only one of the loves in our lives. Too often we let it dominate us; we behave as though bringing up children were the whole purpose of our existence. As a result, we suffer and they suffer; the quality of our love for them suffers.

This becomes especially clear when they are approaching adulthood. Having invested ourselves too heavily in our children, we become possessive; we are unable to let them go. These are the years, too, when our ambitions for them show most nakedly; we can hardly keep from showing our disappointment when they do not gain acceptance to the college or choose the profession or make the marriage we dreamed of for them.

During the first half of our children's lives, parents are often faced with the difficult task of maintaining their children's love as they unavoidably say "no" to them. During the second half, parents are faced with the even more unpleasant problem of taking "no" for an answer from their children. Parental love has thus been called a tragic love. It is a love that demands the most from us and gives the least return; it is a self-liquidating love that must end in giving up possession of the loved one. But this need not be so, if we have not used our parental love more as a form of self-love than as love of the child. When we place too heavy a burden of our own hopes and ambitions on the child, when we wear the child as a garment to reflect credit on ourselves—then we are not really loving the child, but using him.

All forms of love make some demands on the loved one, even the love of friends. Romantic love makes the most extravagant demands—and it is the most evanescent form of love, partly for that reason. Either it matures into married love, or it perishes and becomes enshrined in our memory.

Ideally parental love should be the least demanding form of love. The demands we make on our child should be for his own development, his own welfare, not for ours. The extent to which we can submerge our own needs and attend to the needs of the loved one is a measure of our maturity in love.

How well we can do this in our love for our children depends upon how well we can satisfy our own needs in other aspects of our lives. Obviously we do better in our parental love if we are happy in our married love, if our marriage satisfies enough of our emotional needs.

But it is not necessary to make the quality of our parental love dependent upon the quality of our marriage, or on its continuance. Divorced parents and widowed parents can also be good and loving parents.

Who, then, are the best parents, the ones most successful in their parental love?

We come back to our theme: we have many loves, and our success in any one of them depends upon how well we harmonize them all. The parents who are happiest in their parental love may well be those who combine it best with all the other loves in their lives—with marriage, with friends, with work, with love of the arts or intellectual pursuits or whatever else has the power to absorb them and give them satisfaction. When we live a life of our own, of which our children are a part but not the all-absorbing, all-devouring part, then we may be happiest in our parental love—and we may make the best parents.

CHAPTER SEVENTEEN

Freedom to Love

WILLY-NILLY WE ALL develop countless attachments in life. These are our loves. Only few of them reflect rational choice. Accident and unconscious need dominate our selections. Fortunately for us, this represents only half the story of love in our lives. What we do with our choice is often at least as important as the choice itself. As we grow, we enjoy the potential of greater freedom both in choosing and in cultivating our attachments. Love, rising from our natural needs, can come to bear ideal fruit.

Like a weed, love can flourish anywhere. Even the most barren craggy rocks can nourish an occasional flower. But specimen shrubs or prize-winning flowers require a rich healthy soil. Personal freedom is the healthy ground for ideal love and this is what we nowadays call emotional maturity.

It is how emotionally grown-up or mature we are which determines the quality of our love life. Our loves all bear our personal stamp. We may be attractive enough to whet the appetites of many people but how well we can continue to satisfy them depends on more than our initial appearances. We too are often and easily charmed by others but how well we reach them depends on more than the desires ignited in us. Some people window-shop and dream of love all their lives; others create the love they want and really live with it.

Of course, it would be highly desirable to enter this charmed circle of people who are capable of achieving love but emotional grown-upness is not easy to come by. In many ways, it is a lot easier to promote the maturity of our special talents than it is to improve our more general ability to live with ourselves and others. A mathematician can seclude himself with his slide rule, a musician with his scales and arpeggios, a designer with her sketches and each can eventually return to the human race a better mathematician, musician, or designer. Learning to live better or love better does not come as a result of some equally specific kind of practice.

Limitations of Freedom

We foster our growth first of all by trying to free ourselves from the limitations of our own childhood. The boundaries of childhood are best recognized by its twin signposts: dependency and parents. So long as parents continue to play the primary role in our lives—positively or negatively—our dependency feelings remain strong and our attachments elsewhere weak. One thing to do is to work hard at becoming financially free of our parents. We can then establish our own residence and enjoy the warmth of the child-parent relationship with what time is left over from the rest of our pursuits. Wise parents encourage their children, by the time they graduate from college, to accept this way of life.

A second major limitation of our freedom stems from our smallest, everyday failures to achieve the emotional satisfaction we seek. We all have neurotic tendencies and perhaps know them better merely as bad habits. What we often do not know is really how bad they are. We dismiss our excesses, for example, with a patient shrug and blandly admit we work a little too hard, perhaps drink too much, spend somewhat more than we can afford, and eat a little more than is good for us.

The fact is that nothing we do is unconnected with the rest of our behavior and anything we do in excess suggests two things about us. It means, firstly, that we are being driven, that we have been dislodged from the driver's seat, that some force inside of us is impelling us to do more of something than we admit is good for us. Secondly, something else about us suffers or pays the price for our excess. Either we feel guilty for it or suffer some physical or emotional discomfort as a result. The excess and its aftermath both have an enslaving effect upon us. They occupy too much of our time and energy, they spoil our mood, and thereby disturb many of our relationships.

Unfortunately our long-standing neurotic needs escape our recognition by disguising themselves in "sheep's clothing." An insecure woman who craves more attention than anyone can give her is bound to erode her love rapidly away. Yet she feels guiltless about her marital unhappiness. From her point of view, it is only her husband who fails her. In superficial social situations, she remains seductive enough to win flattery. She cannot see how she attacks everything in her husband's life as competitive with herself. At home, where we let our hair down, she soon irascibly demands what she tries to win elsewhere. Her own wants and needs, whether they are successfully expressed in a glittering social performance or unsuccessfully expressed in an infantile cry of protest, are the basic subject of her life. This imprisonment in the self necessarily dilutes the quality of any attachment.

There are, of course, neurotic elements large and small in all of us. If the wounds of growth fail to heal, we may be left with little more security as adults than we had as youngsters. This would make us sensitive and easily hurt. Our reaction would be to recoil, withdraw, and once again to become the major subject of our attention. *Our* feelings, rather than someone else's, usurp our thought.

Self-concern makes it difficult for us to nurture an attachment to another human being. Any *excess* of personal sensitivity or fear, even of desire, tends to increase self-awareness and anxious preoccupation with the self. Love is a way of reaching *another* person. Ideally it is a most intimate and total reaching of someone else, requiring a genuine departure from self. This ability to give someone else the attention required by love takes great freedom from self. But freedom is not something which comes to us easily.

Our Unfree Past

No matter how strongly we may desire it, we do not spontaneously embrace it. It were as though something in the very marrow of our bones held us back. It might well be tradition.

For thousands of years, freedom and wealth were distributed very differently from the way they are now. A tiny insignificant portion of the human race enjoyed these possessions and the huge majority of people suffered great deprivation, and worked hard merely for their survival. The religions of the world helped people to adjust to this socio-economic condition by demeaning the value of material goods. Goodness meant holiness and this, in turn, meant otherworldliness, sacrifice, prayer, and the acceptance of the inscrutable ways of the Lord. These were all accepted as primary virtues and the necessary condition for entrance into the Kingdom of Heaven. Life on earth was not supposed to be heavenly. Man was encouraged to accept himself as humble, godfearing, and not primarily given over to the expression or the indulgence of those "instincts" and desires which were carnal or joyful in any way.

Social Change and Freedom

With minor exceptions this was the general condition of man for many hundreds of years. The first major change came with the American War of Independence. The Declaration of Independence was important not only in expressing the freedom of one nation from another, but also in extending the same to individuals, underscoring their right to ". . . liberty and the pursuit of happiness."

Subsequent events in history translated this dream into reality. Freedom required not only legislation but economic change. Within another century, much of this was accomplished. The opening of the frontier, the Industrial Revolution, and the growth of cities all played an effective part in the redistribution of wealth. Personal freedom had become enough of a political, social, and economic reality to attract many, many others to American shores.

The rise in the general standard of living encouraged people to think better of themselves. *This* life became constantly more promising. Theological principles dictating self-abnegation were more and more seriously questioned. The promise of greener pastures became less tempting the freer we were to enjoy ourselves now.

Psychological Change and Freedom

Finally a slow revolutionary change in our thinking occurred, marking more clearly than ever the meaning of what is so boldly proclaimed in *The Rubaiyat:* "Behold, myself am heaven and hell." We finally began to see that our position in the world and our opportunity for growth and improvement are one thing. The way we regard ourselves and come to handle ourselves are still another. Our external or social freedoms failed to liberate us entirely. Like Spinoza before him, Sigmund Freud described the devious ways our emotions enslave us. Only unlike anybody before him, Freud accomplished this task with infinitely greater and more realistic detail.

The body of knowledge he set before us has grown in impact since its original appearance at the turn of the century. Art, literature, everyday thought have all been strongly influenced. We now know that good health, both mental and physical demands a certain amount of freedom—freedom to express ourselves without the burden of inner conflict. We are constantly menaced in our growth by unwholesome attachments to desires, feelings, parts of ourselves, even people around us. Any and all these attachments have the potential power of arresting our growth, dominating the rest of our inclinations, and keeping us bound to what we rationally would rather reject.

It is not that we cannot love under these circumstances. We do, but we cannot love well. Not all our needs and desires are equally good for us. Worse yet, not all of the ways we suppress them are good for us. The freedom we are coming to enjoy in the outside world is not yet matched by an equal harmony of forces within us. We still feel more than a merely occasional irrational tug which keeps us from ideal choices and attachments. And we still feel the force of equally irrational inhibitory agents, such as guilt and fear, within us.

More clearly than ever we realize that the blind, unreasoned suppression of desire is no better for the individual than the suppression of free speech is for society. Not that we are encouraged to express ourselves with psychopathic indifference to others. Emotional anarchy is no better than political anarchy. Just as freedom of speech is not meant to encourage libel, greater freedom of personal expression is not meant to encourage fickleness, perversity, or disregard for others.

There is a balance still to be developed within us between these warring forces. We are in better position than ever before in our history to achieve this. First we really believe at long last that we have an inalienable right to freedom and happiness. Secondly, we know from the findings of modern psychology that freedom and happiness are not idle dreams but the necessary conditions for a healthy, symptom-free life.

Social and economic changes have given us a chance to move about more and current psychological theory has laid bare for examination what our inner conflicts are. Yet we hesitate and continue to tie ourselves up, keeping ourselves from the ideal choice and cultivation of our important loves.

The Bad Habit of Hard Work

The very socio-economic tradition which aims to free us often has just the opposite effect. On the one hand, we believe that we no longer need be what we were at birth. Among our most common biographical themes are the tales of farm boy to president, or rags to riches. The sky is the limit—provided we are willing to work hard enough. The result is that many people work so hard first at school and then at their careers that their success never really frees them. They continue to work just as hard, if not more so, after they are successful. Although they are well regarded and appear to be free, it is only their label and appearance which have changed. They remain harnessed and driven by strong subtle forces which permit them little time for the cultivation of deep human relationships.

People who grow up with unresolved feelings of guilt are often quick to accept the virtue of hard work. What better way for anyone to overcome his guilty feelings? Guilt leaves us with the need for punishment, sacrifice, the performance of those acts which bring expiation and forgiveness. We hear again and again that hard work is virtuous and one of the best signs of good character.

The snag in all this is that hard work is obviously hard. It is distinctly easier *to talk about* how hard one's work is. People worry about their work, beat their breasts, complain, speak of how driven they are, constantly expect the worst to happen—in short, they develop the habit of grief. It is as though they were making public announcements of having been punished.

Just as dependency and neurotic drives thin out our relationship with others, guilt thins out our attachment to ourselves by lowering our sense of self-worth. All three conditions combine to rivet our major attention uneasily onto ourselves. Love at its best requires freedom from the self. Maturity leaves anxious preoccupation with the self behind in one's growth so that, in our adult life, we can enjoy concentrating on our relationships. We take ourselves and our survival for granted when we are ideally grown up and refocus our attention on the adult adornment of life.

Some Wayward Judgments

Unfortunately we do not find grownupness in people ready-made. People do not sort themselves out so neatly. They do not fall into mutually exclusive categories labeled "mature" and "immature." Most of us reach marriageable age with only a better or a poorer prospect of achieving maturity. At best, none of us is likely to become ideally mature in all areas of the complex human personality. Probably none of us can hope to be or to meet an individual who is totally mature.

The best we can do is to make as mature a judgment as possible of whom to fall in love with. And this is not easy either. The state of mind connected with falling in love has little room for judgment of any rational kind.

When we are in love we make judgments freely enough, perhaps too freely for our own good. The lover sees every characteristic of the loved one in its most flattering aspect. If our beloved is touchy and easily hurt we say she is tender and sensitive. If she is superficial and possibly a little silly we say she is gay and young, a breath of spring, and never consider that such a spring may forecast an early autumn.

If a man is inclined to be stubborn, the woman who is attracted to him admires him for having the courage of his convictions. A stuffy and pedantic person is transformed by loving eyes into an intellectual, and a humorless person into a serious one. A hyperactive, driving person may drive right through the unfortunate lover, but in the lover's eyes such a person is intense and alive.

The categories can be continued ad infinitum: a carping, critical man is described by his sweetheart as devoted to the truth, a stingy man is thrifty and conservative, and a ruthless man is a man of strength.

Sometimes this wayward judgment goes deeper than the temporary aberration of falling in love. It may tap neurotic tendencies. A man with an unconscious wish to be mothered will see a woman as tender and loving because she expresses so much concern for him during their courtship, but what he will get in marriage is domination and control—which is what he may have wanted in the first place. Another man, whose need is to be lord of the manor, will describe a weak, docile woman as sweet and loving, and in fact she is sweet and loving in his terms because she is a total and willing follower.

These are not so much blind judgments as judgments guided by a single dominating—although unconscious—need. This single need by its very compulsive power reveals itself to be neurotic. Yet the same individual has other needs, and if the whole force of his attachment is spent in satisfying only the one need, then the other needs go unsatisfied.

Detouring Our Neurotic Drives

None of us, of course, is entirely free of neurotic needs. This gives us all the more reason to try to protect ourselves from having our most important attachments made by them. We might learn to detour around some of our unconscious drives. Take the case of a young man who falls head over heels in love at first sight. If he is immature, he will want to run right off and marry the girl. If he has some maturity, he recognizes that he has just fallen head over heels in love and he enjoys it, but he does not take final action on it. He may experience the whole scale of romantic feelings from ecstasy to anguish, and yet he does not rush headlong into marriage.

Sometimes we hear a piece of music and find it so intensely appealing that we rush right out to the record shop and buy the recording. We play it and play it, but before long we find we are tired of it and we put it at the back of the record shelf. We may never want to play it again. Or we fall in love with a painting, and feel we must have it. A responsible art dealer, familiar with this phenomenon, advises us to come back and look at it a few times, or he offers to let us take it home for a few weeks. He wants to keep his customers, and he knows that a painting that strikes a viewer too intensely at first sight may not be the one he will want to live with.

Falling in love with a person is not too unlike falling in love with a symphony or a painting. Like a work of art, a man or woman may have great striking effect and yet not be the right choice for one's lifetime.

Something about the setting, the circumstances, the frame of mind in which two people meet may weave a kind of magic, and they feel they were meant for each other. It is Saturday night or they are on vacation in the Caribbean or on some glittering ski slope, or one or the other has just been through a gruelling period of work or trouble or loneliness and is looking especially hard for happiness. There may of course be a strong physical attraction, and while this is all to the good, it is still not enough to build a life on.

Love at First Sight

We need not suspect a neurotic origin in order to be wary of a sudden and striking attraction. When we fall in love at first sight, it is not love that comes over us all at once. It is the feeling which strikes suddenly and overwhelmingly; it is the desire and the longing for love. The love itself, the attachment, takes considerably more time to develop. The feeling can dissipate, for the very reason that there is as yet no attachment of any depth or breadth.

Some people are continually falling in and out of love. They want the strong feeling but they may not want or be able to form the attachment. To be accurate, they have an attachment, but it is an attachment to the feeling or desire for love, not to the person they think they love. As the popular phrase puts it, they are in love with love.

Additionally, feelings of love when they are sudden in onset invariably give us the illusion that, of all our attachments, this is the one really of our own free choice. So many of our relationships are thrust upon us by circumstances, prearranged by life. We do not choose our parents, brothers and sisters, relatives; we do not choose our business and professional colleagues. Many of our friendships begin with the accident of growing up in the same neighborhood, going to the same school, the same college, and many of them continue, as we sometimes feel, sheerly out of habit.

Only in this sudden, wonderful, magical experience of falling in love do we feel that we ourselves have chosen. Either we dismiss the role of accident entirely or we glorify it and call it destiny.

What is the mature way to confront this experience? Must we quench the romantic glow and pour cold water on our rhapsodic feelings? Surely not. There is no harm in enjoying to the full an exaggerated, possibly even somewhat neurotic, but certainly delicious attraction that has sprung up between two people. The harm lies only in making a decision on the strength of these feelings, and slipping into a relationship that may have a narrow and tenuous basis. If it has little more than a neurotic underpinning of infantile need, it may well end in early divorce. Sometimes such a relationship endures for a lifetime but it cannot result in a mutually satisfying marriage.

Falling in love is an experience not to be missed. But the lovers also need time to be together in a more commonplace setting, among family and friends who know them as they are, not as they seem when transformed by a romantic dream. We detour our neurotic drives by recognizing that falling in love and staying in love can be very different from each other. Almost anybody, given half a chance, can fall in love with another human being easily enough. But basically this is little more than saying that we all have desires which can be ignited by others. How well we can keep the fire going is another matter. We must admit that many of our desires, no matter how deeply felt, are short-lived. And we all have other desires which would do us more good if they were short-lived. All in all, raw desires cannot be trusted. Harnessed by a memory of consequences and steered by the consistency it maintains with the rest of our daily life, desire is the beginning of all pleasure in life. But free to act on its own, desire is unreliable and just as often "brings us grief and pain for promised joy."

We need not be suspicious of our desires; we need only learn to label them for what they are. Short-lived desires can be enjoyed; so can neurotic desires, and even silly, irresponsible, and ridiculous ones. "It is not wisdom to be only wise." There is no fun in a ponderous life lived by the book. If we do not follow our inclinations, we are not living *our* life. The difficulty we have is in combining all the elements of it. Of prime importance is knowing when to stop so that we can turn to the pursuit of other of our needs and their fulfillment. Labelling any one desire as more important than it actually is turns satisfaction into slavery. We lose the freedom to maintain balance, harmony, and diversity—and finally we even lose the over-evaluated desire which crowded out the other needs and desires which form a legitimate part of our lives.

This evaluation of our desires rarely derives its validity from thought alone. The fact is that few of us are capable anyway of such a cool, dispassionate look at ourselves. And it is just as well. Life teaches us best by living—*and*—reflecting on it. Experience alone is as untrustworthy as are untested ideas. Additionally, experience is habit forming; it is true that there's no fool like an old fool. The best method, then, of evaluating our desires and our choice of love objects is to give them both a chance—a chance to affect our experience and a chance for us to reflect on our experience. We can enjoy the reality of our most exaggerated desires in the present without making ourselves prematurely dependent upon their future fulfillment. The trick is to enjoy what we have and let it season or age somewhat, giving ourselves a chance to think, instead of couting our chickens and plunging precipitously into a poorly sampled future.

There is one additional precaution or condition for the proper evaluation of our loves. It is an extraordinarily difficult one and stems from the simple fact that time itself does not solve our problems but what we do in time might. Having fallen in love, young people generally allow themselves also to fall out of circulation. They justify this by reporting their lack of interest in other members of the opposite sex. Also, is not the exclusiveness of their relationship more typical and representative of marriage and therefore a better sample of it? Even if this is true, they suffer the danger of acting on their feelings too soon. Falling in love and being in love ideally do not exclude dating other people. Later on, people learn that no man can get along well with his wife and poorly with the rest of the female world. It is understandable for a man not to enjoy his other dates so much as the woman he loves, but if he cannot enjoy them at all the future of his love is doubtful indeed.

Attachments Also Mature

An attachment that has begun in an immature form may of course mature. Indeed this is what happens with many an attachment that flowers into a rich and satisfying relationship. There are immature and mature forms of our attachments other than those we have toward people. A baby begins his love for music by banging a dishpan with a spoon. It is hard to see in this noise-making stage the eventual adult music-lover, and, of course, not every pan-pounding baby grows up to appreciate the more complex arrangements of sound we call good music. Yet for those who do, the attachment follows a clear path of development, from the baby's purely auditory pleasure through the young child's appreciation of rhythm, to the adolescent's pleasure tinted with feelings, emotions, and imagery. Finally we have the adult music-lover who adds to this the intellectual enjoyment of following the structure of the music as he listens, perhaps the skillful playing of an instrument or the pleasure of dancing to music, reading music history, or even discussing music with fellow music-lovers. The more mature his love, the more varied his pleasures in it, the more facets his attachment can encompass.

Our attachments to people mature in a somewhat similar way, developing more and more facets from which we draw satisfactions. To be sure, the child's first attachment to another human being is more complex than his first attachment to sound. Yet with all its complexity it still has one major dimension. The child's attachment is primarily a dependent one.

Dependency is very different from mere sensory attraction, the binding force is the growth of a love of music. Dependency is different and stronger than most other forces which promote attachments. As a result, the relationship between a child and his parents remains influenced by this powerful force and often maintains much of its limited, infantile quality.

The helplessness of the child's early years is eventually replaced by the strength, the skills, and the understanding which growth makes possible. Yet, this does not guarantee the dissolution of his feelings of dependency. A person can be competent without feeling his competence. He may be able to stand on his own two feet without believing that he can. The growth of our abilities, in short, does not guarantee the growth of our belief in them. Dependency is difficult to give up and we do, in fact, need the attractions of many other relationships to help wean us away from the primary one we have with our parents.

Young Love

Fortunately for us, we have many loves at many levels which add their contribution to our maturing ability to love. The many relationships of a child tend to increase his experience and expand his learning in forming and sustaining an attachment. Children have to live through many attachments to people before they are capable of mature ones. They have playmates, teammates, schoolmates, roommates, friends, a rising scale of attachments of increasing variety and complexity. Their relationships to parents and siblings at home also change and become more complex, with both more and less satisfactions. And finally as adolescents or young adults they develop still other attachments they call love.

What this means is that the young person is sufficiently attracted to some member of the opposite sex so that both long to reveal to each other and enjoy together the various facets of themselves as members of the opposite sex. But in this youthful love they often discover that their attachment is almost as one-dimensional as the infantile attachments of babyhood. The first strong attachment that they feel for someone outside the family summons up the only other strong attachment they have experienced, and they tend to express their attachment in the most familiar ways they know, the infantile ways of wanting, demanding, of peaks and depths of feeling, fierce angers and quick hurts. The attachment may be intense, and it usually has the added excitement of sexual attraction although not necessarily overt. Yet it remains an extremely limited kind of love.

The modern custom of pairing off—going steady—from an early age tends to confirm many of these tentative first attachments of boy and girl, if only as a mutual habit of social dependence, of being able to count on a steady date. Almost automatically, a good many of these primitive young loves drift into the demanding relationship of marriage.

When young people barely out of their teens jump into the well together, whether they are childhood sweethearts or have just met and fallen in love, they bring with them all their still unresolved infantile attachments. A boy who has not had time or experience enough to outgrow his strong attachment to his mother ends by developing the same kind of attachment to his girl-wife, and she brings similar infantile needs into her attachment to her husband. Neither has yet learned enough from their other attachments to improve the relationship they develop with a person of the opposite sex; neither yet knows a mature way to love. It is not easy for two such young people to grow up together and convert their love into a more mature, freer form. The probability is that their infantile needs will cling, and their youthful love will develop only into neurotic love.

The Testing Ground of Love

Marriage demands the most mature expression of a love between man and woman; it is the testing ground of love. No other relationship is like it; no other prepares us entirely for it. Most other relationships that we have with people are either transient or fragmentary. The predominantly one-dimensional attachment to parents, the competitive attachment to siblings, the occasional intensity of a friendship or a youthful sexual affair—none of these alone gives us the practice we need for the many-sided loving and working together of marriage. But all of them together might.

Young people who have not yet shed their dependency are not ready for the single strong love that will engage their entire personalities. They have little chance to resolve their infantile attachments in a love that demands so much of them and in which they must invest so many of their hopes and desires. The chances are small indeed for anyone to make the transition from childhood to maturity in one fell swoop. The first teenage love of some couples may take seed and ripen to mature fulfillment but this is the exception rather than the rule. People need three, four, five or any number of lesser loves, lighter and thinner loves, out of which they can extract the sweetness and pleasure of love without expecting satisfaction for their deeper needs. The experience of such attachments, especially if they are attachments of some variety, provides people with the most worthwhile raw material for reflection. Instead of dealing exclusively with their desires when they think about themselves, they have a chance to evaluate what actually happens in their relations with others. The young lover can then increase his understanding of himself and others so as to become more ideally ready to form an important attachment on an adult level.

CHAPTER EIGHTEEN

Mature Love

THE PHRASE "MATURE LOVE" sounds like a tired love, a warmed-over love with all the flavor cooked away. There is a sneaking suspicion that when people can no longer enjoy the ecstasies of passion and romance they call their love mature, as though mature love were the sour grapes of the elderly.

Yet if we take the phrase apart and call it, instead, the love of mature people, we bring more clearly into focus that which helps us understand love best, namely, the lover himself. What are the characteristics of this lover, who brings maturity to his love?

Some Myths Unveiled

To begin with, we might examine some of the myths about maturity, and there are many. One is that a mature person is necessarily an old person. We know from observation that this is not so. There are of course many old people whose maturity sparkles with a special quality of lighthearted tolerance and wisdom. But other old people are just as petulant and demanding as they were in their teens, only now their immature behavior is even less attractive than when it was clothed in youth. By contrast, we often encounter young people who show considerable emotional or intellectual maturity despite the fact that their experience is still limited. Evidently, then, age alone does not confer maturity.

It would be difficult to designate a minimum age for emotional maturity. This is a difficulty encountered elsewhere as well. Young men in the United States, for example, are regarded as old enough to fight and die for their country at the

279

age of 18 but are not privileged to vote until they are 21. The age of sexual maturity or consent varies from one state legislature to another. From a more distinctly psychological point of view, maturity is ideally that phase of growth following adolescence. This does not mean that mature judgments cannot be made until one is past one's teens. Even pre-school children are often capable, partly out of their very naïveté, of seeing things more clearly than we do. This does not make them mature individuals any more than a single robin makes a spring. We would expect a certain amount of knowledge of people, experience with them, and sufficient physical and emotional growth to allow a person no longer to be dependent on someone else's care before maturity is reached. Although we need hardly be old for all this to have taken place, it is unlikely that the mature individual will not be past adolescence.

If we equate maturity with good judgment, then we encounter another myth, the myth that mature people are dull and only neurotics are interesting. Many neurotics are indeed interesting—for an evening or two. But to live a life with a neurotic is likely to be wearing if not actually destructive.

Nor is maturity necessarily dull. Dull people are dull, whether or not they are mature. Interesting people become increasingly interesting as they mature. Mature people can be merry; they can be adventurous without being reckless. They welcome change, variety, surprise. They can be daring and even take risks, since they know how to measure the values to be gained against the hazards to be faced. When they make a mistake they can afford to cut their losses and go on without repining; they emerge bruised but cheerful, with no tiresome tale of blame for others or pity for themselves. They can enjoy nonsense and foolishness; they can get drunk without having to apologize for it. They know how to play. They maintain their capacity for being enthusiastic, zestful, curious, through the inevitable periods of pressure, disappointment, and even tragedy with which life attacks us again and again. Maturity, ideally, is not the eroded remains of youthful pride and vigor; it is the more weathered, enduring monument to life's potential.

The immature have nothing like the range and capacity for enjoyment of those who have liberated themselves from the problems of growing up. Mature people are free to enjoy themselves because they are no longer governed by infantile needs and hedged about with infantile fears. They are not restricted by infantile ignorance and the distortions of infantile understanding. To the mature, the only limitations are those of reality.

A Look Backward

We might define a mature person as one who has found his way through the confusions of growing up to the point where he has established a rational order in his life. This does not mean that he is forever stopping to think and decide whether this or that is rational. It means that making good choices and reaching for good values have become habitual and automatic with him—and "good" in this context means good for him, bringing him positive satisfactions.

We understand maturity when we look back over the road we must travel to reach it. We see what it is like to be mature by remembering what it is like to be immature, to be a child or an adolescent.

A young child has no awareness of consequences. Drawn by the brightness of a match flame or a lighted electric bulb, he will stretch out his hand to grasp it. This is simple ignorance of the properties of fire and heat; he does not know that they will burn him. When he is a little older, he may run out into the street for his ball. Even though he has been warned, he is still governed by his first impulsive wish, still unable to stop and consider its possibly dangerous consequences. The same immature behavior may persist in the adolescent who fails to prepare for an exam; he knows what the consequences may be but some momentary pleasure prompts him to behave as though he did not know.

As adults we sometimes indulge in the same wistful ignorance of cause and effect. We overeat, knowing very well that we are likely to suffer distress; we eat more calories than we expend, knowing that we will surely put on weight. When we follow the same pattern in our relationships with people, when we ignore the consequences of our behavior in our attachments, then our loves, too, are immature.

There may come a point when the inability—or the unwillingness—to take consequences into account becomes a dominating pattern. It governs the individual's behavior; it compels him to do what he does, and invites consequences that cause grief and pain—and at that point we call his behavior neurotic.

Know Thyself

"Know thyself," that great Socratic principle as important today as it was in ancient Greece, is another pointer toward maturity. The child does not know himself, does not know his capabilities and his limitations. He spends the first years of his life bruised, bleeding, and sometimes broken, physically and in his image of himself as well. His lack of self-knowledge leads him into situations which he is far from able to manage comfortably or even safely.

Many an adult behaves much the same way. People we call "accident-prone" are constantly doing themselves in. If we stop to think of it, most of the mistakes we make are mistakes we have made before. This strongly suggests that in adulthood it is not through simple ignorance of ourselves that we fall into error. Rather it is an unwillingness or inability to assess our limitations. We cling to the infant's sense of omnipotence, of being able to do everything and have everything, simply by making the demand for it.

The child has even less insight into others than he has into himself. He cannot foresee how they will behave toward him. He has no idea how they feel. He is limited to his own narrow experience of pleasure and pain and cannot empathize with the pleasure or pain of another. He does not know how it feels to be pushed or struck until someone pushes or strikes him, and even then he may not relate his own pained outrage to the protest of another child whom he has pushed or struck. He is limited in experience, in his ability to relate cause and effect, and most significantly in his ability to feel for others. His feelings are still only for himself.

We see the first awkward attempts of a child to feel for another person when he approaches his sleeping mother. He tiptoes and he whispers, because she had taught him that we do this out of consideration for someone who is sleeping, and he wants to be considerate. But he also wants what he wants. And so, still whispering, he makes his request. Naturally he wakes her. He wanted to wake her. He cannot subordinate his wish for what he wants to his wish for his mother's comfort and rest. If his mother awakens annoyed with him, he shows the further immaturity of not understanding why she is cross.

Many an adult shows the same inability to understand another's irritation with him, or another's hurt feelings at something he has done. A man who finds himself short of cash borrows money from a friend, and at the moment the money has enormous value for him because of his urgent need. He expresses effusive gratitude to his friend, and makes firm promises about repaying the loan. But once his immediate need is met, the whole transaction loses its importance and he lets months go by without paying the money back. If his friend reminds him, he cannot understand why the man no longer acts like a friend, why he has to be importunate about the loan. He has every intention of paying, but why can't the man be a good fellow and wait? Is money more important than friendship?

The fact is, the borrower has forgotten how important the money was to him when he borrowed it. Now it is no longer important to him, and he cannot imagine or perhaps is unable to care whether or not it is important to his friend. He understood his own need but he cannot understand another's need. The inability to empathize with another person is endlessly damaging to relationships, and in the end it is damaging to the immature individual himself.

The same man would have been outraged if his friend had refused him the loan he asked. No matter if the friend was in a bind and did not have the cash to spare; no matter how good the reasons his friend gave for refusing him. The simple fact of being refused something he wants is enough to embitter him against his friend. Like a child, he cannot take no for an answer. The child wants what he wants, and he wants it now. He cannot weigh the validity of his wish or consider it in relation to another's wish. When he cannot have what he wants, he cries. When he is somewhat older he no longer cries openly but he does it inwardly, by feeling sorry for himself.

A child cannot endure postponement of his desire, because he does not appreciate the reality of tomorrow. He has little sense of past and future; his world is limited to here and now. I once casually tested the time sense of a group of children between the ages of eight and eleven. We were spending a summer afternoon around a swimming pool, and I called them out of the pool and asked them what time they thought it was. The answers ranged from eleven in the morning to six in the evening; one boy, taking a rational approach to the problem, asked, "Did we have lunch yet?" In actual fact the time was four in the afternoon.

Many adults behave as though they still had no belief in the reality of tomorrow. Like children who squander all their allowance the day they get it, some people habitually spend their week's salary over the weekend and are left with nothing for the rest of the week. It takes time, and patient teaching by his parents, for a child to learn that if he wants something that costs more than this week's allowance, he must give up some present satisfactions and save for a greater future satisfaction.

This ability to plan for long-term goals is something a child must learn in both work and play. He learns that to enjoy the water he must first learn to swim, and to fly a model plane he must first patiently build it. He learns to drudge at learning a language or a subject in order to have the rewarding use of it later.

With increasing maturity, he learns to apply this knowledge to his attachments to people; he becomes able to sustain a friendship, a love, through frictions, hurts and misunderstandings in order to arrive at a more rewarding, mutually understanding relationship.

Finally, the child is shaken by a change, by surprise, by anything unpredictable in his environment. He himself is unstable and unpredictable. He functions on the impulse of the moment, and whatever happens at the moment is either wonderful or terrible; his responses are entirely out of scale with the facts. At the same time he needs the reassurance of a calm and stable world around him, an orderly routine, an environment in which things and people are where he expects them to be and behave as he expects them to behave. Surprises, as we have noted, are more often alarming than pleasing to children.

The fear of change, of the unexpected, is true also of some adults. The man by whom you can set your watch may be one of those who need an unchanging, dependable routine to give them a feeling of security. To such a person the world may still be as frighteningly unpredictable as it was in childhood.

Maturity in Liberation

The literature that pictures youth as a springtime of lyrical happiness, of rhapsodic joys and glorious griefs does not lie, it simply does not tell all the truth. Childhood and youth are full of pain as well as joy, and by a remorseless principle of growth it is mostly the pains of youth that immature people tend to carry with them through life. They suffer the restrictions, the limitations, the hazards and frustrations without any of the privileges of childhood. They pay a heavy price for their failure to mature.

The finest gift of maturity is its freedom from these pains. By understanding the consequences of his behavior, by being able to exercise control and restraint, by being able to make choices that are in his deepest interest not only for the moment but in the long view, the mature individual is liberated to make the most of his life. He can enjoy the present and still believe in and plan for the future. He is free enough of his infantile needs to pursue a variety of attachments to work, to recreations, to ideas, and especially to people.

As a result of his awareness of others' needs as well as his own, his empathy for others' feelings as well as the high value he places on his own, he has also developed some special skills of maturity. He knows not only what is worth wanting but also how to get it.

No for an Answer

The most difficult lesson a child has to learn in life—and many of us struggle with it forever—is to take no for an answer. He must have what he wants, and have it now. The same is true of the immature adult. Children and adults both who are victimized by the tyranny of immediate desire are usually fickle and incapable of long term satisfaction. The child who gets every toy he demands rarely enjoys any one toy for long. The immature adult who must have whatever he finds attractive marries in haste and frequently more than once.

Unlike the child such a person does not openly cry when he has to take no for an answer. His crying takes another form. He complains and charges the people who have refused him as unfair or wrong. His resentfulness can scarcely be concealed by such accusations. It serves only to lose his audience so that any other request has even less of a chance. His defeat and failure are real enough to lead to brooding and depression, which are every bit as painful as the child's unhappiness when he cries.

The mature person does not welcome disappointment or

frustration. He does not like to take no for an answer any more than anyone else. But instead of bemoaning his luck or the cruelty of the world, he takes the trouble to cultivate the art of persuasion. He develops insight, foresight, and an intelligent use of hindsight. He draws upon the resources of maturity to help him get the answer he desires.

There is a fairy tale about a little boy who is hungry, cold, and lost in the woods. He comes upon a creature even worse off than himself, an animal caught in the cleft of a rock. The waif goodheartedly frees the animal, and the animal of course turns out to be a representative of the fairy queen. Her reward to the boy is an extraordinary power, the power to make people unable to deny him any request. He awakens the next morning in a bakeshop and is soon well fed, by afternoon he is handsomely dressed, and before the day is out he has won the hand of the princess in marriage.

The ability to win yes rather than no, from people and from situations, is not so magical as it is complex. It requires great willingness to give as well as to receive. People who must too often take no for an answer are usually unwittingly asking for it. They create the setting for their own frustration. They are thoughtless, abrupt, or perhaps they demand too much. They give too little consideration or none at all to the other person's state of mind, his situation, his needs and how the demand will coincide or conflict with them. Such people have the primitive understanding and the awkward timing of children. And since they have often been bruised by the wrong answer, they come with their responses primed for it. They are hypersensitive or hostile; they are quick to be hurt, quick to strike back.

The mature person can afford to wait for an appropriate moment, to consider the reasonableness of what he wants, to trim his expectations according to the situation and the needs of the person to whom he addresses himself. He can afford to take a modified yes, which may not be all he would like but still is better than nothing. He can yield a little, and the other may yield a little, and out of a flexible approach may come some positive result.

A story is told about the Swiss psychiatrist Eugen Bleuler, famous for his work in schizophrenia toward the end of the last century. The students at his hospital had come upon a schizophrenic who had deteriorated so far that they could get no response from him whatever, and they called Dr. Bleuler. While he went into the patient's room they waited outside, gloating in advance over what would surely be the great professor's failure. After about twenty minutes the door opened and the professor and the patient walked out arm in arm, tears streaming down the sick man's face; obviously he had experienced a genuine emotional response and a catharsis. When the dumbfounded students asked Dr. Bleuler by what profound scientific method he had reached the patient, he answered, "I cried a little, and he cried a little, and that's how it happened."

The mature person can also cry a little with another, in the sense that he can appreciate the other's situation and genuinely sympathize with it. This breadth in his capacity for feeling works for him whether he wins or loses. If he suffers a rejection, he does not have to blame himself or the other— there is no blame involved. In some situations he is able to say with conviction that if he were in the other person's shoes he also would have given a negative answer.

In another situation he may not find the rejection so justifiable, but again he is not crushed by it. He does not feel that because one man or woman has said no to him the whole world is against him. All that has happened is that one individual has said no, and there may be a better way, a better time, or perhaps a more suitable person to ask for what he wants.

A Mature Recipe for the Good Life

Philosophers since ancient times have sought guideposts to the good life, and many of their ethical standards reappear today in our psychological concept of the mature individual. The Greeks, for example, talked of the value of harmony and balance in living—"nothing in excess" was an age-old precept quoted by Aristotle.

The mature individual lives by this rule although he may never have heard of it or consciously applied it to himself. He maintains, or tries to maintain, a harmonious combination of his many needs, drives, and interests. He may be more absorbed by one or another for a period, but he manages on the whole to put his eggs of satisfaction into not one but many baskets.

He is free to do this, free to be absorbed for a time in work, for a time in play, for a time in courting a woman and making her his own. He is free to cultivate a diversity of attachments to people and a major attachment to one person. No attachment takes control of him and obsesses him to the exclusion or neglect of others. He is free to live a well-rounded life.

The philosophers also, and Spinoza in particular, observed that the man who achieves a good life is a man who has learned to like what is good for him. This too is a mark of maturity, although it is not always easy to see. We see the reverse clearly enough in a person who likes more food or more alcohol than is good for him. A mature person may thoroughly enjoy food and drink, and at the same time he can take them in moderation because he also enjoys having a trim, healthy body and a clear and active mind. Similarly, a woman who enjoys her youthful, slender figure may find it a chore, but not an overwhelming one, to watch her weight.

It is also characteristic of such people to make these choices unobstrusively, without calling attention to them, and so we are often unaware that they are showing us the mature trait of liking what is good for them. We note, too, that they have the freedom to make these wholesome choices. They are free of an obsessive craving for food, liquor, or whatever may be bad for them in excess. We may call habitual excesses immature or neurotic. We may make moral judgments and say they reveal weak character or lack of will power, as many believe. But we would all agree that these harmful habits are not characteristic of a mature individual.

The freedom to choose what is good for him is the mature individual's privilege also in love. Literature is full of characters who are enslaved by a love that is clearly not good for them. Often tragedy is deepened by the fact that the victim knows his attachment is destroying him and yet can do nothing to save himself. In Thomas Mann's great novelette, *Death in Venice*, the victim of a degrading love is a man of highly developed intellect and sensibilities. Yet despite the maturity of these facets of his personality, his emotional life never enjoyed the same degree of growth. As a result, he is not free and becomes trapped by a single enslaving attachment that leads him to his ruin.

The case of Philip in Somerset Maugham's *Of Human Bondage* is a classic illustration. Philip knew very well that his love for the prostitute Mildred was not good for him in any way, and yet he could not free himself from her; hence the author's choice of title. Interesting enough, this is the same title given by Spinoza four hundred years earlier to that section of his Ethics having to do with our emotions and their relationship to the achievement of maturity and the good life. Philip was suffering human bondage, or slavery; he was compelled against his will to pursue an attachment that was not in his interest.

A mature person is free not only from harmful attachments to others but also from the nagging, absorbing attachment to oneself created by physical illness. He is likely to have a good health record, partly for the reason that he likes what is good for him physically as well as in other ways. There is a more profound reason, besides, for his comparative freedom from illness. Good health might at first glance seem to be an organic and medical matter, independent of psychology and the emotions. Today we know better, for psychosomatic medicine points to many physical ills which are emotional in origin. Deep-seated, unresolved emotional problems are often expressed in physical symptoms for which there is no organic cause.

The mature individual remains reasonably immune to such symptoms, not because he is free of emotional difficulties but because he tends to deal with them effectively on a behavioral level. There are times when a single deed is worth more than a thousand thoughts and feelings. He is not likely to push his dissatisfactions out of sight and bury them where they may fester and find their way into his body in the form of headache, backache, fatigue, or chronic indigestion. He treasures his physical and emotional well-being; he has far more interesting things to do in life than nurse symptoms. Rather than live with discontent, he prefers to seek and find a satisfactory way out of an emotional log jam that may have occurred in his life.

Neither All Work nor All Play

We said earlier that youth cannot match the mature individual's capacity for enjoyment, and now we can extend that statement. His life is filled with enjoyment, because he has learned to enjoy so much of what he does. He likes to play, and he likes to work. The mature person is a productive person, not out of a compulsive drive to achieve, to win recognition and material success. These rewards are agreeable, but they are not his primary goal. He accepts the necessity to work in our society, and that is part of his maturity. An 18th-century European nobleman, a Roman patrician or a Greek aristocrat in antiquity could escape the economic necessity of working since tenant farmers, serfs or slaves did the work for them. And yet we note that many of them worked intensely at intellectual, literary, and scientific pursuits or in the public welfare. True, they had the choice of working or not working, and they also had a fairly free choice of what work they would undertake to do.

Today most men and many women work not from choice but from necessity, and their choice of work is narrowed by many factors beyond their control. It is mature to accept this reality, and find satisfactions in work that is perhaps not ideally one's choice. It is like the song in *Finian's Rainbow*, "If you can't be near the girl you love then you love the girl you're near." If you cannot have the job you would like then you make the most of the job you have.

Work does not absorb all of a mature individual's life, and his choice of play activities is his own. Between work and diversified play he manages to meet the many needs of a well-rounded personality.

In both his work and his play there is a constant factor: he not only enjoys what he does but he enjoys doing it with people. He both works and plays well with others. Some activities are solitary but at some point even writing, painting, cabinetmaking, stamp collecting become social, if only in sharing the pleasure of the completed work with others. And although reading, listening to music, and viewing paintings and sculpture require no company, we eagerly share these enjoyments by talking about them.

The solitary who eschews human companionship may have great achievements and great satisfactions but his satisfactions are on a single plane. They do not have the variety, the give and take of working with colleagues and playing with friends. Most mature people relish some solitude, and some actively seek it from time to time. They are not dependent upon companions, not even upon the single most important companion of their lives, for every satisfaction they enjoy. At the same time they also welcome the social side of life. They make acquaintances, cultivate friendships, find common meeting ground with people of many kinds.

The Essential Strength

The mature individual gives an impression of strength—not the strength of a driving force nor the strength of a rigid rock, but the strength of a well-built structure that withstands stress and serves its function with grace. A good boat, a good plane, a good building have this kind of strength. If we were to seek the source of this strength in human terms, we would find it in the mature individual's attitude toward himself and the world.

He values himself and believes in the world. This is the reverse of smugness or star-spangled optimism. His belief in the world is not blind; he is in touch with reality. His value of himself is equally realistic. He knows his limitations and accepts them as he accepts his talents and skills. He is able to say that he plays a terrible game of golf but he enjoys it anyway. He is able to admit to ignorance or error, and does not have to win every game or every argument. He can lose without feeling diminished. He is like the captain of a sound ship who knows her seaworthiness. He has confidence in his ship's ability to encounter fierce winds and buffeting seas and yet come safely to port.

This kind of strength does not depend upon uninterrupted success and good fortune; quite the contrary. This kind of person is not an undefeated champion. Indeed, his belief in himself is reinforced by the knowledge that he has taken defeat and loss, and has survived them. He knows life is not so niggardly that it does not offer second chances.

He also knows how to make do. If something is not perfect, he does not spend his time mourning its imperfection. An accountant does not look only at the red entries in the company's books, and jump to the conclusion that the firm is bankrupt. Nor does he look at the black entries and decide that the firm is riding the crest of a runaway prosperity. He makes a judgment on net balance.

The ability to look at both sides of a situation and make a judgment on net balance indicates maturity. Adolescents characteristically magnify either the bleak or the bright side, and often on no other basis than their mood of the moment. A teacher is either great or awful, a course is marvelous or unbearable, a girl is the most or else she is a complete washout, and from one minute to the next life is both pure heaven and pure hell.

These spontaneous judgments based on feeling are all very well for adolescents, most of whom still live in a fairly sheltered world and have no very crucial decisions to make alone; they still have their elders to advise and protect them. But in the adult world, with actions to take and attitudes to adopt that affect one's own and often others' well-being and happiness, such judgments will not do.

To make a more balanced judgment requires not more time, essentially, but more readiness to weigh the many elements of a situation, an issue, a person. Not many things in life are all good or all bad. It is part of maturity to see both the bad and the good, and to decide whether the good is worth the emotional cost of accepting the bad that comes with it. We are not always in the position to make a choice or a decision, or to take action. But we are always in the position to make a judgment. The important thing is for that judgment to represent our best interests.

When it is possible to take action, the mature person is generally in favor of it. An immature review of the world is either the rosy one of dreams or the black one of disappointment and despair; there is no middle ground on which anything can be done about anything. People who live in a world of dreams that are never fulfilled, that probably never can be fulfilled, are likely to be forever mourning their disappointments, forever taking inventory of their failures. They almost never do any celebrating, for they almost never experience anything worthy of celebration. Behind them there is likely to be no track record of decisions made, action taken, results accomplished.

Perhaps the most eloquent warning of the consequences of excessive thought was that of Hamlet. At the end of his famous soliloquy his introspective brooding reminds us:

> "And thus the native hue of resolution
> Is sicklied o'er with the pale cast of thought;
> And enterprises of great pitch and moment,
> With this regard, their currents turn awry,
> And lose the name of action."

Clinical psychologists have a saying, "I'd rather be wrong than doubtful." Such a dictum has much of value. Doubt is the psychological equivalent of pain. Worse yet, it inhibits us from testing alternatives so we remain no wiser for all our thought.

In matters affecting our own life and those we love, action must be direct. The captain is not one to sit helplessly by or to retreat in panic to his cabin. He takes his bearings, lays out his course, and follows it to the best of his ability. Mature men and women, and preferably a mature man and woman together, tend to manage their lives the same way. Their emotional stability enables them to take their bearings and choose their directions with both sensitivity and appropriateness. They repeatedly do those things which are best for them. Although initially they may have selected each other for the beauty they found in each other, it is their maturity which stabilizes the relationship and allows their love to become ever more satisfying. They remain free to enjoy life, themselves, and each other.

When Love Is Mature

How do these mature people express their love? Their freedom allows them the greatest variety of expression imaginable. One curious characteristic of mature love is that it exists only in the plural. The attachment we develop for a member of the opposite sex can be mature only if we already have other mature attachments—to ideas, friends, pleasures, to work, and to leisure interests.

The central love of our life, the love of a wife or husband feeds on and is enriched by these other loves. The mature lover does not spend his time gazing lovingly into the eyes of his beloved. This may be agreeable for a while but sooner or later it will pall on the loved one if not on the lover. The mature lover has a rich feast of other loves to spread before the loved one. He brings interests, enthusiasms, enjoyments into their life together for her to share.

Unlike the romantic phase of love, the mature and life-long love does *not* demand full-time devotion. A Johnny-one-note lover who has nothing to offer but a repetitive "I-love-you, I-love-you, I-love-you" cannot keep this up for a lifetime. His love can have richness and fullness only if he keeps his life rich and full—that is to say, only if he keeps his other loves alive. No matter how deeply two people love each other, they make the most of their love if they retain their separate individualities. As Kahlil Gibran put it in *The Prophet*, in an ideal love the lovers do not drink from the same cup. After years of marriage in which a strong, mature love has flowered, the lovers do not lose their indentity; they discover a harmony between them.

Mature Expressions of Love

Mature lovers have not one but many ways of expressing their love for each other. They find expression for it not only on Sundays and holidays, not only in play and leisure time, but in their everyday working life. A young husband may help his wife with dishes and baby chores without being asked, because he likes to be with her in the kitchen or nursery or wherever her tasks are, not only in the living room or the bedroom. Or he does not like to think of her alone with the pots and pans like paid household help; he is aware that with all her love for her family, an endless round of household duties can become monotonous and wearying, and companionship lightens the task.

This is especially so during the intensive years of child-rearing. Social observers have noted the boredom and discontent of young wives immured in the house with their babies, and have drawn from this observation a criticism of modern marriage. Others have suggested that when husbands share the housework and baby care there is danger that the roles of the sexes are becoming blurred. Some point out that modern young wives tend to demand a husband's help with a "See how overburdened I am" attitude, an implied complaint that this is the consequence of having married him.

All of this may be true. It is also true that married partners today tend to concentrate childbearing and child-rearing into a short, intense period. A loving husband recognizes these years as especially stressful for his wife, and it is a mature way of expressing his love when he does his share to ease the stress. A young wife similarly expresses her love in a mature way when she empathizes with her husband's equally heavy burden during the same period. His activities may be more varied and stimulating than hers, but he does carry a heavy load of responsibility for his young family's welfare, usually at the same time that he is taking the anxious first steps of his lifetime career.

Under these stresses the infantile needs of both can come to dominate their relationship. It is also possible that these very stresses can be consciously recognized and turned into motivations for greater maturity in their love. It is immature to measure one's own work load against the other's, and demand sympathy and help as compensation. It is equally immature to give the sympathy and help as an appeasement of one's own guilt. These are infantile demands and infantile responses. They tend to occur in young marriages but older lovers are far from immune to them. Mature lovers also give sympathy and help, but the attitude, the accompanying music of feelings, is altogether different. Neither is driven by a compulsive need to demand or to give. Both are able to give generously and voluntarily, since they are free of the clutching, clinging needs of immaturity.

Small but thoughtful attentions often have large value in the expression of mature love. A single daisy can be more soulful and significant than a dozen long-stemmed roses. Mature people enjoy their sensitivity to each other's needs and desires, their moods, their feelings, their unexpressed longings, the whole rhetoric of their rich inarticulate inner life. Sometimes this may involve a reckless extravagance but, more often than not, costliness never matches the virtue of appropriateness. Understanding and acceptance tend to express themselves best by sharpening our ability to be emotionally apropos.

Contrary to the popular complaint of husbands about extravagant wives, more than one loving husband is convinced that his wife spends not too much but too little on herself. Through the early years of high family expense and limited income she has stinted on her wardrobe, and the habit may persist even when the income can stand a little extravagance in clothes. A man who goes shopping with his wife in this spirit is reminding her that she is worth spending money on; he is dressing up not only her outer but her inner person, her self-image, and this is a profound expression of mature love despite the fact that it takes the apparently superficial, material form of money and fashion.

A wife also has mature ways of expressing her love, sometimes so subtle and interwoven in the fabric of their life together that her husband basks in the warmth without knowing precisely how it is created. She may do it simply by being happy, showing him that his love makes her happy. An observant writer of another century remarked that a woman's greatest beauty is her capacity for happiness.

There are times when a woman tiptoes around her husband, knowing that he is troubled and trying to solve some problem in his working life. She encourages him to enjoy some pleasures that may not include her, and spares him any feelings of guilt by having some enjoyments of her own to turn to when he goes fishing or hunting with men friends. Mature lovers enjoy sharing most of their pleasures and interests, but they do not insist upon sharing them all.

Mature Love Has Many Roles

Mature lovers play many roles in each other's lives. One may lean and the other provide the emotional support the loved one needs. A husband, however manly, now and then needs comforting, and in a mature relationship he suffers no shame in accepting it.

Mature lovers act as sounding boards for each other to air problems of work and of other relationships. They ask and give advice. They sustain each other in making family decisions. They disagree, and work with each other toward agreement.

And still, although they meet most of each other's needs, neither demands or expects that the other can meet them all. If they are well-developed, complex personalities, they need and maintain friendships, working relationships, companionships of shared interests with other people.

A mature love accommodates all these. It is not exclusive, not voracious of the lovers' attentions. It is secure, and has no need to be competitive or jealous.

A Realistic Love

People of maturity enjoy a realistic appreciation of love. With the richness that they bring to it, they yet see love as only a part of life, perhaps the heart and core of life but not the whole of it. They do not see love as solving problems. They see that they have problems in their lives that must be solved in order to maintain their love.

Mature people treasure love as something valuable, a sturdy plant that grows and flowers but nevertheless must be cared for and cultivated. They work at nurturing it because they believe in it and derive pleasures and satisfactions from it that they know can come from no other attachment. Besides loving each other, they enjoy the feeling of being in love. They keep alive a romantic feeling for each other by thinking of ways to give each other pleasure, finding new enjoyments to share, new places to be together, new experiences to explore together.

Mature love has a rich sexual side, the physical expression of a rich love. Romantic love in its sexual expression tends to be hasty and sometimes bungling. A purely sexual attachment may be physically satisfying but it has little more to express than its physical aspect. Mature lovers bring to their sex life the whole range of their attachment to each other. Their physical expression of love does not stop with physiological climax, with the mere physical release of sexual tensions. They also take physical pleasure in each other even in non-sexual situations. Their physical awareness of each other enhances all the other pleasures of their companionship.

Misunderstandings, disagreements, times of melancholy, times of worry, times when outside pressures mount or energies are low and irritability is close to the surface—these do not shake mature love. The attachment has survived bad times and will survive them again. It is stable and little threatened by changes of mood and occasional distempers.

One of the signs of maturity in married lovers is the manner in which they argue. In the midst of a full-fledged disagreement, both are aware that they are very much upset at having to disagree and perhaps hurt each other. At the same time, they are bound to have it out. They argue, not to win the point or have the last word, but to find a way to come to an agreement. They battle with a minimum of hostility and wounding words, because their goal is to work out their difference and get it out of the way. Their disagreement does not contaminate the quality of their love.

Love Versus the Desire to Love

The love that we have been describing is clearly very different from the love that a man talks about in terms of longing and desire for a particular woman. We ordinarily take his word for it that he is talking about love, but in fact he is talking about something else entirely. Usually a man talking this way scarcely knows the woman, has spent very little time with her and has surely not developed more than a superficial relationship with her, however promising it may appear to be. What he is talking about is not love but his desire to love and be loved.

It is easy to develop desires. Desiring is as natural as breathing and is just as much a sign of life. Still there remains a vast difference between wanting something when we do not have it, and continuing to want it when we do have it. Continuing to desire and cherish what we have means that we have established a relationship, that we have formed an attachment—that we do, in fact, love.

This involves altogether different aspects of ourselves. It involves flexibility, staying power, a willingness to work for long-term goals. It involves a dependable set of values. In order to make the human relationship we call love permanent, our dreams and fantasies must yield to our ability to deal with the realities of life. This involves our skills of living no less than of loving.

This is why only maturity brings genuine freedom to love. When we are mature we are not driven by some single desire that has come to be more important to us than anything else in life. When we are mature we place our highest value not on accomplishment, power, material possessions, not even on our work. We like all these aspects of our lives, but we are not obsessed by them. We are not driving along a superhighway with no exits except toward one single goal. We hold human relationships more precious than any of these, and most precious of all is an enduring and satisfying love between a man and a woman.

When mature people believe they have such a love, they nurture it. They give it their best. It is a sign of maturity to cherish something good when you have it, and to know when you are happy.

CHAPTER NINETEEN

The Ability to Love

How CAN THE ability to love maturely be recognized? We all take our own ability to love very much for granted. We do not question it, examine it, or compare it with other people's ability to love. We assume that when the right person comes along, we will love.

We do sometimes wonder about other people's ability to love. Often we find others more complex than is good for them. But most of us see ourselves as understanding, giving, and generally loving, even though the facts frequently fail to support such a handsome picture of ourselves.

The ability to love can not be measured by a computer. There is no psychological test that could be relied on to tell us our Love Quotient, as certain familiar tests can reasonably estimate our Intelligence Quotient. Yet there are circumstances in the lives of all of us when we need to know more about our ability to love, how it grows and what defects it may have and how we may perhaps improve it by understanding it better than we do. And for this understanding we do have some facts.

Three Facts about Love

The first fact worth noting is not obvious to us among adults but it becomes very clear indeed when we are observant with children. And that is, that we are not born with some fixed, finite ability to love.

Love is something we learn. It is the product of a host of experiences, most of which take place early in our lives. Some of us may remember from childhood the experience of love for another person, perhaps a teacher or a first best friend. A certain grownup or older child may be forever enshrined in our memory for having done a kind or comforting act. But these are exceptional experiences. Our first steps in loving, like our first steps in walking, are shrouded in those early years before words and before memory. We have noted how Freud interpreted these initial infant stirrings of love.

These first experiences, as we have seen, are associated with the vegetative functions, with eating, eliminating, sleeping. We all go through the same stages of development in these functions. And yet for each of us these experiences have individual effects.

Each of us is born with a certain set of parents and siblings, a certain set of living conditions. Besides all this, there is the element of chance. Some experience that would be quite tolerable at one stage of development might be painful at another. An illness or an accident may occur at some period of childhood, or the illness or absence of a parent, or the death of a loved grandparent. A young child does not understand absence, or death. When someone he loves disappears from his life, many a child feels that that person has gone away and left him because that person no longer loves him.

We must reckon all these individual experiences as part of our learning to love. And each experience has its peculiar influence depending upon what kind of person is experiencing it, at what age, and with what other knowledge and experience. Obviously no computer has yet been invented that could measure and evaluate this highly individual sum of experience.

And this is our second fact: no two people reach adulthood with the same capacity to give and to receive love.

It is important to recognize this fact, in ourselves and in those we love. Our success in love, marriage, parenthood, to some extent our success in a job or business or profession may at some time depend upon how well we understand these differences, these individual differences, in the kind and quality of love each of us can give.

The third fact, one which Freud illuminated for us, is that any particular love we may have today is influenced by our previous loves.

We can readily see this in a young man, for example, who has just suffered an unrequited love affair. He is prone to look at the next girl with distrust, as a burnt child dreads the fire. If he finds himself about to fall in love again he will approach the new love guardedly, afraid that the same thing will happen, that he will be rejected again.

This is a most obvious instance of the way love is influenced by a previous love. But Freud meant it in a much deeper sense. He meant that any love in later life is affected by the quality of love we enjoyed—or suffered—early in our lives.

To extract the full significance of these three facts about love, and the ability to love, we should remember the definition of love as we derived it earlier. Ordinarily we think of love as a special kind of attachment to a particular human being. But we have taken Freud's suggestion and defined love in larger terms, as any kind of attachment, whether to a person, an idea, a place, an object, an activity, even to oneself.

We are using this definition because it gives us a new and more profitable way of looking at love. It teaches us, among other things, that the way we relate ourselves each day to people, places, and events is an integral part of our life. Our ability to love is expressed in and is affected by *all* our relationships; not merely the rare, romantic one we isolate as good enough to call love.

The Lover's Illusion

When we first enjoy the delights of falling in love, we feel our love so acutely it is easy to believe that it is also boundless. It is not easy, however, to know how big a reservoir lies behind that love.

It may be like fireworks brilliantly illuminating the nighttime sky but gone before the dawn arrives. The first dazzling days of falling in love are a difficult time to tell whether we can count on our love for the long haul of a lifetime, the long partnership of a marriage. There is great charm in riding a bicycle on an occasional Sunday afternoon but most of us would prefer an automobile to this method of locomotion for a cross-country tour. A longer journey requires something more substantial than what we might choose for a brief romantic trip through the park.

At just such times, just when it is hardest to stop and think and evaluate clearly, it may help to remember the three facts about each one's ability to love, our own and another's: that love is learned, that no two people grow up with the same capacity for love, and particularly that our love of today is shaped by all our loves that have gone before.

We assume without thinking that the intensity of a person's love depends upon whom he loves. Having chosen "right," his love will be boundless, and the one he loves must love him with the same depth and devotion.

In this we could not be more mistaken. No matter how lovable, no matter how worthy the object of his love, the lover can love no more than he is able. And this ability is already developed in him by the time he has reached adulthood.

This does not mean that this development is complete and unalterable. Change can and does take place, but we are easily disillusioned when we count on it. If change comes, generally it comes slowly. Insight and understanding may come in a moment of illumination, but revising old patterns of behavior is slow and often difficult work. In a more innocent era than ours, many a nice girl married a rake or a drunkard in the dewy-eyed belief that she could reform him. All he needed, she was sure, was the love of a good woman, and she of course was that woman. Nowadays we are realistic enough to know how little chance that hope has of coming true.

It is the lover's traditional illusion that his love will change the loved one, that it will transform the loved one into the ideal image in the lover's mind. The loved one will be as deeply, richly, enduringly able to love as we believe we are ourselves. When disillusionment comes, it can be painful indeed.

Then is it best not to fall in love? Not at all. The fact is most of us cannot prevent ourselves from it anyway. We fall in— and out—of love as though forces beyond our control were driving us. And there are such forces. The threat of loneliness is one. It creates more anxiety in the human breast than people can readily put into words. This is especially true of young people, emerging out of their adolescence, marriageable people. A second powerful force is exerted by the hidden machinery of society which presses us all together into the same mold; namely, we are sooner or later obliged as men and women to seek each other out, become attached to each other, in short, love and marry. Finally, our very own biological impulses promote attachments between us almost independently of rational decision.

Part of the challenge of life is to try to direct our comings and goings in such a way that we get the most out of them. Most of us are sufficiently interested in our happiness, no matter how little many do about it, to examine the worthwhileness of some attachment or love we may be forming. Surely we know that the happiness we feel on falling in love is known to breed some fairly unreliable predictions about future happiness.

Recognizing the Ability to Love

Perhaps the first realistic consideration is to accept as inevitable the existence of defects in our ability to love as well as in anyone else's we choose to love. Since nothing human is perfect, we cannot reasonably expect perfect love, of ourselves or of another.

There are signs which might help us recognize and evaluate the ability to love in others and in ourselves. The difficulty is in remaining dispassionate enough to look for them. Once we get emotionally involved, we suffer the tendency to see only what we want to see and we remain blind to what else is there. Beauty in the person we are beginning to love may be accompanied by narcissism, success by insensitivity, and devotion by neurotic dependency. Speak to a lover about this and you are impatiently dismissed. Reality, for someone falling in love, is easily transformed into an exclusive preoccupation with one's feelings for the person loved. His feelings are so important to him that his interaction with other people becomes less and less meaningful.

The Enjoyment of Friends

There is a clue in this of great importance. The more substantial our attachments are to others, the less likely will it be for any new love to dissolve the others away. Surely a person's strongest heterosexual ties with others may fade as he falls in love, but friends, family, interests, aspirations—most of the rest of his attachments—ideally remain intact. These represent the fact that he can and does love. The love we yearn for or promise has none of the tangible reality of the positive contacts we daily enjoy with people.

This ability to get along well with people is the most promising sign that you can get along well with some one other person. This does not mean having a million "friends" to whom we do little more than wave as the social merry-go-round spins us by. The quality of our relationships with people is best revealed in our mutual enjoyment of each other and in the sense of freedom we have to reveal ourselves to each other. Do they seek our advice over and above their automatic complaints about "the evils the flesh is heir to?" Do we confide equally in them? Additionally, are our relationships satisfying enough to be maintained over the years? Or do we constantly touch and go, never preserving and ripening the ties we have to others?

There are some people whose friendships are constantly being replaced. Others fall in and out of love constantly. They never maintain and develop a relationship. Such a record strongly suggests that they are very attractive people. It also strongly suggests that they cannot or will not preserve the attachments they attract.

The history and quality of our attachments to others certainly give us a reasonable indication of how we relate ourselves to people. After all, what tells us more about an individual than his own record? Everyone has good intentions, probably in excess of good deeds. We must count the latter if we want to know how a person will behave. Love is promised often enough, but its continued existence cannot be guaranteed by promise or desire. Only a record of performance will do.

The Enjoyment of Family

The earliest and one of the most telling portions of this record is revealed in our relationship with our parents. If we grow up having enjoyed our parents and home, we are left with positive and favorable feelings toward them. Our oldest and longest attachment and association, then, has been a good one. We are not wary and defensive as a result, but open and ready to accept other human attachments.

It should be clear that thinking well of our parents and getting along with them are not the same as being dependent on them. Nor is this to be confused with their dependence on us. The unmarried thirty-five-year-old man who continues to live at home with his widowed mother does not get along well with her no matter how devoted to her care he may be. Getting along well means that we enjoy the relationship without having to make any considerable sacrifice no matter how willingly. There is a big difference between being proud and being possessed. This difference shows up even in small ways. It is one thing for a man to be enthusiastic about some of his mother's cooking, but quite another to think nothing can match it.

Spontaneous Acceptance

People who have enjoyed their family attachments while growing up manifest their ability to love in still another way. Not only do they think well of their parents, but their spontaneous remarks about people in general are more often favorable than critical. They can and do recognize shortcomings in people and they may learn to dislike them for their faults. But their initial reaction is one of acceptance and friendliness. More often, additionally, it is their prevailing reaction. They are flexible enough to get along with others as they are instead of correcting, convincing, and otherwise trying to change everyone into their own image. Not only do they accept differences in people, they may even be charmed by them. At the least, they are not critically uncomfortable about them.

A History of Love

This makes it easy to be attracted to others and to fall in love. Anyone with the ability to love has been in love. The absence of several heterosexual loves in a person's past is grounds for suspicion. If he or she is as attractive as you say, why have not others been attracted and attachments formed? Certainly there are extenuating circumstances and suspicion is not tantamount to conviction. Suffice it to say, people who are loving have overcome mighty obstacles in the path of love.

A Happy Lover

And love, for the person who has the ability, is not the cause of suffering. It is ennobling. It makes him happy. He feels expansive, open, accepting. Life seems good rather than cruel and threatening. Although parting remains "a sweet sorrow" to him, he is left strongly able to function. The anguish and melancholy thoughts of death described in romantic literature are not to be taken literally. The color and appeal of poetic exaggeration would then give way to a drab clinical picture.

A Happy Person

Another important sign of the ability to attach oneself favorably to another human being is to enjoy favorable feelings about oneself. Unlike conceit, a good self-image leaves room for humility at the same time that one entertains a deep-seated conviction of his basic adequacy. Such a person forms attachments to others not out of desperate need but for the pleasurable give and take he soon establishes. You recognize such people in many ways. They are genuinely interested in you. They are sincere and realistic about their ambitions. They do not feel that they must be entertaining. They are interesting to be with because they let you be yourself.

Renovating Our Self-Image

Sometimes being ourselves can be fairly gloomy. Many of us come to maturity with some doubts about our own adequacy. Even if we emerge from adolescence with no very dark bruises, as young adults we encounter many pressures that tend to throw us back into infantile forms of self-love. In a world that presents many challenges, we all suffer feelings of helplessness and dependency from time to time; we all tend to lash out childishly sometimes at unfeeling fate.

When ideals of achievement and material acquisition are thrust upon us from all sides, our efforts to maintain a healthy, outgoing self-acceptance are too often undercut. Too often we succumb to one or another form of narcissism, whether it is a drive to compete more ruthlessly or a need to find excuses, to complain, to be taken care of. And as our self-love falters, our ability to give and receive love is also impaired. Our discontent with ourselves sheds a miasma of discontent over all those nearest to us. As we have less satisfaction with ourselves, we perversely withdraw more and more into that same unsatisfactory self. Whether the form of our withdrawal is self-aggrandizing or self-pitying, it is all one and the same—it is all self-centered. Feeling poor in love, we have less love to give.

What can we do about this? How can we protect a good self-image, or nourish and strengthen a wavering one? How can we renovate our self-love against the wear and tear of living?

More often than not, people drive themselves even more strenuously in the belief that some new accomplishment will bring them favorable attention. And if others respect them, of course, they will like themselves better. All this is plausible, but unlikely. Driving oneself harder has the immediate effect of increased wear and tear on the ego. Success is by no means guaranteed and public recognition is even more unreliable and fickle. Finally, no one achievement lasts forever. As a famous general once put it, "There is no security, only opportunity."

We do have the opportunity to treat ourselves better, to behave toward ourselves as if we did have a good and sturdy self-love—in other words, to take the trouble to enjoy ourselves more.

In our way of life we are not really very good to ourselves. We make great boasts about our high standard of living, and yet what do we really get out of all our abundance, beyond an array of durable consumer goods, bright and shiny automobiles, dishwashers, home laundries, hi-fi and television sets? We polish and pamper our cars but we do very little pampering of ourselves. It is a somber heritage of our past to look upon enjoyment as a Saturday night reward for a week's work, something that has to be earned rather than a value in itself.

It is possible to develop the *habit* of enjoyment, just as easily as so many of us, without realizing it, develop the habit of anguish, of worry, of thinking constantly about bills, taxes, indigestion or lower back pain. It is possible to enjoy oneself a little every day, not only on Saturdays, holidays, and two or three weeks of vacation each year.

Every ordinary day is rich with the opportunity for enjoyment, if we only take the trouble to become aware of this. Even our most prosaic daily activities can be brightened into small sources of pleasure. A few pennies more for a cake of soap can add the delights of scent to the otherwise prosaic task of washing ourselves. In our culture, we hardly make enough of the sheer physical pleasure of performing the bathroom functions.

In our cities it is hard to cultivate the simple sensory pleasures of sight and sound, touch and smell, but it is not impossible. A clean west wind blows now and then even among the towering cave dwellings of a metropolis. The sun still sets and the young moon still shows its slender curve in the western sky. It is possible to notice weather, to enjoy a brisk fall morning or a balmy spring afternoon even in a city street. Plenty of people do; anyone who seeks these uncomplicated no-expense enjoyments will find company. Some people even enjoy rain and snow.

Cultivating the habit of enjoying a little pleasure every day may seem a minimal way to bolster up a faint and failing self-image. Each moment of enjoyment may increase our good feeling for ourselves by only the merest fraction. But the fractions add up day by day, and before long they are contributing measurably. Our bodies need only minimal quantities of vitamins and minerals, and yet without them we lose strength and may even fall ill. Small moments of pleasure, taken at frequent intervals, act the same way; they are the psychological vitamins of a healthy self-image.

Achievement brings its satisfactions, but achievement alone does not sustain self-love; the successful man or woman often lives in terror of losing success, and some have literally gone to pieces with the fear of falling from its dizzy height. Nothing else has quite the power to refresh our self-image as enjoying *ourselves*. The parting wish, "Enjoy yourself!" with which a friend sends us on a vacation reveals a homely truth: only as we learn to enjoy ourselves do we come to love ourselves as we would have others love us.

As enjoyment becomes more habitual, so does love. This is how we come to love with greater pleasure, constancy, and depth. The best lovers do not merely enjoy each other. They enjoy themselves by enjoying the world together. Love, for them, is a luxury. They do not need their attachment to each other in the imperative way we need air to remain alive. Certainly they find solace in each other, but this is not the major function of their relationship.

The desire they have for each other, no matter how great its initial romantic urgency may have been, becomes part of their more general desire for and love of life itself. They do not necessarily feel that this is the best of all possible worlds nor do they smugly feel that the world stands by merely to do their bidding. What they do feel is that, on net balance, life is good

—and even better when they share the goodness they find.

Such people, in their protestations of love, essentially invite us to become part of their cherished world. It is a real world of joys and of sorrows. There are dark episodes but, on the whole, life remains worthwhile. When people enjoy enough freedom from themselves to explore life together this way, they slowly but surely come to be the most important part of life to each other. Their love is thus deeply reinforced not by mere desire or promise but by life itself. It becomes stronger and constantly more fulfilling.

The ability to love has not been easily recognized and remains one of the least heralded accomplishments in our history. It has been accorded no important social recognition, no Nobel prize, not even a gold watch after fifty years of devotion. Romantic literature is largely recognized for what it is: fictional, imaginative, sweetly untrue. Who, then, in history if not in fancy have been the great lovers? We can find them only if they distinguished themselves in the exercise of some ability in addition to love. If they unified an empire or wrote outstanding poetry, we might recognize also how well they loved. But their monuments bear no inscription about their love.

Who are the great lovers today? People frequently mistake the stars of stage and screen for them. Granted, they are good-looking, generally attractive, and repeatedly appear in amorous roles. Their private lives are often another matter. Or reference is made to men and women who figure prominently in gossip columns as great lovers. Their frequent involvement in scandals and divorce suggest a basic instability in life highly inimical to love.

The fact is we do not know who the best lovers are because we neither recognize nor measure the ability to love publicly. Yet, without knowing it, some of the best lovers may be very close to us indeed. We approach the task of picking them out by a small change of reference. The ability to love is not some special talent but the largest part of our ability to live. We cannot have one without the other, the way someone might have great musical memory and yet be color-blind. Living and loving are so much a part of each other that our performance in one is the most tell-tale indication of how we perform in the other.

Our ability to love is established not so much by fervent

promise as by often repeated deeds. Perhaps it is more helpful to think not of the ability to love, but of the ability to remain loving. This emphasizes its history and presently continuing character. It stresses the reality of the daily pleasure we find in human relationships. This constantly reinforces our ability to love, freeing us more and more from the prison of the self. Life runs more smoothly, leaving less to impair the ideal growth of some special love of our choice.